THE OTHER BISHOP BERKELEY

THE OTHER BISHOP BERKELEY

An Exercise in Reenchantment

Costica Bradatan

Fordham University Press

New York   2006

Library of Congress Cataloging-in-Publication Data

Bradatan, Costica.
  The other Bishop Berkeley : an exercise in reenchantment / Costica
Bradatan.—1st ed.
     p.   cm.
  Includes bibliographical references and index.
  ISBN-13: 978-0-8232-2693-1 (cloth : alk. paper)
  ISBN-10: 0-8232-2693-X (cloth : alk. paper)
  1. Berkeley, George, 1685–1753.   I. Title.
 B1348.B73   2006
 192—dc22   2006034078

Cover Art by Cosmin Bumbut

Printed in the United States of America
08 07 06 5 4 3 2 1
First edition

To
Cristina and Anastasia

Is that not a useless undertaking, to dig up earlier opinions about things and go into them at length? Is this fruitless business . . . not ultimately a flight from what is today required of us? Are these safe promenades in the old gardens of earlier conceptions and doctrines not a comfortable avoidance of responsibility in face of the demands of the day, a diversionary spiritual luxury to which we no longer have any right?

—Martin Heidegger

Contents

Acknowledgments

In writing this book I have accumulated many intellectual debts and I have benefited from the broad-mindedness, generosity, and friendship of many people. It is with great pleasure that I acknowledge these debts here and thank these generous friends and colleagues. I am particularly grateful to Giuseppe Mazzotta for the friendship, generosity, and constant encouragement he has shown me over many years. His work and vision, fundamental optimism, and solar personality have inspired me and taught me what it means to be, in a meaningful way, a humanist scholar in the twenty-first century. I am very grateful to Branka Arsić for the instrumental role she played in bringing this project to life. Apart from being the most interesting Berkeley scholar I know, Branka is always a caring and understanding friend. I am grateful to Peter Harrison for reading the whole manuscript and providing me with priceless feedback. This book was born out of a doctoral dissertation. I take great delight in thanking David Cooper for guiding me, with unique kindness, patience, and grace, through my doctoral studies at the University of Durham, in England. Special thanks go Andrew Louth and Stephen Clark, members of my dissertation committee, for their important comments, recommendations, and advice. Thanks to the generosity of all these people this book is improved. Needless to say, I am the only one responsible for its shortcomings and weak points.

I finished writing this book while holding postdoctoral positions at two U.S. universities. I am grateful to Jonathan Monroe, director of Cornell University's Knight Institute for Writing, and to Karen Dawisha, director of Miami University's Havighurst Center for Russian and Post-Soviet Studies, for their institutional support and their personal friendship. Helen Tartar, of Fordham University Press, has played an essential role in the publication of this book. I am very grateful to her. Nicholas Frankovich and Dorothea Halliday took very good care of the book's editing, for which they have my deepest gratitude.

I also own special thanks to some good friends who in many important ways and on various occasions have helped me over the last few years: Sorin Antohi, Aurelian Craiutu, and Stephen Thornton.

Above all, I am grateful to my wife for things that are so numerous and so important that they cannot be listed here.

Earlier versions of some of the materials in this book have been published before in journals or collected volumes. I am grateful to the following editors and publishers for allowing me to reproduce these materials: Stephen Thornton, editor of the electronic journal *Minerva*, for "Berkeley and *Liber Mundi*," published in *Minerva—An Internet Journal of Philosophy* 3 (November 1999); the Society for the Utopian Studies for "Waiting for the *Eschaton*: Berkeley's 'Bermuda Project' between Earthly Paradise and Educational Utopia," published in the *Journal of Utopian Studies* 14:1 (spring 2003); Palgrave Macmillan for "'One is All, and All is One': The Great Chain of Being in Berkeley's *Siris*," published in *Ordering the World in the Eighteenth Century*, ed. Frank O'Gorman and Diana Donald, Studies in Modern History Series, 2005; Instituti Editoriali e Poligrafici Internazionali (Pisa, Italy) for "Alchemists or Ecologists? Some Remarks on the Philosophy of Alchemical Transmutation," published in *Acta Philosophica: Rivista Internazionale di Filosofia* 14: 2 (2005); the Peeters Publishers for "George Berkeley's 'Universal Language of Nature,'" published in *The Book of Nature in Early Modern and Modern History*, ed. Klaas van Berkel and Arjo Vanderjagt (Leuven, Belgium: Peeters Publishers, 2006); and Blackwell Publishing for "Rhetoric of Faith and Patterns of Persuasion in Berkeley's *Alciphron*," published in the *Heythrop Journal* 47:4 (October 2006).

While a doctoral student at Durham, where this book was actually begun, I benefited from the financial support of several institutions and foundations, for which I am very grateful: the University of Durham, the University of Durham's Department of Philosophy, the Committee of Vice-Chancellors and Principals of the Universities of the United Kingdom, the Open Society Institute in New York, and the Ratiu Family Charitable Foundation.

THE OTHER BISHOP BERKELEY

Introduction

The ultimate objective of this book is to propose a new way of looking at the philosophy of George Berkeley (1685–1753). Namely, to assess Berkeley's thought from its roots, rather than from the point of view of the various developments that this thought has triggered in modern philosophy; in other words, from the perspective of *its past* rather than *its future*. The most fascinating thing about such a shift in perspective is the fact that what we see when we look at George Berkeley from the perspective of his past is strikingly different from what we see when we consider him from the perspective of our own time. It is as if there were two Berkeleys, separated from each other. One is the Berkeley of today's mainstream (analytically minded) scholarship, the Berkeley taught in schools, dissected and debated in journals, and occasionally even turned into a source of philosophical humor, whereas the other one is more obscure and humble. One of the major aims of this book is to show not only that this other Berkeley exists (even if he has not been perceived very much in the literature), but also that he is a fascinating character.

In what follows I will, in the first place, deal with a number of specific introductory issues: what are the primary objectives to be attained through the present work, why these particular objectives rather than any others, what are the main guidelines and principles on which my approach is based, how is this work related to the existing scholarship, and what precisely a reader should *not* expect from this book. In the second place, in light of the fact that the book is intended to be, above all, a study in the history of philosophy, I will advance some general considerations of the nature and significance of the historical research, of the role that the past plays in the configuration of the present, and, very briefly, of the philosophical significance of the study of the past. Finally, the philosophical past will be specifically considered, along with a number of issues in the history of philosophy. These rather general considerations are intended as an attempt at delineating a theoretical context within which, I hope, my own approach will reveal its scholarly significance.

A characteristic trait of today's mainstream (analytically minded) Berkeley scholarship is its tendency to single out from the whole of Berkeley's thought only those features, topics, problems, and questions that seem to have a certain importance for today's philosophical debates. There is a certain inclination in this scholarship to consider Berkeley interesting only insofar as he has something relevant to say about the problems that *we* are concerned with, and only as long as he is able to solve what *we* consider significant philosophical problems. (Of course, this is the case not only with Berkeley.) As a result, a certain selection operates throughout the exegesis, teaching—and, consequenctly, common reception—of Berkeley's philosophy: Of the rich variety of arguments, topics, problems, and ideas one comes across when reading Berkeley's writings, only some are, on the criterion of their usefulness for contemporary philosophical debates, taken seriously and given the "right" to be considered really "philosophical." Accordingly, in today's mainstream scholarship, Berkeley seems to be considered an "important philosopher" because of, among other things, his anticipation of the "linguistic turn" in philosophy (hence, his significant contribution to the advancement of analytic philosophy), his contribution to the development of the empiricist tradition, his "linguistic" approach to problems of traditional metaphysics, his anticipation of pragmatism as a distinct philosophical position, his contributions to the philosophy of mathematics, the philosophy of science, economics, and even twentieth-century physics.[1] The topics of monographs dedicated to George Berkeley today are discussions of, say, his doctrines of vision, perception, abstraction, meaning, realism, other minds, the distinction between primary and secondary qualities, intentionality, or causality. These are topics about which Berkeley certainly had something significant to say, and they are popular in today's philosophical debates, too. Needless to say, the fact that Berkeley could still be found useful from the point of view of the various contemporary philosophical concerns, and that he can still offer answers to our own philosophical interrogations, testifies to his greatness as a philosopher and to the sharpness of his thinking. I admire those mainstream Berkeley scholars (most of them of analytic orientation) who, whether knowingly or unknowingly, make the link between Berkeley's writings and our own philosophical concerns—looking to Berkeley for solutions to *our* problems. Of course, contemporary philosophy must take over, reinterpret, and make use of arguments borrowed from past philosophers (Berkeley's arguments included) for its own purposes: this has always been the case, and this is how philosophy, and knowledge in general, advances. If there is already a body of knowledge available, it would be absurd to simply ignore it and start everything anew. There is nothing wrong with having a critical, selective attitude to what has been said in the past. However, this must be done *in full awareness of the situation*: that is to say, with the understanding that, when doing so, we do *not* do historical work, but simply deal with our own (present) problems, we do not (even try to) discover what such and such historical figures wanted to say, but we seek to *use* what they said (sometimes even before realizing what they really meant to say) for our own benefit. The most important thing about such a historical awareness is that, in its absence, we run the serious risk not only of missing the real significance of the past, but also of systematically *inventing* a past that has never existed and taking it for the real one. Not only do we miss the target, but we simply aim at something else, without even knowing it.

Nevertheless, my book is not necessarily intended as a criticism of what the mainstream (analytic) Berkeley scholars have done. My only intention is to do justice to the historical truth, as far as this is possible, by pointing to the existence of *another* Berkeley, as it were, one in general unaccounted for by the mainstream analytic scholarship. The central idea of the present work has been born precisely out of the realization that today's mainstream Berkeley scholarship, valuable as it is, does not deal with the *entire* Berkeley (and, what is worse, in some cases it even claims that there is no need to do so), but only with certain segments of his philosophy, namely with those that, in some way or other, prove to be useful in *our* debates, and interesting from the standpoint of *our* current concerns.

Of course, this is not the case with the entire Berkeley scholarship. For there are also excellent monographs dedicated to George Berkeley's historical background, predecessors, and past influences. There are studies trying to place him within a broader and more complex historical context and to relate him, in a meaningful way, both to the past and to his own time. A. A. Luce, T. E. Jessop, Charles McCracken, David Berman, Harry Bracken, Stephen Clark, Stephen Daniel, and more recently Branka Arsić, to give only very few examples, have published over the years excellent scholarly studies, in which Berkeley's philosophy is approached with a sense of awareness of its historical roots and its predecessors, with a deep understanding of how Berkeley relates to his epoch and how his thought shaped the birth of modern thought. The numerous references that I make to the writings of these scholars throughout my book testify to my deep indebtedness to them.

Yet, beyond that, there is (I dare to say) something definitely new about my book. Its novelty comes, I suggest, from its program to consider the whole of Berkeley's philosophy in relation to the past; from its plan to look at George Berkeley systematically from the perspective of his various intellectual ancestors, rather than from that of his "descendants" (which is commonly the case with the mainstream scholarship); from its constant focusing on a number of traditional roots of Berkeley's thought, some of which have never been previously considered (quest for the "Earthly Paradise," utopianism, Cathar-like attitudes), while others have been only briefly discussed (*liber mundi*, archetypal knowledge), as well as from the accompanying attempt to place Berkeley's thought within a much broader framework of spiritual and religious traditions, cultural archetypes, perennial patterns, and bold utopian projects. I hope that, as a result of all these endeavors, a more complete and more faithful image of George Berkeley's philosophy, and of his place in the history of European thought, will be presented.

The first thing I should emphasize at this stage is that it is not my intention in this book to undertake a critical analysis of Berkeley's philosophical theories, arguments, and concepts. What I am concerned with here is not whether Berkeley is right on such and such a point, nor whether his philosophical arguments are good, or valid, ones and his theories "empirically justified." Precisely because there are already plenty of excellent works dealing analytically with Berkeley's arguments and theories,[2] I have chosen to take an approach significantly different from the other current (analytical) ones.

I would very briefly characterize my approach as being:

1) *Genealogical.* The roots of Berkeley's thought that this book seeks to explore are traditional topics, or clusters of topics, whose individual "stories" are narrated, and whose "genealogies" are followed in some detail, before discussing the specific way in which Berkeley incorporated them into the texture of his own philosophizing. For instance, a chapter of the book is dedicated to Berkeley's notion that nature is the visual language that God speaks to us. In order to better understand this notion and its deeper theological significance in Berkeley, I embark on a genealogical study of how such a notion emerged in the European culture and then how it developed over the centuries, with some special emphasis on its presence in St. Paul, Augustine, Dante, Alan of Lille, Thomas Browne, and Descartes. As

a result, once the reader has undertaken her journey into the labyrinthine history of this notion, she comes to grasp the deeper significance of its presence in Berkeley's writings, and what exactly the employment of such a topic by the philosopher means. It is precisely this genealogical type of approach to the roots of Berkeley's thought that plays a central role throughout my research. This is why a good part of it might well be seen as a study in the genealogy of philosophical ideas.

2) *Comparative*. In this book I constantly "confront" Berkeley's philosophy with various other systems of thought, modes of thinking and worldviews. In an attempt to discover who his intellectual ancestors and inspirers are, I constantly look at Berkeley's philosophy as if it were a voice within a *larger conversation*. For instance, in the chapter dedicated to *Siris*, Berkeley's last published work (and one of those of Berkeley's writings that always embarrass his modern commentators), I discuss Berkeley's treatment of tar water as a universal medicine in close comparison to the alchemists' treatment of the *lapis philosophorum* as a panacea. As a result, Berkeley's philosophizing is being projected into, and mirrored by, the sophisticated universe of the alchemical operations and proceedings, and thus *Siris* is rendered more comprehensible for the modern reader.

3) *Interdisciplinary.* Apart from the specific fields of history of philosophy and history of ideas, which are the two main areas into which this research is to placed, there are also frequent "journeys" into issues and topics, and employment of protocols and techniques, belonging to other humanistic fields: history of religions, religious studies, literary history, comparative literature, symbolic geography, and utopian studies. To give only one example, Berkeley's project to build a theology college in the exotic setting of Bermuda is connected to the long tradition of the quest for the "earthly paradise" and of the millenarian expectations, and therefore analyzed with the tools provided by the history of religions; then, the *Proposal* that Berkeley wrote for that purpose is deconstructed in light of, among other things, the observations that literary theorist Northrop Freye once made on the utopian discourse.

In terms of writing procedures and rhetorical protocols, the method I have chosen in this book is based on a creative dialogue between my own text, on the one hand, and, on the other hand, Berkeley's writings and the authors to whom I seek to relate him. Hence I constantly employ quotations from Berkeley's works as well as from his philosophical ancestors. I had at least two reasons for doing this. First, one of the findings of this book is that, toward the end of his philosophical career (especially in *Siris*), Berkeley came to see his philosophizing simply as part of an ample, ongoing conversation in which philosophers, mythmakers, poets, and sages from different epochs are engaged. He constructed *Siris* in such a polyphonic manner as to give ample space of manifestation to the noble figures of the past (Orpheus, Parmenides, Plato, Hermes Trismegistos, and Ficino); he conceived of his role in the book not so much as an author but as a humble moderator and harmonizer, someone whose presence is not immediately visible but is precisely what makes possible and visible the presence of others. Somehow inspired by the spirit of Berkeley's late method of philosophizing, and as a tribute to his philosophical humbleness, I have tried to take, at the textual level, a step back, as it were, and leave the floor to the other voices (Berkeley's and his philosophical ancestors'). Second, what lies behind this technique of juxtaposing texts by Berkeley and texts by those who, even if many centuries before him, shaped his thinking, is my belief that, in some way or other, even Berkeley's stylistic inclinations, literary (formal) preferences, and rhetorical devices betray deep affinities with those authors, traditions, and modes of thought in which the very substance of his philosophy was rooted.

Let me also add that, given the obvious necessity of focusing this research only on a limited number of topics and areas of study, I have been compelled to leave provisionally aside, with some exceptions, George Berkeley's significant contributions to the fields of ethics, politics, economics, philosophy of mathematics, and philosophy of science. The discussion of such contributions in this book, important and interesting as they are, would have made it unreasonably lengthy, and consequently weakened the main argument it proposes.

The structure of the book derives to some extent from the character of the approach: each of the chapters explores, historically or structurally or both, a certain topic—or cluster of topics—and then seeks to determine the precise role that particular topic plays in the configuration of Berkeley's thought.

In chapter 1, I advance the idea that there is in Berkeley's early writings an entire network of Platonic features, attitudes, and mind-sets, and that however allusive or ambiguous these Platonic elements might seem, they form a coherent whole, playing an important role in shaping the essence of Berkeley's thought. In other words, I suggest that, given some of the ideas contained in his early works, it was, in a way, unavoidable for Berkeley, in virtue of the inner logic of the development of his thought, to arrive at such an openly Platonic and speculative writing as *Siris*.

Chapter 2 is dedicated to discussing the issue of archetypal knowledge (I call it "philosophy as palimpsest") in *Siris*. One of the fundamental theoretical presuppositions behind it is precisely the notion that the source of our knowledge does not lie in the limited faculties of the individual, nor in the empirical observations of the world around, but in the ancient books, legends, and myths, privileged containers of all important revelations and embodiments of an immemorial tradition. In the first part of the chapter I explore some elements of the Platonic tradition pointing to the existence, throughout it, of a conception of philosophy as palimpsest. In the second part I show how this archetypal knowledge works in *Siris*.

Following the chapters dealing with Berkeley's Platonism, chapter 3 is a systematic attempt at considering Berkeley's immaterialist philosophy in close connection to the topic of the Book of the World (*liber mundi*), with the twofold objective of pointing out, on the one hand, those medieval implications of the topic that Berkeley preserved in his philosophy, and, on the other hand, the "novelties," or at least some of the major changes, he brought forth in his use of the topic.

The central idea in chapter 4 is that in his *Siris* Berkeley comes to employ and make extensive use of alchemical terminology and arguments. Berkeley's arguments and notions in *Siris* are discussed by constant reference to alchemical notions, writings, and authors. It is the objective of this chapter to show that, apart from its being under the strong influence of the Platonic tradition, Berkeley's thought, as it is revealed in *Siris*, seems to have been also marked by some intellectual inclinations, spiritual concerns, and mindsets characterizing the alchemical tradition.

Chapter 5 proposes a consideration of Berkeley's thought from the standpoint of the Christian apologetic tradition, and my objective is to show that one of the roots of Berkeley's thought could be found precisely in this tradition. This chapter deals mainly with *Alciphron* as an apologetic writing, in an attempt to place this book in the long tradition of Christian apologetics. Chapter 5 also discusses some of the rhetorical tools Berkeley employed against freethinkers, and the "pragmatism" of Berkeley's apologetics: Berkeley sees the beneficial practical effects that the adoption of an active Christian attitude might have upon people's morality and social life as an argument for the Christian faith.

In chapter 6 I show that not only was his philosophy rooted in some ancient or medieval traditions of thought, but Berkeley was also, in a serious way, under the modeling influence of the past even when designing such a practical endeavor as the "Bermuda project." More specifically, this chapter offers a discussion of Berkeley's project to build a theology college in the islands of Bermuda, in light of some traditions and patterns of thought governing the Western representations of the "happy islands," "earthly paradise," and *eschaton*. I also point to a certain symbolic relationship that might be established between the substance of Berkeley's immaterialist philosophy and the utopian character of his "Bermuda project."

Finally, the last chapter (chapter 7) undertakes a comparative analysis of some of the ideas professed by the medieval Dualistic heresies (Catharism in particular), and George Berkeley's denial of the existence of matter. The central notion in my comparative approach is the idea that, in both cases, matter comes to be regarded as the source of evil. What I will try to show is not necessarily that Berkeley was a modern Cathar, but simply that his attitudes to the material world echoed certain Cathar theological anxieties and patterns of thought.

One of the central suppositions on which my research is based is that there is something called "the past," something objective, exterior to us, and different in several ways from us, and from our personal perspectives and interests. As such, if this is granted, historical scholars—as truth-seekers—must be guided in their enterprises by the principle that what they should focus on is precisely this objective reality called "the past," their mission being to try to locate it and offer the best possible description of it, leaving aside, for the time being, the various ways in which their historical knowledge might be used by other people for purposes alien to the historical scholarship. Even if such things as "historical truth" or "historical certainty" are sometimes difficult to attain, this is not at all a reason for ceasing to pursue them. Even if one is aware (and any historian should be aware) of the fact brilliantly outlined decades ago by Hayden White that history is, above all, a form of writing, a "literary genre," and is therefore inseparable from the categories of narrative, or fictionalization, this does not mean that we should give up our historical investigations. On the contrary, such a fact must serve as a starting point for a process of increasing our self-awareness as historians: "Strictly speaking, the question of 'how it really was' can only be answered if one assumes that one does not formulate *res factae* but *res fictae*" (Koselleck 2002: 15). Once this is acknowledged, the historian can gain the confidence that she is on the right track.

However, this is not the only way of seeing the nature and role of knowledge of the past. There is another position, according to which knowledge of the past cannot, and should not, be pursued for the past's sake, but for satisfying our own current intellectual needs and interests. Since the past is already dead, is not anymore, we should not be vainly concerned with "how it really was," but we should rather look forward and pursue historical research only insofar as in doing so we gain something we can use for better dealing with the present or the future. An important consequence of this view is that, if the results of a particular historical research cannot be translated into something interesting for us, then we do not in principle have any reason to pursue that research further. In other words, there is no such a thing as gratuitous historical research. What this position upholds has been expressed, analogically, as follows:

> The anthropologist is not doing his job if he merely offers to teach us how to bicker with his favourite tribe, how to be initiated into their rituals, etc. What we want to be told is whether that tribe has anything interesting to tell us—interesting by *our* lights, answering to *our* concerns, informative about what *we* know to exist. Any anthropologist who rejected this assignment on the grounds that filtering and paraphrase would distort and betray the integrity of the tribe's culture would no longer be an anthropologist, but a sort of occultist. He is, after all, working for *us*, not for *them*. (Rorty, Schneewind, and Skinner 1984: 6–7)

As such, history is seen as the business of the present, whose pursuit must always result in a better dealing with the present—and future—states of affairs. Historical research is, of course, to be encouraged because it supplies us with excellent means through which we can be more successful in our various undertakings. Someone who has (some) knowledge of the past is certainly in a better position to understand what is going on, and can, if not foresee the future, at least say why certain future developments are more likely than others. Then, thanks to our knowledge of the past, we are able to articulate our views on various subjects better. For example, we customarily appeal to historical arguments for supporting our current positions and undermining our rivals' positions. Someone with historical knowledge has a broader perspective and can give relevant examples from the past; such a person can always find illustrations in support of the various opinions she might have.

And this is the case with every discipline that has known historical developments. If one knows sufficiently well the "historical background" against which a certain theory, or view, or argument, appeared, then one is much better prepared to defend, or challenge, it than those who do not possess such knowledge. Moreover, different types (or degrees) of historical knowl-edge within a given disciplinary field will produce different "versions" of the past of that field. In philosophy, for example, various versions of the philosophical past are often used to support various contemporary philo-sophical positions. Depending on the camp or school or "tradition" to which one belongs, one is bound to use a certain version of the past. Each "historian of philosophy is working for an 'us' which consists, primarily, of those who see the contemporary philosophical scene as he does. So each will treat in a 'witchcraft' manner what another will treat as the antecedents of something real and important in contemporary philosophy" (ibid.: 7). As such, the "past in itself," the past as it really was, does not concern anyone anymore. According to this line of thought, it would not be of any use, for anyone, to know this "past in itself." The real value of the past actually lies in its flexibility and wonderful capacity for supplying us with various argu-ments we might need for our current purposes. This past is rich and gener-ous: anyone can take anything from it, and it still has plenty to offer for the coming generations of scholars. The past "as it really was" should not con-cern us; not necessarily because it is inaccessible (that is another story), but above all because knowledge of it would be useless. Pushed to its limits, this position comes to assert that the idea of "the truth about the past, uncon-taminated by present perspectives or concerns" is like the idea of "real es-sence, uncontaminated by the preconceptions and concerns built into any human language." It is "a romantic ideal of purity that has no relation to any actual enquiry which human beings have undertaken or could under-take" (ibid.: 8).[3] As a result, history becomes *instrumental*, and does not have an epistemic value per se: it acquires a certain (pragmatic) value only when the arguments it provides are successfully employed by others, in other fields.

The problem with this position comes, I suggest, from a certain confu-sion it makes between the actual conditions under which such and such historical research takes place, on the one hand, and the principles guiding the historical research in general, on the other hand. It is often true that the historical research is, to various degrees, "contaminated," or "impurified," by the researcher (which is to say, by his personal and cultural background, particular "prejudices," ideology, idiosyncrasies, mind-sets, etc.), but that research would be utterly impossible as a serious intellectual enterprise if the researcher began his work with the conviction that there is no such thing as "historical truth," and that the past is not "out there," but rather is ulti-mately the result of some human invention. In spite of the individual taste, subjective propensities, or ideological makeup of the historian, he draws closer to a transsubjective historical truth, free of any personal interests or subjective proclivities. This is something that derives structurally from the very definition of knowledge: any process of knowledge, however simple, involves a subject that, due to some felt insufficiency or ontological lack, seeks to transcend itself. As such, it opens itself up toward something else, in this way overcoming itself, discovering and recognizing its otherness.

Serious historical research cannot be done in the absence of an ideal of truthfulness. Of course, we all have our personal inclinations and preferences, certain perspectives and affinities, but this does not necessarily mean that we have to remain eternally, in MacIntyre's words, "prisoners of the present in our ostensible renderings of the past" (MacIntyre 1984: 33). There are ways of freeing ourselves from the prison of the present, and our sheer awareness of the fact that the past objectively exists might be a good starting point. The evolution of the historical disciplines, the successive internal crises and their overcoming, the alternation of historical "schools," historiographical theories, orientations, and currents of thought, the various methodological revolutions that have taken place over the centuries—all these are an implicit recognition of the fact that there must be a "historical truth," and that, through all these endeavors, the historical disciplines have tried to draw closer to the past "as it really is."

Needless to say, historians know that some results of their work might be interpreted and "used" for a better dealing with present states of affairs, but this does not prevent them from performing the specific tasks that their profession requires them to do. Historians get inside the world they are studying, allowing at the same time others (nonhistorians) to benefit from their work, just as, to use the same analogy, the anthropologist "wants to know how primitives talk to fellow-primitives as well as how they react to instructions from missionaries. For this purpose he tries to get inside their heads, and to think in terms which he would never dream of employing at home" (Rorty 1984: 50). Even if the historian realizes that, say, such and such ancient beliefs she studies are *wrong* ("wrong," of course, by standards current in the world from which she comes), this realization cannot change her attitude to them.[4] It is not her mission as a historian to assess the truth value of those beliefs, nor to express her personal views on them, but only to unearth them, place them in the appropriate context, describe the role that those beliefs played within that particular context, and so on. And, it might be further observed, the less she lets her personal proclivities and idiosyncrasies interfere with her work the better a historian she is.

Above all, it is a matter of intellectual honesty, to say the least, not to try to interfere with the past, and "change" or use it for one's own purposes. Properly speaking, the past does not, and cannot, belong to us: it is a reality outside us, much greater and "older" than ourselves. The past is a foreign country where one is only accepted as a guest. The best thing we can do about the past is to simply take it as such, and, as far as we can, try to understand it. And understanding the past means precisely acknowledging its character of otherness. Surely, in our everyday encounters with the world, we always come to establish certain relationships with this otherness, but this fact does not make it ours. With or without us, the past remains what it has always been: a solid, deeply rooted and irremovable other. In a way, I suppose we must have toward the past an "ecological" attitude: we do not have any right to "use" the past, the less so to "abuse" it.

The alternative to this "ecological" attitude to the past is what we encounter, in its extreme version, in Orwell's *Nineteen Eighty-Four*: the permanent rewriting and updating of the past in the (ever-changing) interests of the present. With supreme literary talent, Orwell grasps the entire absurdity of the situation, and shows how (just like in that old joke, once very popular in Eastern Europe) it is not the future that is impossible to predict, but precisely the past:

> Day by day and almost minute by minute the past was brought up to date. In this way every prediction made by the Party could be shown by documentary evidence to have been correct. . . . All history was a palimpsest, scraped clean and re-inscribed exactly as often as was necessary. . . . Books, also, were recalled and re-written again and again, and were invariably reissued without any admission that any alteration had been made. (Orwell 1987: 42–43)[5]

This tendency to "correct" the past and to "adapt" it to the various needs of the present is manifest in the field of philosophy, too. The fact has been noticed with concern by numerous philosophers, historians of philosophy, and intellectual historians, and it is regarded as having given birth to a certain crisis in today's philosophical world. For one of the distinct flavours of a larger and larger part of today's philosophy is precisely a large-scale "de-historization": a consideration of philosophers, no matter the epoch in which they lived or the culture in which they were formed, as if they were all contemporaries and were all speaking the same language, using the same terms (of course, with the same meaning), determined to philosophize by the same reasoning, puzzled by the same problems, visited by the same visions, and haunted by the same anxieties. Yet, I should add, this is a rather utopian, overoptimistic description of the crisis. In fact, for reasons of economy and saving time, there is no round table where all philosophers are invited (as contemporaries), but only some of them, namely, the most "fashionable" of them. More than that, not even their entire philosophy is debated, but only some parts of it, the most "interesting" ones; and sometimes not even parts of it are debated, but only what some modern commentator or other believes might be a "hot" topic in their philosophy.

As a result of this tendency, philosophers of the past are commonly considered "philosophers" only insofar as they seem to "understand" and are able to answer our own questions: "Past authors may be read, but they are treated as if they were contemporaries. They earn a right to enter the dialogue because they happen to offer good formulations of one or another position which is worthy of a hearing. They are not explored as origins, but as atemporal resources" (Taylor 1984: 17). Certainly, there is something deeply narcissistic in this attitude toward the past: we do not look into the past in order to get knowledge of it, but only to learn more about ourselves; the past is a mirror into which we endlessly project ourselves, our own uncertainties and our own anxieties. From time to time we return to the great dead only to take from them what we think we need in order to deal with our problems successfully, without paying attention to what the great dead are like aside from how they are useful to us. In other words, we reinvent and recreate them; we make them "fashionable" and "hot"; by taking their words out of context we attribute to them things they never said; we "use" them again and again in a process that we call "actualization" or "reconsideration." As Alasdair MacIntyre ironically puts it, the great dead should even be proud for having been helpful to us in this way: "we shall admit the philosophers of the past to our debates only in our own terms, and if that involves historical distortion, so much perhaps the better. We shall have paid the past the compliment of supposing it to be as philosophically acute as we are" (MacIntyre 1984: 39).

According to a widespread view,[6] this situation has been triggered especially by the dramatic process of redefinition of philosophy, and of the "genuinely philosophical problems," that has been undertaken by the analytic philosophy during the last one hundred years or so. Rorty, Schneewind, and Skinner describe in detail how the new definition of philosophy has had as a result the emergence of a divide of the entire philosophical past into two main categories.[7] Criticizing the analytic philosophers' tendency to consider themselves "the first to have understood what philosophy is, what questions are the genuinely philosophical ones,"[8] Rorty, Schneewind, and Skinner describe the process through which this self-representation of the analytical philosophers resulted in an attempt "to tease out the 'genuinely philosophical elements' in the work of past figures, putting aside as irrelevant their 'religious' or 'scientific' or 'literary' or 'political' or 'ideological' concerns" (Rorty, Schneewind, and Skinner 1984: 11). As a result, the past philosophers have been clearly divided into

> those who anticipated the questions asked by contemporary analytic philosophers and those who held back the maturity of philosophy by diverting attention to other questions. Such an attitude produces a history of philosophy which eschews continuous narrative, but is more like a collection of anecdotes—anecdotes about people who stumbled upon the "real" philosophical questions but did not realise what they had discovered. (Ibid.)

Strictly speaking, as the analysis made by Rorty, Schneewind, and Skinner in their book shows, even if references are made in their writings to past philosophers, the analytic philosophers do not have a genuinely historic interest in studying the past, but they make use of various philosophical arguments of the past, taking them out of context, and depriving them of any historical specificity. Certainly, analytic philosophy as a school of thought has merits difficult to overestimate; what I am talking about here, in the footsteps of Rorty et al., is only the way this school of thought has considered some of the problems of history of philosophy, historicity, historical nature of knowledge, and our knowledge of the past. For in the analytic tradition the history of philosophy has a meaning only insofar as it prepares the advent of analytic philosophy; otherwise, it is only a collection of irrelevant stories about philosophers and anecdotes about their lives. But, as Rorty et al. ironically say, "stories about people who almost stumbled upon what we now know to be philosophy are like stories about people who would have discovered America if they had just sailed a little further. A collection of such stories cannot be a *history* of anything" (ibid.: 12). Thus, it could be said that, as a result of the analytical (re)definition of philosophy, the problems with which the past philosophers have been concerned are either "genuinely philosophical problems," and in this case they do not have anything to do with history, or simply pseudoproblems, in which case they do not have anything to do with (analytical) philosophy.[9]

The programmatic tendency—the big ambition, actually—of analytic philosophy to single out "philosophical problems," to take them out of their historical and cultural contexts, and then "solve" them forever, its constant focusing on things "as they are in themselves," separated from any cultural setting whatsoever, has gradually determined the rise, among its supporters, of a certain impatience with what appear as sophisticated "stories" that have been uselessly woven over the centuries around the "genuinely philosophical problems." Hence, the emergence of a certain dismissive attitude, among the analytic circles, toward the history of philosophy as such and toward historically minded philosophies in general. Historical figures are studied, but ahistorically: not as thinkers who emerged and worked at a certain point in time, and whose works bore the marks of their respective epochs, but as some ethereal angelic creatures, with no connection to their historical worlds. Their thinking is analyzed from a strictly formal-logical point of view, leaving aside anything that, by today's standards, might appear "exotic," "outdated," or simply "uninteresting." It is this attitude among many analytic philosophers that makes Richard Popkin talk about "a very strong tendency among philosophers, especially those of our century, to reject any historical study of the subject, to reject any historical interpretation, and to reject the historians of philosophy as part of the philosophical enterprise" (Popkin 1992: 325).[10] Yet, I should add, the history of philosophy is not simply neglected or "rejected." What is even worse, the history of philosophy is often manipulated, "hijacked" for purposes alien to serious historical research.

On the other hand, this lack of a more serious interest in historical issues is certainly one of the causes of the criticisms that analytic philosophy has had to face over the last decades. Analytic philosophy has come to be seen as lacking in historical self-awareness, unable to understand genetically the unfolding of Western philosophy, prone to misrepresentations and anachronisms of all kinds, and ultimately driven by some unreasonable "arrogance." The fact that problems with which some of the greatest philosophers of the past were concerned (but which are considered pseudoproblems from the analytic perspective) are still debated today in various circles—philosophical or not—is taken as a clear sign that the analytic project has, at least in part, failed. By simply decreeing that something is a "pseudoproblem," one cannot persuade people that it is not worth considering. That problem comes back, over and over again, until it becomes part of our thinking. The "genuinely philosophical" is not what some school or other decrees so at some moment or other: there is something supremely rich, uncontrollable, and spontaneous about the definition of the "genuinely philosophical." And any attempt to legislate strictly what is "genuinely philosophical" and what is not is damaging, first of all, to philosophy itself. Rorty et al., for example, decry the fact that

> analytic philosophers have tried to think of themselves as the culminating development of a natural kind of human activity ("philosophical activity"), rather than simply as participants in a brilliant new intellectual initiative. This attempt has had bad effects. . . . on philosophy itself. For the disciplinary matrix of analytic philosophy has made it increasingly difficult for those within it to recognize that questions once asked by great dead philosophers are still being asked by contemporaries—contemporaries who count neither as "philosophers" nor as "scientists." (Rorty, Schneewind, and Skinner 1984: 13)[11]

It seems to me that the analytic philosopher's dismissal of the history of philosophy—and of any historically minded philosophy—as dealing with "stories" about things, and not with "things are they are" (which, for the analytic philosopher, should be the real job of a philosopher) betrays a certain misunderstanding on his side. For what concerns the historian of philosophy (or the historically minded philosopher) is not a futile thing at all, but something serious and objectively existent: just like the analytic philosopher, the historian of philosophy deals with things as they are, which is for him the past. The historian's job is not simply "story telling," he does not seek to "tell stories" for their own sake, or look for entertaining "anecdotes," but his object of research is the historical truth, and those "stories" he sometimes tells are the particular modality through which this truth reveals itself. Anyway, it is highly ironic that analytic philosophers dismiss history of philosophy precisely on the ground that this is simply "story telling." It might well be argued that, thanks to their taking philosophers and philosophical problems out of their historical contexts, thanks to singling them out and using them only insofar as they can offer a response to our concerns, and arguments in our debates, it is the analytic philosophers that, in fact, abundantly use "stories" and "story telling" in their enterprises. They do not even dream of discovering the historical truth as such: what they want is producing some nice "versions" of it, to be conveniently used in their philosophical debates. But what are, in fact, these "versions" of the truth other than "stories," interesting fictions about the past?

Finally, in light of these introductory and general considerations, I would like to point out that, in a sense, this book itself comes as a response to the crisis in today's philosophy I mentioned earlier on in this chapter. By showing the various ways in which George Berkeley's philosophy is connected to a set of ancient theological traditions and neglected modes of thought, and by revealing the crucial role that these traditions and modes of thought play in the formation and identity of Berkeley's philosophizing, I hope to point also to the tremendous importance of the historical scholarship for a better understanding of the philosophical thinking itself. It would be foolishly naïve to claim that what this research will have offered its reader at the end will be, as it were, "the whole truth" about Bishop Berkeley. All I want to say is that what I have all the time borne in mind when working on this research was the belief that there must be a truth about Bishop Berkeley, and that through what I was doing at least I would not go too much astray from it.

1. *George Berkeley and the Platonic Tradition*

There is already a certain amount of literature dedicated to the presence in Berkeley's early philosophy of some typically Platonic topics (archetypes, the problem of God's mind, the relationship between ideas and things, etc). Based on some of these writings, on Berkeley's own works, as well as on the examination of some elements of the Platonic tradition in a broader sense, I suggest that, far from being just isolated topics, loosely scattered in Berkeley's early writings, they form an entire network of Platonic features, attitudes, and mind-sets, and that however allusive or ambiguous these Platonic elements might seem, they constitute a coherent and complex whole, playing an important role in shaping the very essence of Berkeley's thought. In other words, I suggest that, given some of the ideas displayed in his early works, it was in a way unavoidable for George Berkeley, in virtue of the inner logic of the development of his thought, to arrive at such an openly Platonic and speculative writing as *Siris* (1744).

THE PLATONIC TRADITION

Defining the Platonic Tradition

"Platonism," or "the Platonic tradition," is not easy to define. The more so in a chapter dealing not with Platonism as such, but primarily with Berkeley's philosophy and with a possible connection between the latter and certain elements of the Platonic tradition. It seems to me at this stage that a reasonable (if oblique) solution to the difficulty would consist in simply starting out this discussion without attempting to give a complete, fully satisfactory definition of Platonism, but rather provisionally outlining some general information about it. I hope that by constantly seeing the development of Berkeley's thought in light of the Platonic tradition, by "checking" Berkeley's though against a number of Platonic topics and ways of thinking—in other words, by setting the two terms "face to face"—a more complete and concrete understanding of Platonism would result.

Very schematically put, by "Platonism," in accord with a long usage of the term, I mean a certain line of metaphysical thought originating in Plato, and subsequently developed by such diverse figures as Philo, Plotinus, Proclus, Dionysius the Areopagite, Marsilio Ficino, Giovanni Pico della Mirandola, the Cambridge Platonists, and many others. There are authors who draw a clear-cut distinction between Platonism (strictly understood as Plato's doctrine), and Neoplatonism (the subsequent philosophical schools and currents inspired by Plato's thought). For reasons of simplicity, in this book I will use throughout the term "Platonism" in a rather broad sense, that is, as covering also the meaning(s) of any "Neoplatonisms." Moreover, I will sometimes use the phrase "the Platonic tradition" with more or less the same meaning as "Platonism"; even if it might seem a little loose and lacking in historical rigor, the phrase "Platonic tradition" conveys well enough the complex of traditions of thought, schools, and various authors born out of, or clustered around, Plato's philosophy along the centuries.

On the other hand, just as this philosophical tradition that Plato inaugurated did not take over the whole of Plato's thought,[1] so it acquired, with the passing of time, new elements, Christian or otherwise, some of them more or less alien to Plato's original ideas. In fact, what is most interesting about the Platonic tradition is not so much its core of Plato's ideas as its remarkable openness toward other philosophies, worldviews, and systems of thought. Platonism is indeed an open school of thought; moreover, as has repeatedly been said, at its most remarkable it represents the openness, pluralism, and dialogism of thought. I would even venture to say that what explains the longevity and special aura of the Platonic philosophical tradition is precisely its impressive capacity to interact, communicate, and enter into spontaneous dialogue with various other philosophical systems, with various humanistic disciplines, and with sometimes exotic ways of thinking and cultural forms. Various links have been established, whether profound or superficial, temporary or long-lasting, for example, between Platonism and theology (be it Christian, Jewish, or Islamic), Platonism and various forms of mysticism, Platonism and Gnosticism, Platonism and all kinds of Esotericism, Platonism and poetry/literature, Platonism and the arts (icon painting, for example), Platonism and politics, Platonism and theosophy, Platonism and the utopian tradition, and so on. All these alliances have sometimes resulted into new cultural or disciplinary entities: subcurrents, sects, heresies, various schools or mini-schools of thought, philosophical clubs and societies, various intellectual fashions, or marginal ideological

groups. And the most fascinating thing about this whole situation is probably the fact that, pervading all these "alienations," alliances, and combinations, whether in a visible manner or in a more subtle way, there almost
always remains a distinct "Platonic" flavor, some ingredient that ultimately
reminds us of "the spirit of Plato's thought." Yet, the question is: what is
precisely the essence of this "Platonic spirit"? What is it that makes something (some school of thought or just some intellectual fashion) "Platonic"?
What is ultimately "Platonism" in this broad sense?

Due to its excellent synthetic qualities, I have chosen to borrow this description of the "Platonic spirit" from Andrew Louth:

> It is fundamental to Platonism, in virtually any guise, that this world, the
> world we perceive through the senses and about which we hold a variety of
> opinions, is not the real world. This world is a world of change, decay, and,
> for all of us, death; all of which bear the mark of unreality. The real world is
> changeless, incorruptible, a place of enduring life: it is, for Plato, the realm
> of the Forms. (Louth 1994: 54)

Platonism is, then, about a primordial duality, about an ontological gap between a realm of plenitude and perfection, of enlightenment and complete
understanding, on the one hand, and a realm of precariousness and imperfections, of ignorance and erroneousness, on the other. And being human is
precisely to dwell in this uncomfortable ontological space, and at the same
time to long to overcome the gap and gain access to the ultimate reality.

Another issue to recall before discussing the problem of the Platonic influences on Berkeley's thought is that of the specific Platonism-Christianity
relationship. Very early in the history of the Christian church there was a
sense that Christianity and Platonism had something essential in common,
making their "marriage," in a way, unavoidable. And this privileged relationship between the Platonic tradition and Christianity should play an important part in any discussion of the Platonic tradition within the European
context. For, as many scholars have noticed, of all ancient philosophical
schools, sects, and currents, it was probably Platonism that had the strongest
and most durable influence on the initial shaping and then on the development of Christian theology. A certain Platonic substance was poured into
Christian theology at the moment of its inception and then became an un-
distinguishable part of it. As (among other things) a moral philosophy, Platonism had always encouraged an emphasis on man's spiritual side, on the
noblest longings of man's soul; the Platonic philosophy had touched on a

region "where the clear air of the knowledge of God was attained by self-denial, subjugation of the flesh and the cultivation of the intellectual purity, and man's soul could rise above his baser nature" (Evans 1993: 25). Thanks precisely to its ascetic drives and to some of its basic metaphysical presuppositions, Plato's philosophy would be in a position to make ample room for Christ and give him a unique philosophical role to play: "Christ could be seen as the highest Reason, God's Wisdom" (ibid.). As Andrew Louth rightly observes, the story of the influence of Platonism on Christian theology "goes back at least to the second century of the Christian era, if not earlier, and became so pervasive that it is almost impossible to envisage Christian theology apart from its Platonic dress" (Louth 1994: 52). And the main reason this happened is simply that "Platonism and Christianity had so much in common." In terms of both doctrine and apologetics "Christian theologians soon came to look to Platonism for arguments with which to defend Christianity" (ibid.).[2] At the same time, Christian notions, attitudes, and beliefs influenced to an important degree the further development of Platonism itself—Dionysius the Areopagite, John Scotus Eriugena, Marcilio Ficino—the Cambridge Platonists being only the most notorious cases from this point of view. There was a mutual influence involved here: "the traffic between the Platonic tradition and Christianity was not all one way" (ibid: 59).[3]

This marriage between Platonism and Christianity was to put a clear imprint on the development of European thought. Calling Plato a "Christian before Christ" is to recognize a fundamental truth about the ultimate physiognomy of the European mind. Platonism helped the Christian faith acquire its doctrinal, theological identity, rooting it in an old and venerated school of philosophical thought, and subterraneously connecting it to the mystical traditions of ancient Greece, ancient Egypt, the Middle East, and beyond.

Seeing Berkeley as a Platonist

It was within this particular metaphysical, Christian-Platonic context that the rise of George Berkeley's philosophy took place. Yet, there is no agreement among the Berkeley scholars as to the exact extent to which Berkeley was a Platonist. Some scholars even deny that he was one at all. Before the second half of the twentieth century if Berkeley had sometimes been perceived as a Platonic thinker, this had only been with regard to his last work *Siris*, as the earlier works were not generally considered from a Platonic point of view. For instance, in his history *The Platonic Tradition in Anglo-Saxon Philosophy* John Muirhead, on the occasion of one of the very few mentions of Berkeley in the entire book, talks about how "the seed" of Platonism, replanted in Britain by the Cambridge Platonists, "failed to show above the ground except in the pale form of the later speculations of Bishop Berkeley" (Muirhead 1931: 13). Moreover, Paul Shorey even felt that "Berkeley's earlier writings are apparently at the opposite pole from Platonism" (Shorey 1938: 207). Until well into the twentieth century Berkeley's early philosophizing was in general still perceived in the strict context of the "new philosophy," and his thought unproblematically placed within the thematic, methodological, and programmatic repertoire of "British empiricism." For most of the scholars and philosophers of the first part of the twentieth century Berkeley was nothing more than a convenient bridge between Locke and Hume, a natural logical step in the development of British empiricism from the former to the latter.

During the last thirty years or so, however, several studies have been published dealing precisely with the presence in Berkeley's earlier writings of some specific topics that could be seen as belonging to the Platonic tradition.[4] The problem is that these topics are in general seen as isolated Platonic notions or patterns of thought only accidentally scattered in Berkeley's earlier work, and no systematic and sustained attempt has been made until recently to establish some "necessary connection," on the one hand, between these topics as they appear within the early Berkeleian writings and, on the other hand, between their presence in Berkeley's early writings and his avowed Platonism in *Siris*. It is true that Peter Wenz, for example, wrote some decades ago that "the neo-Platonism of the *Siris* should be viewed as compatible with, rather than as a reversal of both the empiricism and the attack upon abstract ideas present in the *Principles of Human Knowledge*," (Wenz 1976: 542) pointing explicitly to such a connection, but without following it up in detail, or considering it otherwise than in light of the archetypes—"abstract ideas" relationship. Subsequently, some other authors took over Wenz's insight. It was Stephen Daniel who, in a recent article (Daniel 2001), took a decisive step forward, proposing a systematic consideration of the *Principles* and the *Three Dialogues between Hylas and Philonous* in light of Berkeley's "Christian Neoplatonic metaphysics," and suggesting that "that metaphysics is already present in his early works" (ibid: 239–40).

In a certain sense, my approach here might well be seen as a continuation of Daniel's efforts to offer a Platonic reading of Berkeley's earlier philosophical writings. Nevertheless, I will try to move this discussion forward, by bringing forth new Platonic elements in Berkeley (for example, the likeness relationship between the human mind and the divine mind, or the topic of the *liber mundi*). Moreover, I will try to enlarge this discussion significantly by pointing to an entire network of Platonic topics, patterns of thought, and mind-sets in Berkeley's earlier works (a network within which the archetypes discussed by Daniel and others represent only one "knot" among others). However allusive, ambiguous, or vague these Platonic elements might seem, they form a coherent whole, which played a crucial part in shaping the essence of Berkeley's thought as he displayed it in his earlier philosophical writings. Finally, I will argue that once Berkeley started following this line of (Platonic) thought, the speculations in *Siris* were not only possible, but, in a way, unavoidable.[5]

In what follows I will outline some of the "knots" of this Platonic network.

PLATONISM IN BERKELEY'S EARLY PHILOSOPHICAL WRITINGS

The Likeness Relationship: The Human Mind—The Divine Mind

One of the central arguments employed by Berkeley in order to supply his immaterialist system with logical soundness, metaphysical depth, and eventually with a serious means of refuting any accusations of solipsism is that the existence of sensible things is based in the last instance on their being continually perceived (conceived of) by God, or—in other words—on their being in God's mind. Simply stating that *esse* is *percipi* is not enough; an essential addition is required: perceived not only by us, but also (and more importantly) by God. We perceive things in the world and this fact makes them existent, existent *to us*. Yet, outside us, in our absence, before our birth, and after our death, or when we are not awake, things must be, so to speak, "cared for" by some infinite, uninterruptedly active spirit, that is, God:

> sensible things cannot exist otherwise than in a mind or spirit. Whence I conclude, not that they have no real existence, but that seeing they depend not on my thought, and have an existence distinct from being perceived by me, *there must be some other mind wherein they exist.* As sure therefore as the sensible world really exists, so sure is there an infinite omnipresent spirit who contains and supports it. (Berkeley 1948–57, 2:212 [*Three Dialogues*])

As it were, as far as we human beings are concerned, things exist only insofar as we perceive them, according to our limited faculties, and—in some sense—"for our own sake," but as far as things themselves are concerned, they must necessarily be thought of by an infinite mind, according to its infinite powers, and for their own sake. Their ontological completeness is assured only by their being perceived by the divine mind. To put it slightly differently, in order for things to exist objectively and autonomously God's existence and workings are necessary. God is what gives things a stable ontological status and makes them truly real "things" (*rei*). In a similar passage, Berkeley stresses that when

> I deny sensible things an existence out of the mind, I do not mean my mind in particular, but all minds. Now it is plain that they have an existence exterior to my mind, since I find them by experience to be independent of it. There is therefore some other mind wherein they exist, during the intervals between the times of my perceiving them. . . . And as the same is true, with regard to all other finite created spirits; it necessarily follows, there is an *omnipresent eternal Mind*, which knows, and comprehends all things, and exhibits them to our view in such a manner, and according to such rules as he himself hath ordained, and are by us termed the *Laws of Nature*. (Ibid: 230–31)

The most important fact to notice here is that the underlying supposition behind Berkeley's line of argumentation is that there is a fundamental likeness and a similarity of function between the human mind and the divine mind, that in this process of "realization" of things the human mind and the divine mind perform in essence the same function. True, the human mind is endowed only with limited powers, has a limited scope, and is deeply marked by a character of dependence and finitude. Yet—despite all its imperfections—in Berkeley we encounter a fact that will never be overemphasized, namely, that *the human mind performs exactly the same act as the divine mind actually does*: perceives, or conceives of, objects, thus (according to Berkeley's immaterialism) conferring upon them existence and intelligibility, and ultimately rendering them real. Even if on a much more reduced scale, the human mind mirrors the activity of the divine one: it faithfully reflects, according to its powers and complexity, the processes of "realization" of things that take place in the divine mind. The question is, of course: why this similarity of function? What made Berkeley postulate this similarity? What is the source of this line of thought?

In light of the fact that Berkeley saw philosophy as having preeminently religious and apologetic[6] functions and objectives,[7] and considering the entire theological background against which his thought emerged, as well as Berkeley's own formation as a churchman, I propose here the hypothesis that this notion of a fundamental "similarity of function" between the human mind and the divine mind has to be considered in direct connection with a certain biblical insight, that we come across in the book of Genesis (1:26, 27): namely, it is the notion that God made us in his "image and likeness," that he created us *like* him: "And God said, Let us make man in our own image, after our likeness. . . . So God created man in his own image, in the image of God created he him." Simple and unproblematic as it might seem to some at a first sight, this theological notion supplied Berkeley with an ingenious and elegant model on which he molded his complex philosophical argumentation about the similarity of function between the mind of God and that of man. Needless to say, our being made "in God's image" is too complex a theological issue to be satisfactorily treated, even *en passant*, in this chapter, but all I am concerned with is to point to a possible theological (extraphilosophical) source of Berkeley's argument. Even in terms of personal background and biographical formation, there are enough reasons to believe that this is a reasonable hypothesis to advance: Berkeley was formed as a theologian, he served as a bishop of the Anglican Church, and throughout his life he considered that what he was doing must serve faith and theology to the highest degree, to the point that that he conceived of his chief mission as a philosopher as to "utterly destroy" atheism and free-thinking. Therefore, that he borrowed a theological notion on which to build one of his central arguments seems quite plausible.

As such, in virtue of the fundamental fact that we are made "in God's image," our mind, through all its processes and working patterns, must remind us of what happens in God's mind. According to this line of thought, by carefully examining ourselves we might analogously get a glimpse of what the divine world is like. True, although God created man "in his image and likeness," due to several causes, "the image of God in us" (*imago Dei in nobis*), as the medieval writers used to put it, has become corrupted and unclear. "The image of God in us" is always in danger of being tainted by our sinfulness and error, in other words, by our tendency to forget in whose image we are actually made. St. Anselm, among many others, expressed with excellent poetic force the deep anxiety caused in him by the realization of this fact and the longing for an inner renewal and for spiritual rebirth:

> Lord, I acknowledge that I thank thee that thou hast created me in this thine image, in order that I may be mindful of thee; but that image has been so consumed and wasted away by vices, and obscured by the smoke of wrong doing, that it cannot achieve that for which it was made, except thou renew it, and create it anew. (Anselm 1962, 6 [*Proslogion*])

Nevertheless, the fact remains that, despite all its imperfections, errors, and bad inclinations, the human mind still bears on itself the mark of God, the original imprint of its creator. This is to say that, thanks precisely to such a mark, by the sheer fact of being human we have the capacity of overcoming the distance, however huge this might be, that separates us from God: "immediately after the soul is born from God, it turns toward him as its parent by a certain natural instinct, just as a fire created on earth by the power of higher things is immediately directed toward the higher things by an impulse of nature. Having turned toward Him, the soul is illuminated by his rays" (Ficino 1985: 75).

As far as Berkeley's philosophy is concerned, this divine mark impressed upon the human mind by God at the moment of creation manifests itself precisely through the fact that the human mind functions as a God *en miniature*. The notion that, within Berkeley's system, the human mind perceives things and thus renders them existent (*esse est percipi*) does nothing but precisely confirm that it is indeed created "in the image of God," and "after his likeness," insofar as, according to Berkeley, the supreme mission of God himself—the main reason for his existence, so to speak—is to do exactly the same thing, namely, to perceive things and thus render them existent: "Men commonly believe that all things are known or perceived by God, because they believe the being of a God, whereas I on the other side, immediately and necessarily conclude the being of a God, because all sensible things must be perceived by Him" (Berkeley 1948–57, 2:212 [*Three Dialogues*]).

At the same time, this privileged relationship between the human mind and the divine one is a crucially important topic in Platonism. We touch here on one of those points where ancient Greek philosophy turns out to be extremely closely connected to, or intertwined with, some of the theological ideas coming to us from the biblical tradition. As in the Judaic-Christian *Weltanschauung*, within a Platonic context the two terms are not at all indifferent to each other, but there is a permanent dramatic drive, on the human side, toward the divine realities, an unstoppable longing for the realm of ontological plenitude and ultimate happiness that is the unique feature of God's world. And this longing is structurally possible precisely by virtue of the above-mentioned "ontological" likeness between the human and the divine. A central doctrine in Platonism is clustered around the belief in "a world of higher realities, beyond the fallible realm of sense-perception; the belief that the soul belongs to that higher world and can find its way back there" (Sheppard 1994: 17–18). The human mind, through all its endeavours, efforts, and undertakings, permanently looks for its divine origin

as a place of transfiguration and redemption, as a place where it can fulfil all its potential. This dynamic drive is, according to the Platonic view, embedded in the deepest structures of the soul as one of its defining characteristics. To live a "good life" means precisely to let oneself be guided by this innate drive of the soul toward the realm of ideas.

What makes one particularly well prepared for the encounter with the realm of unchanging realities is dying a "good death." In Platonism the experience of death is a central metaphysical experience: death is above all seen as an initiation and as a great beginning, not at all as a loss or an absolute end. If death is the end of something, it is only the end of an existence marked by decay and precariousness, an impoverished existence during which the soul is always tainted, to the point of embarrassment, by its proximity with the body. Owing to the same proximity, the mind is always short-sighted and dependent on senses. Only in death can our soul get rid of all the imperfections brought about by our existence as embodied creatures and meet its divine model. For instance, in *Phaedo*, Plato has Socrates imply that his being ready (and happy) to die is in fact a required part of an ampler scenario of redemption, a scenario at the end of which the human mind/soul is to encounter and find rest in its divine counterpart:

> there is good hope that on arriving where I am going, if anywhere, I shall acquire what has been our chief preoccupation in our past life, so that the journey that is now ordered for me is full of good hope, as it is also for any other man who believes that his mind has been prepared and, as it were, purified. (Plato 1997: 58 [*Phaedo* 67b–c])

This is why philosophy, as the supreme form of spiritual achievement, comes to be seen in the Platonic tradition as a "training for death" (ibid. [*Phaedo* 81a]), death thus meaning a fundamental initiatory experience by means of which the ultimate truths are completely revealed to the human mind, the latter coming to see its divine counterpart "face to face" (*facie ad faciem*), as St. Paul would later say. In other words, "the soul's gaining the spiritual world is experienced as a homecoming (*nostos*)" (Louth 1994: 54). In a smooth continuation with Plato's meditations in *Phaedo*, Plotinus would famously claim later that "our fatherland is whence we have come, and there is the Father" (Plotinus 1966–88 [*Enneads* I.6.8.21]). In this way, philosophy comes to be nothing else but a sophisticated *ars moriendi*, and this will become a distinctive feature of the Christian-Platonic philosophy of all times. St. Augustine (1963 [*Confessions* 10]) faithfully echoes Plotinus when exclaiming in this much quoted passage: "Thou hast made us for Thyself,

O Lord, and our heart is unquiet until its rests in Thee" (Fecisti nos ad te, Domine, et inquietum est cor nostrum donec requiescat in te). As such, in the Platonic system, endeavouring to get beyond all that the sensible world gives us, in order to comprehend as much as we can of the intelligible realities (in the hope of a final "rejoining" with them), is the most important task of one's mind throughout one's lifetime. This drive toward the divine is in fact what ultimately defines us as human beings, and what gives meaning to our lives, making them worth living: "an eternal love by which the soul is always drawn toward God brings it about that the soul always enjoys God as a new spectacle. The same Goodness of God that also makes the lover blessed always kindles this love in the soul" (Ficino 1985: 80).

This is not, of course, an easy task: a common concern among Platonists was that "the human condition is a perpetual struggle between a debasing materialism and an elevating spirituality" (Evans 1993: 95). Nevertheless, it is only through this difficult struggle that we can free ourselves from the "prison of the body" and of the material world in general, and through which we can reach what is most appropriate to us. And the "place" where human reason can most properly be said to be "at home" is only where Reason resides. Hence the prevalence, within the Platonic-Christian tradition, of the ideal of "reason transfigured, able to see clearly the supreme Reason which is its pattern and to enjoy purely intellectual joys untainted by the urgencies of the demands of the flesh" (ibid: 95). Therefore, to be "at home" for our mind means coming to rest in Christ as the Reason (*Logos*) of the world. The individual reason returns and dissolves into the divine Reason, thus reaching such a stage that it almost does not imitate its processes anymore, but becomes one with it, "flesh and blood" of it.

In view of these brief considerations, Berkeley's account of the relationship between the divine mind and its human counterpart acquires, it is hoped, a more complete understanding, and a more appropriate contextualization. For his argument was not at all a piece of brilliant sophistry, or just some philosophical device ingeniously employed in order to dismiss accusations of solipsism, but—when using such an argument—Berkeley actually followed an ancient and consecrated pattern of thought. This was a pattern whose feasibility and strength had already been tested by a long tradition of Platonists and Christian thinkers who took basically the same view as Berkeley: a view according to which the human mind actually functions as some *speculum Dei*, as a living mirror of God. And it is precisely this function that gives the mind ("the Candle of the Lord" in us, to use Benjamin Wichcote's phrase) a very special character, transforming it into a privileged realm. Our perceiving of things, in the very special sense that the word "perception" has in Berkeley, is our profoundest way of "imitating" God. Made as we are in "His image" and "after His likeness" we faithfully reproduce, *en miniature*, the divine process through which the world comes into being.[8] Thus, Berkeley's philosophy seems to hide theological gems never accounted for yet.

The Archetypes

Yet, the sheer assertion of God's mind as a "place" where things exist is not enough: there must be some immediate *modality* through which God's mind can perceive objects, or—in other words—a means by which objects exist in the divine mind. Hence the introduction of the ancient notion of archetypes. In the Christian-Platonic tradition archetypes are plastically defined as the "thoughts of God" or "the thoughts occupying God's mind" (pensées dans l'intellect d'un dieu suprême [Dillon 1997: 107]). They form an ideal order of things, an ideal version of what we see in the sensible world. Actually, the sensible world is made possible precisley by the fact that the archetypes of sensible things exist in the divine mind. As the Renaissance Platonist Giovanni Pico della Mirandola put it, God

> produced everything, because in that Mind He produced the Ideas and Forms of all things. There is, therefore, in that Mind the Idea of the sun, the Idea of the moon, of men, of all the animals, of the plants, of the stones, of the elements, and in general of all things. The Idea of the sun being a truer sun than the sensible one, and so on, it follows not only that God has produced all things, but also that He has produced them with the truest and most perfect being that they can have, that is, ideal and intelligible being. (Pico della Mirandola 1986: 16)

In his article on the archetypes in Berkeley published in 1976, Peter Wenz writes that: "there is good reason to believe that Berkeley was . . . a Christian neo-Platonist, one who holds the view that abstract ideas exist in the mind of God and that the world was created by God using these ideas as models or archetypes" (Wenz 1976: 537). Even if there are still some problematic aspects in this identification, in the sense that Berkeley's attack upon abstract ideas might be seen as an attack against the divine abstract ideas as well,[9] and even if Berkeley's immaterialism does not fit in absolutely every detail into the traditional pattern of using the notion of archetypes, it could be however shown that the existence and function of the archetypes (a Platonic topic *par excellence*) is crucially important in Berkeley's thought, as well as for understanding the development of his philosophy from his early writings through *Siris*. As a matter of fact, the employment of the notion of archetype is simply necessary and unavoidable for accounting for the way in which God's mind comprehends and makes intelligible the things in the world. It is not enough to say that "things exist in God's mind": an account of *how* they do so is also required. As Steven Daniel clearly pointed out, "if God's perception of things is . . . Berkeley's way to avoid the solipsistic implications of his doctrine that to be is to be perceived, then it would seem that his theory of divine ideas or archetypes would be at the heart of his idealistic immaterialism" (Daniel 2001: 247).

Although the role of the archetypes is crucial to Berkeley's immaterialist system, as they supply it with a relatively nonproblematic—and, we should say, time-honored—means of making things exist in the divine intellect, Berkeley did not in his earlier writings pay a proportionate attention to the theory of archetypes as such. He frequently used the term, but did not seem to rely upon the archetypes theory as much as one could expect. For example, in the *Principles of Human Knowledge* he says:

> whoever shall reflect, and take care to understand what he says, will . . . acknowledge that all sensible qualities are alike *sensations* and alike *real*; that where the extension is, there is the colour, too, to wit, in his mind, and that their archetypes can exist only in some other *mind*. (Berkeley 1948–57: 2:84)

In the *Three Dialogues between Hylas and Philonous* the notion of archetypes is systematically and thoroughly employed, but at the same time one often feels a certain hesitation on Berkeley's side between talking about the perceivable "things" (that is, "ideas") and "their archetypes." For example: "no idea or archetype of an idea can exist otherwise than in a mind" (ibid.: 212–13). Or, in another passage:

> the things I perceive must have an existence, they or their archetypes, out of my mind: but being ideas, neither they nor their archetypes, can exist otherwise than in an understanding: there is therefore an understanding. But will and understanding constitute in the strictest sense a mind or spirit. (Ibid.: 235)

Nevertheless, for all this hesitation, the logical context within which Berkeley employs the notion of archetype is the same as that in which archetypes were employed in traditional Platonism, which is to say, archetypes exist in God's mind, being the favorite divine way of comprehending the created world, in other words, they are "the thoughts of God":

the things I perceive are my own ideas, and . . . no idea can exist unless it be in a mind. Nor is it less plain that these ideas or things by me perceived, either themselves or their archetypes, exist independently of my mind, since I know myself not to be their author, it being out of my power to determine at pleasure, what particular ideas I shall be affected with upon opening my eyes or ears. They must therefore exist in some other mind, whose will it is they should be exhibited to me. (Ibid: 214–15)

Finally, in a (much-quoted and discussed) letter to Samuel Johnson, dated March 24, 1730, that is, some twenty years after Berkeley published his first works, Berkeley comes to openly admit that:

I have no objection against calling the ideas in the mind of God archetypes of yours. But I object against those archetypes by philosophers supposed to be real things, and to have an absolute rational existence distinct from their being perceived by any mind whatsoever. (Ibid.: 292)

This statement is of greatest importance as it allows us to realize that Berkeley was much against the use of the term "archetype" with a Lockean meaning, that is, against "archetype" as referring simply to an external object, to a "real thing," whose mental image (or idea) is reflected in our mind, and which can be said to be the "model," "original" or "archetype," on which that image is molded. Given the then-prevailing influence of the Lockean opinions and language among intellectual and philosophical circles, this explains Berkeley's hesitation and why he was so reluctant to use the term "archetype," yet did not reject it completely. On the one hand, Berkeley was undoubtedly inclined to resort to the term for its metaphysical implications and the problems its employment would have solved in his own philosophy. On the other hand, he was aware that "archetype" still had Lockean connotations he did not want to take aboard. This is exactly what commentators have noticed about the issue in question. T. E. Jessop, for example, says: "On archetypes not as supposed corporeal originals of mental copies but as models in the divine intellect, Berkeley seems to have had an open mind" (Jessop 1949a: 78 n. 1). As it is in general the case with those philosophers who want to assert themselves against a certain intellectual milieu and find their own irreducible way among their contemporaries, Berkeley had to solve a number of terminological problems and had a difficult time before succeeding to create and launch his own philosophical vocabulary.

A very important, not to say decisive, step forward, as far as the employment of the Platonic notion of archetypes is concerned, is taken when

Berkeley, in *Three Dialogues between Hylas and Philonous*, comes to recognize openly that: "I am not for changing things into ideas, but rather ideas into things" (Berkeley 1948–57, 2:244). In other words, things are for Berkeley reified ideas, ideas turned into embodied entities. To put it differently, things exist only insofar as they are the expressions of a higher order of reality—that is, the order of ideas. In a remarkably precise manner, this Berkeleian statement virtually contains, or summarizes, one of the fundamental principles guiding virtually every Platonic school of thought: namely, that this sensible world that we see around is but a reflection of a world of ideas, or archetypes, and that all things in "this world" are—in a sense—but some sort of "embodied ideas," "terrestrial" shades of a higher, "celestial" ontological order. And in the process of bringing things into being it is God who plays the decisive part. Thanks to his intervention, a process of "reflection," or "emanation," or "generation," takes place, a process through which things in "this world" appear as more or less faithful "copies" of the archetypes: "God is the supreme soul, the Mind which knows the intelligible objects but whose function is to create the sensible world in terms of the intelligible model furnished to it by the Ideas" (Feibleman 1971: 28). The world, then, becomes in a way the spectacular "unfolding" of God's thought, a generous, never-ending dissipation of God into his outside, into what is not God. From this vantage point, Berkeley's own understanding of the role of God, and of the use God makes of the archetypes, appears, once again, strikingly similar to that of the traditional Platonism:

> All objects are eternally known by God, or which is the same thing, have an eternal existence in his mind: but when things before imperceptible to creatures, are by a decree of God, made perceptible to them; then are they said to begin a relative existence, with respect to created minds. (Berkeley 1948–57, 2:252 [*Three Dialogues*])

This passage casts an excellent light on Berkeley's usage of the notion of archetypes, and their role in "producing" the sensible world. "All objects" means here of course the archetypes, the "models" of the physical entities we come across in the sensible world around: they have an eternal existence in the mind of God, and only at some point in time, by a decree of God they cause another order of reality to exist—it is, presumably, the primordial event about which we read about in the book of Genesis. This is an order of reality "relative" to our perceiving faculties, dependent on our mind: it exists only insofar as we perceive it. Now, what we do in the course of our encounter with the world is precisely a reconstruction, from our point of view, of the process through which God *in illo tempore* instituted things simply by thinking them: we perceive things and thus render them existent. And by so doing, we can safely be said to be reproducing, even if on a smaller scale, *en miniature*, as it were, the divine process. In other words, in Berkeley's view, we as living beings are always in "God's footsteps." On a longer term, the mission of the Berkeleian subject is to fight permanently the veil of various prejudices, errors, and false images that we mistakenly tend to consider as being the world. Ideally, the Berkeleian subject renews the world every day, in every second, giving it back that virginal flavor that God gave it at the moment of creation. Branka Arsić, touching on this aspect, sees the aim of Berkeley's philosophy simply as "the restoration of everything to the state of an absolutely 'objective' perception, which is the perceived, the restoration of everything to a state of 'virginal' consciousness. . . . Everything is restored to a state without disguises or masquerades, a state of complete nakedness, complete visibility" (Arsić 2003: 131–32).

This being said, it will not be surprising that John Dillon, in a comparative study on Plotinus and Berkeley, comes to conclude that in his using the very term "idea" Berkeley was under a strong Platonic influence, borrowing its meaning precisely from Plotinus: "En se servant du term 'idée,' Berkeley est soumis à l'influence de l'usage du mot grec *idéa* chez Plotin, et dans la tradition du platonisme disponible à Berkeley, il allait de soi que ces *idéai* étaient des pensées dans l'intellect d'un dieu suprême" (Dillon 1997: 107). As a matter of fact, it should be said that, once embarked on his ambitious project of understanding the world as some form of "unfolding" of God, Berkeley could not avoid doing so: thanks to their elegant functionality and explicative virtues, in a way he had to accept the archetypes, along with all the Platonic philosophizing clustered over the centuries around them.

Moreover, there are, in Dillon's view, some other similarities that could be found between Plotinus's idealism and Berkeley's. For instance, within the context of a Platonic theory of archetypes, there must be some individualized modality through which the divine archetypes come to be effective in terms of bringing the sensible things into existence. Plotinus sees the sensible things as been "radiated," or "issued," in some hierarchical fashion, from the One, the supreme metaphysical reality:

All things which exist, as long as they remain in being, necessarily produce from their own substances, in dependence of their present power, a surrounding reality directed to what is outside them, a kind of image of the archetypes from which it was produced: fire produces the heat which comes from it; snow does not only keep its cold inside itself. Perfumed things show this particularly clearly. As long as they exist, something is diffused from themselves around them, and what is near them enjoys their existence. (Plotinus 1966–88 [*Enneads* 5.1.6.27–40)

Even if it would be only in *Siris* that Berkeley would take over, almost literally, Plotinus's way of thinking, incorporating it into the texture of his own cosmology and making an extensive use of it, at this stage (that is, when writing the *Three Dialogues*) Berkeley could be said to be working within a conceptual and thematic repertoire very close to Plotinus's own metaphysical repertoire. Even in the *Three Dialogues between Hylas and Philonous* Berkeley sees the world as being in some way the result of a superabundance of God, of an ever-flowing divine grace:

> *there is a mind which affects me every moment with all the sensible impressions I perceive.* And from the variety, order, and manner of these, I conclude the Author of them to be *wise, powerful, and good, beyond comprehension.* . . . the things by me perceived are known by the understanding, and produced by the will, of an infinite spirit. (Berkeley 1948–57: 2:215)

God is not at all a quiet presence in Berkeley's world, but he continuously and actively reveals himself to our understanding. To put it otherwise, in Berkeley, God constantly assaults us with his sonorous presence. We simply cannot help noticing God; it is enough to just open our eyes and the obviousness of his existence and benevolence will overwhelm us. Berkeley's world is not a cold, unfriendly place; it is a warm and smiling realm, born out of a divine embrace. As such, above all other similarities one might come across in Berkeley and Plotinus, there is this one that makes their philosophies so strikingly akin. Namely, in Dillon's words,

> the point where the two philosophers meet and seem to enlighten one another . . . is their total opposition toward any theory that would create a gap [insérer une différence] between what is given to our senses and that substance beyond them (Dillon 1997: 107).

In both Plotinus and Berkeley what we immediately encounter in the world is the direct overwhelming effect of a generous divinity. There is no place, in either of these two philosophies, for intermediary substances, for sources of alienation, useless digressions, or other things to divert us from our true mission in this world, which is, finding our way back to the unchanging divine realities.

"The Two Worlds"

An immediate logical consequence of the theory that there are archetypes in the mind of God is the idea that there are two worlds: by nature, the world of archetypes (*kosmos noetos*) necessarily presupposes the existence of a world of sensible "copies" (*kosmos aisthetos*), of entities made in the archetypes' image, existing as mere "earthly" imitations of the "celestial" models. "This world, therefore, is produced by that Mind in the image of the intelligible world produced in itself by the first Father" (Pico della Mirandola 1986: 22). A theory of archetypes is thus based on "the recognition of an unseen world of unchanging reality behind the flux of phenomena, a spiritual universe compared with which the world of appearance grew pale and unsubstantial and became only a symbol or even an illusion" (Inge 1926: 7–8). This is another doctrine professed by virtually all Platonic schools, whether ancient or modern, a doctrine with important consequences not only for metaphysics, but also in anthropological and soteriological terms. It is one of those points that make Plato, as it has been said, "the paradigmatic representative of a perennial, 'other worldly' tendency which has never ceased to attract or repel, the emotions as much as the intellect" (Cooper 1996: 107). In light of this twofold state of reality, human beings are now to be defined by their dual nature:[10]

> We human beings belong to both worlds: clearly to this world (which is why we call it *this* world), but in virtue of our possessing (or strictly: being) a soul (strictly: an intellect, *nous*), we belong to the spiritual world. For Plato the whole point of philosophy is to secure our passage to the spiritual world: philosophy is "practising death," *melete thanatou* (*Phaedo* 81a), for death is the separation of the soul from the body. (Louth 1994: 54)

The purpose of all serious philosophical (and, in general, intellectual) undertaking should be, in a Platonic context, precisely the deciphering and understanding of what lies behind the misleading multiplicity of things, in the hope of finding out their eternal "patterns" or "forms." Obviously, our immediate knowledge of the external world is necessarily a knowledge of sensible "copies," it being impossible for it to be otherwise, but the most important thing about this process of knowledge is to understand the true nature of things, to go beyond what is given to us as sensible, and not to mistake the "copies" for their "archetypes." This is sometimes a difficult job because, as has been noted, although the copies "lack the perfection of the Form they are nevertheless regarded as 'imitating' the Form; they are like it even though they fall short of it" (Sheppard 1994: 6). That means that a proper knowledge of the world presupposes, on the Platonic knower's side, an acute awareness of the specific ontological "weight" of each class of things that her mind is concerned with at every given moment. The Platonic knower must at all times show discernment and an increased capacity to distinguish copies from their models, the fake from the genuine, and in general to always know where precisely "this world" ends and where "the other world" starts. Finally, the Platonic knower is an expert practitioner of hermeneutics: she always knows to distinguish the sign from the signified, the symbol from the symbolized, and so on.

Let me also observe, in passing, that, under the massive influence of a Platonizing St. Augustine, this representation of how our knowledge of the world is constituted was to become one of the most widespread notions in the philosophy of the Middle Ages before the rediscovery of Aristotelianism. Important and influential medieval thinkers saw the production of our knowledge of the external world as a progressive and liberating ascension from the sensible level of things to their intelligible source—namely, God, truly the only reality toward which we should always direct our epistemic exercises and intellectual efforts. Coming to know the world meant for them the elaborate ascension of the *scala entis*, from its lowest level to the highest, a progressive mystical movement from the gross engagements with "this world" toward the divine ecstasies occasioned by dwelling in the other:

> Medieval versions of Augustine's account of a progression from sense-perception by way of image-making and abstraction to a truly spiritual and rational encounter with the mind of God are to be found in, for instance, Anselm's *Monologium* and Bonaventure's *Itinerarium Mentis in Deum*; but the notion is widely diffused in many authors. (Evans 1993: 38)

It is this doctrine postulating the existence of two worlds that Berkeley readily admits. As a matter of fact, he could not have done otherwise as this notion was one of the logical results of the very principles on which his whole approach had been based. In *Three Dialogues between Hylas and Philonous*, his mouthpiece, Philonous comes to ask rhetorically

> do I not acknowledge a twofold state of things, the one ectypal or natural, the other archetypal and eternal? The former was created in time; the latter existed from everlasting in the mind of God. Is not this agreeable to the common notion of divines? or is any more than this necessary in order to conceive the Creation? (Berkeley 1948–57, 2:254 [*Three Dialogues*])

In other words, insofar as things are perceived *by us* they are ideas, "second-hand" realities, "imitations," whereas insofar as they are comprehended *by God* they are archetypes, eternal models upon which, and in whose image, sensible things are made.

More than that, in *Alciphron*, written some twenty years later, Berkeley would express views not only consonant with what he said in his early writings, but also Platonic in a much deeper and more far-reaching sense. The fundamental metaphysical attitude betrayed by a passage like the following one is likely to be found in any important writing of the Platonic tradition: "To me it seems the man can see neither deep nor far who is not sensible of his own misery, sinfulness, and dependence; who doth not perceive that this present world is not designed or adapted to make rational souls happy." (Berkeley 1948–57, 3:178). In a sense, it is this kind of existential anxiety and feeling of fundamental discomfort that confers upon Berkeley's thought an even stronger Platonic flavor; in passages like this, one comes to taste the "Platonic flavor" at its most authentic. In other words, whereas in his earlier writings, Berkeley's Platonism was rather theoretical, conceived of just as a sophisticated system of metaphysical notions by means of which he explained the existence and nature of things, in *Alciphron* Berkeley went as far as to allow himself to express some of the specific anxieties and existential attitudes typically accompanying a Platonic way of "feeling" the world.

Granted, there is a certain ambiguity in Berkeley's doctrine of the "twofold state of things," which gives rise to a tension between his own views and the mainstream Platonic views of "the two worlds." This ambiguity originates in his radical denial of the existence of matter. Plato himself allowed matter (*hule*) some sort of existence, even if a problematic, inferior, and obscure one, and so did many Platonists after him, even though some others, Plotinus included, took a view closer to Berkeley's.[11] Berkeley instead did not admit any form of material existence and reduced the traditional Platonic opposition between "the two worlds," one of ideas and the other of physical objects, to an opposition (somehow less dramatic than Plato's) between a realm of archetypes, existing in God's mind, and a realm of sensible objects, occasioned by our perceiving God's archetypes. In this respect, as John Dillon suggests, Berkeley is even more radical than Plotinus:

> For Berkeley, even more than for Plotinus, the external world of the physical objects . . . poses a threat. For him, if we admit the existence of a layer of inferior matter [une couche matérielle inférieure], something possessing primary and secondary qualities, . . . that would defy God's omnipotence and

providence These Lockean material objects would be extramental entities
that would exist in spite of their perception by a mind [en dépit de la con-
naissance de quelque esprit]. They would be entities whose existence would
be completely independent of the mind—even of God' s mind. (Dillon
1997: 100–1)

On the other hand, it should be added that such an ambiguity, or difficulty,
is to be found not only in Berkeley's philosophy. It probably derives from
what Andrew Louth calls the "unresolved problem for Christian Platonism." When God occupies so important a place within a system of thought,
when—according to the most fundamental principles on which such a system is based—God permeates everything and it is only God that renders the
whole of reality intelligible (as God does both in Berkeley and in the Christian Platonists referred to by Louth), then it becomes difficult indeed to find
some proper room for the existence of such a grossly undivine thing as matter, or, for that matter, of any bodily reality. There is a certain sense in
which, in these systems, under the pressure of an invading divine presence
matter tends somehow to "dematerialize" itself.

"The Book of the World"

However dramatic the gap between "the two worlds" might appear in traditional Platonism, there are nevertheless ways of bridging it.[12] One of them
consists, to put it very schematically, in considering the immediately visible
reality ("this world") as an ample system of signs, or symbols, by means of
which God communicates with us, keeping a living relationship with his
creatures and informing them about himself, about his character, his nature,
and his workings. Even if Plato himself did not use the topic as such, in the
Middle Ages the Christian Platonists resorted to a large extent to the topic
in the form of the metaphor of the "book of nature" or "book of the
world" (*liber naturae* or *liber mundi*). As A. E. Taylor has pointed out, behind
the Christian-Platonic usage of this metaphor there was the idea that nature
"is only half-real," and that it pointed to the existence of a "further reality
which lies beyond itself." Nature is "a system of symbols," and our ascension to the ultimate reality takes place as a result of "learning to pass from
the symbols to the non-sensuous realities symbolized" (Taylor 1963: 41–42).
Knowing the world is essentially a process of reading, or, more generally
speaking, of interpretation. We live in the midst of a living book, and in this
book, if careful enough, we can find everything that God wants to let us
know. St. Bonaventure, for example, says that "the creature of the world is

like a book in which the creative Trinity is reflected, represented, and written" (Creatura mundi est quasi quidam liber, in quo relucet, repraesentatur et legitur Trinitas fabricatrix) [*Breviloquium* 2.12]). As we can easily see, the physical world is, so to speak, "redeemed" in the Christian Platonism, being radically transformed into something meaningful to the greatest extent.

It is precisely to this ancient topic of the "book of the world" that George Berkeley resorts most frequently. In the shape of a "divine language," or of an "optic language," Berkeley employs the topic in almost all his important philosophical writings and considers it as properly expressing the essence of his philosophy. In his first philosophical writing, *An Essay towards a New Theory of Vision* (1709), he says that

> the proper objects of vision constitute an universal language of the Author of Nature, whereby we are instructed how to regulate our actions in order to attain those things that are necessary to the preservation and well-being of our bodies, as also to avoid whatever may be hurtful and destructive of them. It is by their information that we are principally guided in all the transactions and concerns of life. (Berkeley 1948–57, 1:231)

Then, in *The Principles of Human Knowledge*, Berkeley talks, in a manner clearly reminding us of the medieval authors, of the proper mission of the philosopher when he is to approach the natural world:

> it is the searching after, and endeavoring to understand those signs instituted by the Author of Nature, that ought to be the employment of the natural philosopher, and not the pretending to explain things by corporeal causes; which doctrine seems to have too much estranged the minds of men from that active principle, that supreme and wise spirit, in whom we live, move, and have our being. (Berkeley 1948–57, 2:69–70) [12]

For George Berkeley the world is thus a book ("an universal language") in a fundamental way, and not merely as a rhetorical device. For him "the whole system of Nature is a system of signs, a visual divine language, speaking to our minds of God" (Copleston 1993–94, 5:248). Berkeley clearly speaks of the existence of an author who has "written" or rather "spoken" the world ("the Author of Nature"), of the existence of an author/subject relationship between him and the world, as well as of the existence of a "reader" whose ultimate aim should be to transcend the "sign," which is the immediately visible world (*kosmos aisthetos*), to the "signified thing," which is the world of the divine archetypes (*kosmos noetos*).

2.   Philosophy as Palimpsest: Archetypal Knowledge in Siris

Although it is possible to talk of an entire network of Platonic notions, "traces," and mind-sets in Berkeley's early philosophical works, their Platonism might still be seen as veiled or somehow hidden behind the (non-Platonic) terminology, methodological preferences, and rhetorical protocols presupposed by the "new philosophy," whose promoter Berkeley was in the early stages of his philosophical career.[1] It is in Berkeley's last published work, Siris (1744), that one comes across the whole repertoire of topics, specific notions, and arguments, and the unmistakable "flavor" of the ancient Platonic style of philosophizing. In Siris Berkeley makes fully explicit and avows openly what in his early writings was sometimes only implicitly Platonic in character. Since Siris is the subject of another chapter in this book (chapter 4) and because the Platonism of Siris speaks for itself, I have decided to focus the following considerations on the literary form rather than the contents of Siris, in an attempt to find out the particular rhetorical procedures through which Berkeley sought to insert himself into the Platonic tradition. Therefore, the main questions that I will try to answer are the following: Is there a sense in which the literary form of this writing comes to betray per se certain Platonic suppositions or ways of thought? Are there specifically Platonic ways of producing, or generating, a philosophical text, some preferred patterns of textual construction that distinguish Platonism from other schools? In trying to answer these questions I have first to discuss in some detail a source-based way of understanding the nature and role of philosophy characterizing the Platonic tradition: namely, philosophy as a systematic attempt at recovering a primordial/immemorial wisdom, or, as I call it, *philosophy as palimpsest*. Then, I will seek to integrate Berkeley's Siris in this tradition.

The "Golden Age" of Plato

In terms of visible embodiments, an understanding of philosophy as a search for an immemorial wisdom manifests itself through texts whose production, as well as inner structure, presupposes necessarily the constant employment of, and reference to, other texts, which are older and supposedly more authoritative and more important. The metaphor of the "palimpsest" seems to me particularly helpful in this context since it suggests, with a certain degree of accuracy, the existence—within one and the same text—of a multileveled, multifaceted discourse, and the notion that, within a given philosophical text, it is possible to come across different fragments, or "strata," belonging to earlier authors or writings. A philosophical palimpsest is, then, a text whose economy requires the existence of, and constant reference to, other, earlier texts, regarded as vehicles of an ancient and authentic knowledge, as the venerated locus of truth. In the absence of these earlier texts, with the whole authoritative aura they bring forth, the palimpsest-text would simply lose its point of reference, and any claim to meaningfulness would be seriously undermined. The "author" of a palimpsest-text does not see himself as really producing or "writing" that text; properly speaking, he does not even see himself as an author, but—more humbly—merely as an interpreter, as a "transmitter" of an ancient tradition of thought to which nothing essential could be added by the present day's scholarship. He is not so much a producer of new knowledge as an archaeologist in search of the primordial knowledge, industriously tracing the roots of the present state of things to their beginnings in the remotest past. What lies behind this way of thinking? What are its origins and reasons? What are its deeper philosophical and historical presuppositions? Its inner mechanisms? To answer these questions, a brief survey of the Platonic tradition will prove, I believe, helpful.

Even a cursory look at Plato's dialogues reveals the perplexing fact that one of the most original and influential philosophers of all time frequently prefers to disguise himself, to resort to various masquerades: rather than simply asserting himself as an original thinker, with a distinct philosophical message, Plato appears, more often than not, to play the modest role of the mouthpiece for others. Not only does he attribute his main philosophical teachings to Socrates, but he often employs mysterious characters to which he attributes doctrines and myths that had supposedly been established a "very long time ago." He repeatedly appeals to figures of the past (real or legendary, Greek or foreign) as preservers, or conveyers, of a perennial wisdom, a wisdom of an almost celestial origin, and compared to which his own philosophy (or for that matter any other philosophy of his time) seem to be, as it were, a mere imitation. For example, Plato is fascinated with ancient (already in his time) Egypt, and, in several of his dialogues, he makes numerous enthusiastic references to the Egyptian world, resting some of his important philosophical claims on a supposedly Egyptian tradition of wisdom, on various Egyptian myths and "exemplary stories." In general, to our amazement—and, anyway, to some of his modern commentators' embarrassment—rather than simply following his own arguments and line of thought, Plato is very often willing to (playfully or not) mix ancient myths, sayings, and "exotic" stories with his own philosophical line of argumentation, and—more than that—he seems to value the employment of such procedures highly.

Most importantly, although this might be seen as a literary technique that brings about powerful rhetorical effects, such an approach to authorship is in Plato more than merely a rhetorical device, some technical subtlety employed for literary purposes only: this practice stems essentially from Plato's philosophy of history, from his specific way of considering the past, as he revealed it in some of his dialogues. Namely, it is the view that history is a process of decay and corruption, that the "best things" occurred sometime "at the beginning," and that, with the passing of time, things will necessarily get worse and worse, until another cosmic cycle starts anew. For Plato, history (historical time) is subject to an uninterrupted process of aging and deterioration. For instance, in the *Statesman*, he has the "Eleatic Stranger" speak at some point of a "Golden Age," of a time when everything was marked by a form of original perfection. The Stranger kindly invites the young Socrates to attend him in his efforts "to explain the origin of our traditions concerning man's life in that paradise":

> A god was their shepherd and had charge of them and fed them even as men now have charge of the other creatures inferior to them—for men are closer to the divine than they. When God was shepherd there were no political constitutions and no taking of wives and begetting of children. For all men rose up anew into life out of the earth. . . . they had fruits without stint from trees and bushes. . . . For the most part they disported themselves in the open needing neither clothing nor couch, for the seasons were blended evenly so as to work them no hurt. (Plato 1961: 1037 [*Statesman* 271e–272a])

What matters here, from the perspective of a history of philosophy seen as a palimpsest, is, of course, not so much the contents of the myth per se, with all their political implications, nor the specific narratives or anecdotes that the myth brings forth, but rather the sophisticated elements of philosophy of history that Plato smuggles into the texture of the *Statesman* with the aid of this myth. For it is precisely in this Platonic vision of history as marked by a primordial fall and then characterized by a continual decay that the notion of philosophy as an attempt at recovering a primordial, "paradisical" knowledge originated. Philosophy as palimpsest is precisely an understanding of philosophy as an effort to reverse (even if only mentally) the process of historical deterioration and decay, and to gain some form of access to how things were at the beginning, at the auroral moment when history was not yet born, and time had not yet started to grow old.

Certainly, the notion of history as a process of decay predated Plato. Not only was it present (or at least alluded to) in some pre-Socratic authors, but in fact, it carried with itself an entire system of mythical thought. And, in fact, as many scholars have observed, it must have been some of the patterns of this mythical thought that inspired Plato as they are easily recognizable in his philosophy. According to this mythical line of thought—characteristic not only to ancient Greece, but also to traditional societies in general—"at the beginning," there was a fundamental communion between gods and men, between heaven and earth, and only as a result of some traumatic cosmic disaster this communion was irremediably broken:

> *In illo tempore*, the gods descended to earth and mingled with men; for their part, men could easily mount to heaven. As a result of a ritual fault, communications between heaven and earth were interrupted and the gods withdrew to the highest heavens. Since then, men must work for their food and are no longer immortal. (Eliade 1971: 91)

What Plato did was precisely to develop this mythical insight into a coherent and sophisticated system of philosophy of history. Even though, thanks to his artistry as a narrator, Plato's version of the myth still bears some of the marks and flavors of the mythical world from which it came, he "translated" the mythical story into a cluster of meaningful philosophical statements and notions, thus establishing the basis for an entire tradition of thought in the field of the philosophy of history. In other words, he made the myth significant philosophically.

Very briefly, according to the myth narrated in the *Statesman*, humanity as we know it emerged as a result of some primordial disaster. The consequences of this catastrophic event are many:

> Bereft of the guardian care of the daemon who had governed and reared us up, we had become weak and helpless. . . . Men lacked all tools and all crafts

in the early years. The earth no longer supplied their food spontaneously and they did not yet know how to win it for themselves: in the absence of necessity they had never been made able to learn this. For all these reasons they were in direst straits. It was to meet this need that the gifts of the gods famous in ancient story were given, along with such teaching and instruction as was indispensable. Fire was the gift of Prometheus, the secrets of the crafts were made known by Hephaestus and his partner in craftsmanship, and seeds and plants were made known by other gods. (Plato 1961: 1039 [*Statesman* 274b–d])

One of the key points in this view of history is that the doctrines professed, as well as the ways of life recommended, by our remote ancestors were necessarily much better and more appropriate than ours, more genuine and fitted for the prosperity of human nature, precisely because the divine imprint on them was still relatively unaltered. This was the case especially before the cosmic disaster referred to by Plato, but even after that, humans were infinitely closer to gods (and to the godly wisdom) than we are today. Whether we realize it or not, time is never on our side, and forgetting is one of our worst enemies. If there is salvation for us, it does not await us somewhere in the future, but—on the contrary—we will have to find it in the remotest past. As such, the best thing for us to do is to try to resuscitate the teachings of that golden past as much as we can, and behave according to the rules established at a time when the memory of a happy communion between gods and men, between heaven and earth, was still fresh in humans. For there are reasons to believe that, as the Eleatic Stranger puts it, "the happiness of the men of that era" might have been "a thousandfold greater than ours" (ibid.: 1038 [272c]). It goes without saying that, as a direct result of all this, one constantly comes across a profound "conservatism" in Plato's thought, whether we consider his sociopolitical philosophy or, for example, his views on the role of poetry in society. At the same time, in view of the above considerations, it should be clear now that his philosophical "conservatism" is not a result of, say, his belonging to the aristocratic class, as several commentators have been inclined to believe, but, I would say, it is rather the other way around: he is conservative in politics because he is conservative and past-oriented in his metaphysical views.

After Plato

Some centuries after Plato, Plotinus—in a perfectly Platonic manner—claimed that what he was doing philosophically was nothing other than a commentary on Plato's philosophy: he insisted again and again that he was only a commentator on the philosophy of Plato, doing nothing more than to explain and clarify Plato's doctrines to his own disciples. However strange this might appear to us today, Plotinus conceived of his mission simply as a humble teacher of Platonic philosophy. In his *Enneads* the references to Plato are numerous and always highly appreciative: "We can scarcely do better . . . than follow Plato" (Plotinus 1966–88, 2 :86); or "We have to fall back on the illustrious Plato, who uttered many noble sayings about the Soul" (ibid., 4:357). As one commentator rightly remarked, "Plotinus would have been surprised at being thought of as the founder of a new school, Neo-Platonism. He considered himself a Platonist, pure and simple, without prefix or qualification—in other words, as an interpreter and follower of Plato." (Paul Henry in ibid.: 1:xxxvii). By doing so Plotinus proves that he learned perfectly the fundamental Platonic lesson about the wisdom that always dwells, not in the present, not in the future, but somewhere back in the past.

Then, as it happened, this sophisticated form of philosophical modesty ended up becoming one of the distinctive features of all subsequent Platonic movements. As a result, not only the authorities cited by Plato or Plotinus were venerated, but also Plato and Plotinus themselves, as well as other supposedly kindred figures, whether historical or fictitious (Moses, Zoroaster, Hermes Trismegistus, and so on). All of them were now seen as forming a "golden chain," linking the wisdom of the remote past to those living in the immediate present. They saw their own role within this chain as limited to simply conveying the received knowledge to their audiences, in an effort to make sure that this knowledge was in no way altered or corrupted, but rather was faithfully transmitted to the next generation of scholars, thinkers, and artists. Over the centuries, this notion of a "golden chain," with Plato playing a most prominent role, strengthened more and more and became central to the Platonic tradition. At the dawn at the modern era, for example, it came to be regarded as so deeply rooted that among the Renaissance Platonists there was a widespread opinion according to which Plato was

> the heir to a line of philosophers going back to earliest times. In this scheme of things, Plato was the conveyor of ancient wisdom deriving ultimately from Adam and shared by others in a line of ancient sages which also included Zoroaster, Orpheus and Hermes Trismegistus. Thus in the Renaissance, the Neoplatonic interpretation of Plato rendered his philosophy at once more systematic as a coherent whole, and more eclectic, incorporating strands of thought not properly belonging to Plato. (Hutton 1994: 70)

In the Italian Renaissance Plato came to be regarded as "the father of philosophers" (Ficino 1985: 35), and the Platonic philosophy in close alliance with Christian theology served as the generous framework for probably the most ambitious philosophical-religious syncretism in the whole history of the West. Astrology, hermeticism, alchemy, magic, numerology, Kabala, Aristotelianism, Islamic philosophy, mysticism, all of these divergent doctrines and modes of thought could coexist peacefully in the work of the same Renaissance Platonic author, on the same page and sometimes even in the same paragraph. Giovanni Pico della Mirandola (1463–94) and Marsilio Ficino (1433–99), to give only a couple of examples, practiced this syncretic style of philosophizing as a matter of routine. Giovanni Pico della Mirandola, for instance, is famously the author of *Conclusiones philosophicae, cabalisticae et theologicae* (1486), nine hundred theses on "all possible subjects," which he conceived as a starting point for a reconciliation of all major religions, philosophies, and doctrines. This would bring about world peace, mutual understanding among people of different religious and political convictions, as well as more spiritualized forms of life. The true wisdom does not come from separation and division, but from synthesis, communication, and from a syncretism of beliefs, convictions, and social practices. In a commentary "on a poem of Platonic love" (Pico della Mirandola 1986), within one and the same sentence, he mixes Greek philosophy and mythology, the Bible, astrology, and Jewish philosophy in an almost breath-taking manner:

> according to the ancient astrologers, whose opinion follows that of Plato and Aristotle and even Moses, according to what Abenaza the Spaniard [probably Abenezra of Toledo, 1093–1167, Jewish grammarian and commentator on the Pentateuch—*trans. note*] writes, Venus was placed in the middle of the sky near Mars in order that she might tame his violence, which by its nature is destructive and corrupting, just as Jupiter tames the malice of Saturn. (Pico della Mirandola 1986: 40)

This is also the working method that Marsilio Ficino followed. He saw in the synthesis of ideas and systems of thought the key to the true revival of spirituality. The truth comes precisely from such a synthesis. For instance, at some point in his commentary on Plato's *Symposium* (Ficino 1985), he puts together, in one movement, Greek poetry, Pythagorean philosophy, numerology, and Christian theology and takes them as instantiations of one and the same truth: "The Pythagorean philosophers believed that the trinity was the measure of all things, for that reason, I think, that God governs things by the ternary number, and also that things themselves are completed by the ternary number. Hence Vergil said, 'God rejoices in the odd number'" (Ficino 1985: 45). Nevertheless, it would be a mistake to think that such reconsiderations of the ancient philosophers, pre-Christian religious beliefs, and even magical practices were intended, as it has been suggested sometimes, as some "return to paganism." In most cases the Renaissance Platonists were devout Christians, and they saw this new synthesis of knowledge and intellectual traditions through a Christian lens. In his *De Vita* Ficino suggests more than one time that this project is to be pursued under Christ's guidance: "Hippocrates promises health of body, Socrates, of soul. But the true health of both is furnished by Him who cries: 'Come unto me, all ye that labor and are under heavy-laden, and I will refresh you. I am the way, the truth and the life'" (Ficino 1989: 107). This syncretism that the Renaissance Platonists were proposing is to be considered in the terms of a Christian philosophy of history, one in which the whole of world history is Christ-centered as it revolves around the historical existence and manifestation of Jesus Christ: "What the Egyptians before Christ thought about the excellence of the cross was not so much a testimony of the gifts of the stars as a prophecy of the power that it was going to receive from Christ" (ibid.: 335). In this way the Christian humanists of the Renaissance are one of the most successful reinstantiations of the ancient alliance between Plato and Christianity throughout history.

The same will be the case with the post-Renaissance representatives of the Platonic tradition too. The Cambridge Platonists, to give the example of one school, shared with the previous Platonic authors the view that there was a "golden chain" connecting them, in a subtle way, to the most ancient sages and doctrines. In spite of the emergence and then prevalence of the new "scientific spirit," in spite of all the contemporary developments in experimentation and empirical observation, and in spite of their contemporaries' increasing fascination with the emerging culture of "innovation" (in technology, science, society) and "discovery" (in geography, anatomy, and so forth), the Cambridge Platonists stubbornly advocated a view about the production and constitution of knowledge deeply rooted in the "conservatism" of the Platonic tradition. As Ernst Cassirer noted, for Cudworth and More, just as for the Renaissance Platonists and, for that matter, for the entire Platonic tradition, Plato formed a link

> that golden chain of divine revelation, which besides him includes Moses and Zoroaster, Socrates and Christ, Hermes Trismegistus and Plotinus. Plato is for them the living proof that the true Philosophy is never opposed to

genuine Christianity. He is the ancestor and patron of that *pia philosophia*, which existed even before the Christian revelation, and which has proved its force and vitality throughout the centuries. (Cassirer 1953: 9)

Ernst Cassirer insightfully speaks of a curious "intermingling of the holy and the profane, of the Christian and the heathen" in the case of the Cambridge Platonists (ibid.: 25). Indeed, the perfect compatibility, or the complete synthesis, of (pagan) Greek philosophy with the (strict) requirements of the Christian faith seemed to be, in their cases, something beyond any reasonable doubt. In light of the unifying principles presupposed by a view of the evolution of knowledge as a "golden chain," Christian and heathen authors, ancient thinkers, and medieval schoolmen, Oriental sages and Jewish scholars, beyond any superficial disagreements that might seem to have existed between them, are taken now as inseparable parts of one and the same tradition. The disagreement is only superficial and inconsequential because an expert eye can always see the unity behind the many. Let us consider only an isolated example: namely, a fragment by John Smith (1618–52), one of the most prominent figures among the Cambridge Platonists. What he says here does not matter so much, but the manner in which he treats the subject is very significant for the purposes of the present discussion:

> When *Zoroaster's* Scholars asked him what they should doe to get *winged Souls*, such as might soar aloft in the bright beams of divine Truth, he bids them bathe themselves in *the waters of Life*: they asking what they were; he tells them *the four Cardinal Vertues*, which are *the four rivers of Paradise*. It is but a thin, aiery knowledge that is got by meer Speculation, which is usher'd in by Syllogisms and Demonstrations; but that which springs forth from true Goodness, is *theioteron ti pases apodeixeos*, as Origen speaks. . . . We may, like those in Plato's deep pit with their faces bended downwards, converse with *Sounds* and *Shadows*; but not with the *Life* and *Substance* of Truth. (Smith 1969: 130)

Following in the footsteps of illustrious predecessors, John Smith finds absolutely no inconsistency in putting together such differing (and, for many authors, conflicting) sources, topics, and terminologies within one and the same paragraph. For, to him, beyond any local differences that might exist between the Persian, Ancient Greek, and Christian authors he quotes, there is a fundamental underlying unity making them active contributors to the same tradition of the true wisdom, to the same *philosophia perennis*. Moreover, as we can easily see, the authors he puts together, making them members of the same school of thought, are separated from each another not only in historical and geographical terms, but also in terms of styles of thinking and methods of argumentation, in terms of epistemic cultures and methodological preferences: some of them use predominantly logic and rigorous reasoning, while others employ nothing but vision and inspiration; some of them are fond of advancing their notions in small steps, exclusively through "syllogisms" and "demonstrations," while others care only how intense their inner sense of truth is, disregarding any logical or empirical verifiability. For John Smith, however, the differences that might exist between the principles, doctrines, backgrounds, and purposes of these authors, are—in continuity with an entire tradition of Platonic thought—decisively overshadowed by their deeper similarities, by their participation in the same ample divine conversation.

SIRIS

A Sophisticated Modesty

A striking characteristic of *Siris* is its purposefully impersonal *écriture*. At the very foundation of this writing Berkeley places, so to speak, an impressive amount of modesty. In *Siris* he is always ready to appeal to ancient authorities and sources (mostly Platonic, alchemical, and esoteric, but also modern), and to report others' opinions on the subject he deals with, without trying very much—especially in the second (Platonic-speculative) half of the work—to express his own opinion of it. We can eventually learn what his views are not so much by reading his text as by gradually realizing what his attitude toward the authors he quotes is.

Almost needless to say, this manner of writing (and practicing) philosophy is in sharp contrast with George Berkeley's earlier style, as it is revealed in such works as *The Principles of Human Knowledge* (1710) or *Three Dialogues between Hylas and Philonous* (1713). As it were, as Berkeley advanced in age, he was drawing closer and closer to the ancient modes of thought. On the other hand, this "conservative" manner of writing philosophy opposed him to most of the promoters of the "new philosophy" (Descartes, Gassendi, Locke, and so on), a school of thought to which Berkeley belonged early on in his career.[2] Based primarily on the supposition that, by virtue of its natural "lights," powers, and abilities, the human mind can grasp, and then faithfully describe, the true "nature of things," the representatives of the "new philosophy" did not feel in general that they had to appeal to ancient authorities in order to endorse the truths about the natural world they were discovering. Indeed, reference to venerated authorities (whether sacred or profane) was then perceived as having been massively discredited by the Scholastic authors, whose excessive bookishness was actually one of the causes of the rise of *la nouvelle philosophie de la nature* in the first place. For instance, at the very beginning of his *Discourse on Method* the reader comes across Descartes's confession that, in his ambitious program of reforming all existing knowledge, he would rely on nothing else but what he receives, with certainty, from his trustworthy intellectual faculties and from *le grand livre de la nature*: "I resolved to seek no other knowledge than that which I might find within myself, or perhaps in the great book of nature" (Descartes 1956: 6). And Descartes was speaking not only for himself: an entire intellectual program was encapsulated in his words.

While in his early works Berkeley did—following the guidelines of the new manner of philosophizing—try to expound his views only by appeal to the "natural light" of reason, and using, in weaving his discourse, the same rhetorical tools, terminological repertoire, and protocols as those employed in shaping the scientific discourse of his day, almost without any references to past authorities, in *Siris* the repeated appeals to venerated authors and ancient sages (who supposedly grasped the ultimate truth of things) becomes Berkeley's main working method. Not that he does not trust the "natural lights" of his mind any longer, but he simply decides to take a totally different approach to the construction of knowledge and to the role that an individual thinker's mind might have to play within this production. In other words, he decides to look for truth elsewhere. His own contribution in *Siris*, as he seems to see it, consists only in a better understanding of how the "great tradition" works, how the ancient authors are connected to each other, and how they understand and complement one another. In this writing Berkeley conceived of his own role as an extremely modest one, and he apparently gave up any ambition to discover and express the "nature of things" by himself, being content only with telling how the ancients, long before him, discovered and expressed the most important truths one can ever attain:

> If we may believe Diogenes Laertius, the Pythagorean philosophers thought there was a certain pure heat or fire, which had somewhat divine in it, by the participation whereof men became allied to the gods. And according to the Platonists, heaven is not defined so much by its local situation as by its purity. The purest and most excellent fire, that is heaven, saith Ficinus. And again, the hidden fire that everyone exerts itself, he calls celestial. (Berkeley 1948–57, 5:103–4)

In light of what I said early on in the chapter, this style of philosophizing is, of course, not some whim on Berkeley's side, or some accident in his intellectual biography, but it belongs to a venerated tradition of thought and spiritual project: Platonism. As shown in the previous chapter, in his earlier writings Berkeley had already employed a large number of specifically Platonic topics and notions. They formed a Platonic net that subtly pervaded those writings, even though, at the level of the literary form and of the rhetorical procedures they exhibited, they suggested a style of philosophizing belonging to the then-fashionable *nouvelle philosophie de la nature* rather than to the somehow old-fashioned Platonism. It is in *Siris* that Berkeley resolves this tension and fully inserts himself into the body of the Platonic tradition both at the level of the philosophical content proper and at that of the literary and rhetorical strategies. Seen from the vantage point of this tradition, what Berkeley does in *Siris* is precisely making his text play the role of a palimpsest: the fortunate occasion on which others' writings come to reveal themselves. It is a sign of a remarkable philosophical broadmindedness and authorial humbleness at the same time.

The fundamental idea behind this rhetorical procedure is that there is—or must be—some fundamental truth "concealed" in all these ancient writings, a truth of which modern authors have unfortunately been deprived, and which could to a certain extent be resuscitated only by a proper reassertion and cultivation of classical scholarship, culture, and learning:

> It was an opinion of remote antiquity that the world was an animal. . . . If we may trust the Hermaic writings, the Egyptians thought all things did partake of life. This opinion was also so general and current among the Greeks that Plutarch asserts all others held the world to be an animal, and governed by Providence, except Leucippus, Democritus, and Epicurus. . . . from all the various tones, actions, and passions of the universe, they supposed one symphony, one animal act and life to result. (Ibid.: 129)

Against a clearly and repeatedly asserted Christian theological background, Berkeley quotes and makes extensive use of opinions of an amazingly diverse nature and origin. And it is precisely this fact that places him remarkably smoothly in the long tradition of thought I talked about early on in this chapter. For what is interesting at this point is that, following exactly the same discursive practices as the Platonic authors discussed above, Berkeley finds it perfectly legitimate to quote, within one and the same sentence, figures belonging to ancient Egypt and ancient Greece and the Hellenistic world, clearly implying in this way the existence of some fundamental agreement between all these authors and, beyond any superficial divergences that might have existed between them, the possibility of their forming one and the same "family of minds," links in one and the same "gold chain." This is why it might be said that *Siris* has a marked character of "intertextuality": Berkeley's own words are constantly echoed by those of the others, just as the others' words are reflected and mirrored in his own phrasing:

> If we may trust the Hermaic writings, the Egyptians thought all things did partake of life. . . . from all the various tones, actions, and passions of the universe, they supposed one symphony, one animal act and life to result. . . . It is a doctrine among other speculations contained in the Hermaic writings that all things are One. And it is not improbable that Orpheus, Parmenides, and others among the Greeks, might have derived their notion of *to hen*, THE ONE, from Egypt. Though that subtle metaphysician Parmenides, in his doctrine of *hen hestos*, seems to have added something of his own. . . . one and the same Mind is the universal principle of order and harmony throughout the world, containing and connecting all its parts, and giving unity to the system. (Ibid.: 128–34)

Yet, the relationships between Parmenides (or the Greek philosophers in general), on the one hand, and the Egyptians, on the other, is of the same type as the relationship Berkeley himself has with all of them. Their joint discourse is reflected within—and harmoniously interrelates with—Berkeley's own text, giving birth to a new joint discourse and so on. Each of the authors Berkeley quotes is, as it were, an important link within a "golden chain" of esoteric knowledge, a chain through which we could possibly get connected with the genuine wisdom of the past, and extract from it a perfectly valid science for coping with the present and the future. Most obviously, the rhetoric of *Siris*, this generous and unprejudiced embracing of past doctrines in view of a broader synthesis, always seeking what they have in common, and paying almost no attention to their disagreements, is reminiscent of the powerful rhetoric practiced by the Renaissance Platonists. A fragment like this, taken from Ficino's *De vita* might well have been written by Bishop Berkeley himself, just as the stylistic flavor of *Siris* could be found in any of Ficino's writings:

> That a specific and great power exists in specific words, is the claim of Origen in *Contra Celsum*, of Synesius and Al-Kindi where they argue about magic, and likewise of Zoroaster where he forbids the alteration of barbarian

words, and also of Iamblichus in the course of the same argument. The Pythagoreans also make this claim, who used to perform wonders by words, songs, and sounds in the Phoebean and Orphic manner. The Hebrew doctors of old practiced this more than anyone else; and all poets sing of the wondrous things that are brought about by songs. And even the famous and venerable Cato in his *De re rustica* sometimes uses barbarous incantations to cure the diseases of his farm animals. (Ficino 1989: 355)

It almost goes without saying that any increase in knowledge (*augmentatio scientiarum*) could under such circumstances occur not in terms of an enlargement of the amount of information we have about the surrounding world (along with, say, a better systematization of it), but only in terms of a more comprehensive understanding of the philosophical past, of the tradition, and through a better interpretation and clarification of it. Ideally, all the information we could have of the natural world is filtered through the ancient doctrines, and, in this way, validated:

Jamblichus declares the world to be one animal, in which the parts, however distant each from other, are nevertheless related and connected by one common nature. And he teacheth, what is also a received notion of the Pythagoreans and Platonics, that there is no chasm in nature, but a Chain or Scale of beings rising by gentle uninterrupted gradations from the lowest to the highest, each nature being informed and perfected by the participation of a higher. (Berkeley 1948–57: 5:128–29)

Something is true about the outside world only insofar as the ancients, who had a much better understanding of nature than we have, endorsed that truth. If they did not happen to say anything about some issue or other we are concerned with today, it is all right: we just have to find a way of translating that issue into something else, into something about which the ancients had something to say.

Before concluding this part of the chapter, let me just add that, by a fortunate chance, there is in the British Museum a catalogue of Berkeley's family library as it was put up for sale in 1796.[3] It is a forty-six–page document, listing over sixteen hundred titles.[4] Such a document is of the greatest importance for anyone studying Berkeley's thought, its formation, sources, and development. A careful and detailed study of this document would massively contribute to a more comprehensive understanding of his philosophical formation and background. As far as the present discussion is concerned, it will suffice to say that this library contained, among other things, four different editions of Plato's *opera* (in Greek, Latin, and French),[5] Plotinus's *Opera philosophica*, Boethius's *De consolatione philosophiae*, some work by Philo Judaeus, two volumes by Origen, two by Moses Maimonides, "Dionysii Opera," Sir Thomas Browne's *Religio Medici*, Boehme's *Aurora,* and many others. As in a mirror, in the catalogue of Berkeley's library we can glimpse his deep immersion into the Platonic tradition. All these books, along with the secret relationships they had with each other, reflect the subtle palimpsest that we come across when reading *Siris*.

How Archetypal Knowledge Works

A couple of general conclusions are in order here.

First, as far as the *authorship* problem is concerned, an unspoken supposition behind this mode of thinking (and writing) is that there must be some primordial, anonymous text, one and the same, not conceived of by a human author, but in some way revealed to humans at some immemorial time (*in illo tempore*), and containing virtually all the fundamental truths at which the human mind could ever possibly, at its best, arrive. This text is "out there," it has some mysterious, yet certain existence, and all what we can do about it is to sharpen our intellectual faculties so as to be able to "extract" it properly, as it were, from the multitude of texts, legends, stories, myths, and other relics that we encounter in our dealings with the past. As a consequence, the crucial mission that the scholars, philosophers, and sages of this world have to accomplish is precisely to preserve, convey, and explain the contents of this archetypal text to those of their fellow humans less endowed to do so by themselves. It almost goes without saying: this view that one is an author only insofar as he participates in the reassertion and recovery of a primordial, anonymous text betrays a conception of authorship deeply marked by modesty and self-effacement.

It is quite tempting to draw a parallel between the notion of knowledge as palimpsest and the function of repetition in traditional societies. Such a parallel could provide us with a glimpse of what is behind, philosophically speaking, this kind of epistemological modesty:

> This tendency may well appear paradoxical, in the sense that the man of a traditional culture sees himself as real only to the extent that he ceases to be himself (for a modern observer) and is satisfied with imitating and repeating the gestures of another. In other words, he sees himself as real, i.e., as "truly himself," only, and precisely, insofar as he ceases to be so. (Eliade 1971: 34)

The pursuer of knowledge (philosophy) as palimpsest shares with Eliade's "man of the traditional culture" the same fundamental vision about the proper place that the individual must occupy in history and in cosmos: both believe that there are bigger and more important things than themselves in the world, that the ultimate (whether mythical or just philosophical) meanings open themselves up only to those who know how to lure them by generosity of mind and humbleness of soul, and that, in general, the human being is just one of the characters, not necessarily the leading one, in God's cosmic story.

One of the fundamental theoretical presuppositions behind this vision of the history of philosophy is precisely the notion that the source of the true (philosophical) knowledge is to be found not in the limited faculties of the individuals (living necessarily in corrupted epochs), nor in empirical observations of (or experiments with) things in the world around, but only in the "old books," in the ancient legends and myths, in the old libraries and dusty manuscripts, all of them privileged containers of the important revelations, as well as the visible vehicles of the immemorial tradition. In other words, in this system of thought, knowledge is not so much produced as administered, not discovered, but preserved and taught. The whole body of knowledge one can ever have access to is already there, complete and flawless. There is no point in trying to increase, change, or reform it; the only thing one can (and must) do is to preserve it faithfully. Therefore, the intellectual faculties one needs to the highest degree for this kind of knowledge are not the capacity of invention or of innovation, nor the capacity of discovering new things or formulating new hypotheses, but only the hermeneutical faculties: memory, the capacity of association, interpretation, and storytelling, of placing things in larger historical contexts and tracing them back genealogically.

Seen in a broad perspective, this whole process is, of course, an attempt at "freezing" time: the future is already contained in the past; the future cannot bring anything "new," anything that one doesn't already know, or know of.[6] Again, what Mircea Eliade says about the function of repetition and the cultivation of archetypes in traditional societies, may well be applied literally to this view of philosophical knowledge as a palimpsest:

> Everything begins over again at its commencement every instant. The past is but a prefiguration of the future. . . . In a certain sense, it is even possible to say that nothing new happens in the world, for everything is but the repetition of the same primordial archetypes; this repetition, by actualizing the

mythical moment when the archetypal gesture was revealed, constantly maintains the world in the same auroral instant of the beginnings. (Ibid.: 90)

Yet, in a way, if we are to observe this tradition of thought, time *has to be frozen. As noted before, when discussing Plato's myth in the Statesman*, historical time is growing old with every passing second. What we have to do as wisdom seekers is to get some form of access to that point in time when history was not yet born, when things were still uncorrupted and men were happy and innocent. Of course this is utopian and unrealistic, but who says that philosophy is the business of realistic people?

Secondly, and as a consequence of what I have just said, this way of thought is Platonic not only in the sense that historically Plato played an important role in its configuration. There is also a deeper sense in which the view of knowledge as a palimpsest is connected to the philosophy of Plato. Namely, this way of thinking is Platonic in the sense that, according to it, any particular piece of local knowledge is possible only insofar as it "participates" in some archetypal knowledge, in something that was revealed "at the beginning," and from which that particular knowledge takes its reality and truthfulness. The archetypes that Eliade talks about in his discussion of traditional societies take in our case the form of the system of knowledge revealed to the human beings by gods, in the way we saw it narrated in the *Statesman*. Just as according to Plato's theory of ideas, any sensible thing exists and is real only insofar as it takes part in its archetype or idea, so, in this consideration of knowledge as a palimpsest, any local knowledge, no matter its object, "becomes real only insofar as it imitates or repeats an archetype" (ibid.: 34). The true philosopher (or scholar, or scientist) does not have to dream of inventing new knowledge, one not already contained or prefigured in what was given by gods *in illo tempore* (she cannot afford to entertain "phantasms" of novelty), but her only concern is to restore the integrity of god-given knowledge and to make sure that it does not contain any unwelcome, alienating additions. And the key to accomplishing this process is repetition: "reality is acquired solely through repetition or participation; everything which lacks an exemplary model is 'meaningless'" (ibid.: 34).

3.   *George Berkeley and the* Liber Mundi *Tradition*

One of the distinctive features of the Platonic-Christian tradition is a consideration of the whole visible world in symbolic terms: namely, as a coherent system of signs, as a sophisticatedly encrypted message that God is continuously sending to his creatures. Born somehow out of the chapters dealing with Berkeley's place in the Platonic tradition, the present chapter is a systematic attempt at considering George Berkeley's immaterialist philosophy in close connection to the topic of the book of the world (*liber mundi* or *liber naturae*), with the twofold objective of pointing out, on the one hand, those of the medieval implications of the topic that Berkeley preserved in his philosophy, and, on the other hand, the "novelties," or at least some of the major changes, he brought forth in his usage of the topic.[1]

The *Liber Mundi* from St. Paul to Modern Times

The Theological Grounding of the Liber Mundi

Liber mundi is one of the most complex and fascinating cultural-philosophical topics of the medieval universe. It seems to belong to that genre of all-encompassing metaphors that eventually come, in some way or other, to "mirror" or "encrypt" entire systems of thought, and carry with them the essentials of entire worldviews. Almost needless to say, the topic predates significantly the Christian Middle Ages. To give only one example, out of many possible, the history of this topic could be traced as far back as the Platonic usage of the ancient notion of *stoicheia*. Initially, the word *stoicheia* (singular: *stoicheion*) meant simply "letters" as part of the alphabet, but later, starting with Plato, it was also used to designate the four elements out of which the entire visible world was made: "Originally the name for the letters of the alphabet, *stoicheia* was a technical term from Classical physics and metaphysics, apparently beginning . . . with Plato's *Theaetetus* and then in . . . *Timaeus*, for fire, water, air and earth and the four elements" (Pelikan

1993: 104). Quite expectedly, this situation has triggered significant difficulties as far as the translation of *Timaeus* into modern languages is concerned. Benjamin Jowett, for example, was forced to resort to some
compromise solution; his rendering of the passage in question goes: "we
speak of fire and the rest of them, as though men knew their natures, and
we maintain them to be the first principles [*archaî*] and letters or elements
[*stoicheîa*] of the whole" (Plato 1961: 1175 [*Timaeus* 48b]).

It was within the theological context generated by the emergence of
Christianity, however, that the topic of the *liber mundi* was given a new,
much deeper significance, *una vita nuova*, as it were. There are at least two
fragments in the New Testament where one can possibly find the theological Christian grounding of the *liber mundi* as it would reveal itself throughout
the Middle Ages: namely, in St. John (1:1–4) and in St. Paul (1 Cor 13.12–
13). What is interesting at this stage is the fact that this "double grounding"
would be preserved and remain easily recognizable along all the subsequent
developments of the topic through the modern day. One of my working
hypotheses in this chapter is that each of these two fragments implies a consideration of the *liber mundi* from a specific perspective. As the idea of "book
of the world" necessarily requires at least two elements (a text to be read
and a reader to do it), I propose to take hypothetically, on the one hand, St.
John's fragment as implying the *liber mundi* "text perspective" (which is to
say, the cosmic text considered in itself, or only in relationship to its divine
author), and, on the other hand, St. Paul's fragment as implying *liber mundi*
"reader's perspective" (which is to say, the cosmic text considered in rela-
tionto its "readers," with their intellectual/spiritual needs, and with their
awareness that their encounter with the natural world around is actually a
process of "reading" and "interpretation"). At the same time, it should be
added that these perspectives are not opposite at all, but, on the contrary,
they are fully complementary, and sometimes sophisticatedly interwoven.

From a strictly theological point of view, we find in St. John's Gospel
the most clearly stated Christian grounds on which the whole philosophizing about the *liber mundi* is based: "In (the) beginning was the Word, and
the Word was with God, and the Word was God. He was in the beginning
with God. All things received being through him, and without him not one
(thing) received being which has received being. . . . And the Word became
flesh" (1:1–14). One comes across, in this short passage, a very fruitful semantic ambiguity at work, since the word "Word," as it is presented in
John's Gospel, is in fact the translation of the Greek word *logos* meaning at

once both "word" (*verbum*) and "reason" (*ratio*). As a result, from a Christian theological standpoint, it would be fair to say that the Incarnation of Christ made the world not only "readable" (since the Word "penetrated" and "inscribed" it), but—more than that—"reason-able," comprehensible (since God as *ratio* brought this world into being). Indeed, as a consequence of this, not only do we have access to the world, but we have good chances of "grasping" it, to know it as it is in itself.[2] In the long run, the fact would play a crucial role in the configuration and development of some of the patterns of rationality characterizing the European mind as one obsessed with knowledge of the world: in this view, the world is considered "thinkable" since it essentially contains "reason" (*logos*), that is, a process of knowledge of the world is always a process of "self-recognition" in the course of which our reason (as a faculty of knowledge) recognizes itself in the ontological makeup of the world (as one that was brought into being by Supreme Reason). It becomes quite interesting, precisely from this point of view, to see how St. John's saying "All things received being through him, and without him not one (thing) received being which has received being" (1:3) would be, many centuries later, rigorously reflected in that cryptic Hegelian statement: "What is rational is real and what is real is rational." In a way, then, what St. John's Gospel did was (echoing a certain Parmenidian idea: *to on = to noeton*) to offer one of the essential theological premises of the European culture, as far as the knowledge of nature is concerned.

On the other hand, there is St. Paul's fragment, offering a grounding of the *liber mundi* that is related to a set of soteriological, ethical, and even "existential" consequences of the fact that the world is seen as a divine message. The Pauline text in question reads as follows: "For we see now through a dim window obscurely, but then face to face; now I know partially, but then I shall know according as I also have been known" (1 Cor 13:12–13). Its Latin version goes: "Videmus enim nunc per speculum in aenigmate, tunc autem facie ad faciem; nunc cognosco ex parte, tunc autem cognoscam, sicut et cognitus sum." As a matter of fact, the Latin version conveys much better than the English the Pauline fundamental idea that, on our encounter with the world, this world is given to us in the shape of a system of symbols we have to decipher: we see the world *per speculum*, which is to say (as if) through a mirror, and have to go beyond the play of appearances. More than that, the text clearly suggests that there is with certainty a significance hidden behind these appearances, and throughout our lifetime we have to try incessantly to "extract" this meaning from the riddle (*aenigma*) of our existence. Of course, in the Pauline text we do not come across such direct words as "letter," "book," "reading," and the like. There is, however, at least one important reason why St. Paul should be placed at the very root of the Christian tradition of the *liber mundi*: as has often been noted, there is a hermeneutic "interchangeability" between the idea of mirror (*speculum*) and that of book (*liber*), and this interchangeability operated to a large extent throughout the medieval culture, and even beyond. Both *speculum* and *liber* point to some clearly determined physical objects, endowed with a special capacity of comprehending virtually unlimited contents. To take only one example, the medieval poet Alan of Lille (1128?–1202), whose place in the history of the *liber mundi* I will discuss in some detail later on in this chapter, simply takes for granted this interchangeability between *liber* and *speculum*, as if these two terms were more or less synonymous: "omnis mundi creatura / quasi liber, et / pictura / nobis est, et speculum" (Alan of Lille [in Dreves] 1909, 1:288). Quite significantly from the point of view of the present discussion, *speculum* came to be in the Latin Middle Ages a very common name for encyclopedias as "books of books." An encyclopedia was seen as "a mirror of . . ."[3] It was a microcosm in itself, ambitiously compiled in the hope of reflecting, or "mirroring," the truths about the cosmos proper: "Encyclopedias . . . are also called mirrors because, as Vincent [of Beauvais] says, mirrors induce speculations and imitation" (Mazzotta 1993: 4.[4]

As such, the whole world comes to be seen in St. Paul as a great, though sometimes confusing, system of signs and messages, of "riddles" and hidden meanings; no one of its parts is insignificant or accidental, but each of them is as it were a letter, a *gramma*, and the whole frame of things constitutes this most interesting "book," that we are actually faced with. The most important thing is to learn how to "read" it, to grasp the rule of its "grammar" and to be able to recognize the meanings of its words. And this cosmic "reading" is not a "cultural practice" among many others, but it plays, in St. Paul's view (and subsequently throughout the Middle Ages) the role of a supreme *praeparatio*: this "reading" of the world is an important stage of an "initiatory process" through which we are given a chance to attain the plenitude of our life (*tunc*). The "reader's perspective" on *liber mundi* mentioned above is massively implied by this Pauline passage; actually, this whole fragment is *about* the "reader" and his inner need to be "saved," about the spiritual benefits that an appropriate and wise reading of the "book of the world" would bring him. It is, finally, about a fundamental promise, the promise that only those who will be prepared to do so will be able to see the face of God, and knowing how to read "the book of the world" is an essential part of this preparation. For, most importantly, the Pauline text testifies to the constant need, on the reader's side, to transcend the mere and imperfect act of reading (nunc cognosco ex parte) and necessarily to link the "reading" of the "cosmic text" to a process of *ascensio coeli* as salvation, in order to reach a state of perfect ultimate ontological transparency (tunc cognoscam, sicut et cognitus sum), an angelic state in which the face of God can be gazed at freely and directly, without mediation and intermediaries. In order to see things divine, the human eyes have to be in the first instance educated and purified through a disciplined application to the understanding of what the cosmic book says.

It was precisely this "existential" component of the *liber mundi* (reader's perspective") that would be further developed to a significant extent by St. Augustine. Augustine was among the first Christian authors to write systematically about this topic, and, moreover, to place it within an ampler system of theological-philosophical speculations. St. Augustine's place in the history of *liber mundi* has been recognized as such and praised by those of the modern scholars who have dealt with the topic. Umberto Eco, to give only one example, simply regards Augustine as the Christian author in whom all the medieval speculations on *liber mundi* originated: "The Middle Ages would borrow from Augustine the idea of a perfect language, that is not a language of words, but one of things, a language of a world which is—as later it would be called—*quasi liber scriptus digito Dei*" (Eco 1994: 11).[5]

One of the passages in which Augustine employs the *liber mundi* topic is in his *Confessions* (13.15.16–18). Here St. Augustine depicts the entire cosmos as an ample text being generously displayed in front of our eyes. It is a text specially addressed to us, written precisely to help us shorten the distance separating us from angels:

> You have extended like a skin the firmament of your Book, your harmonious discourses, over us by the ministry of mortals. . . . Let the angels, your supracelestial people, praise your name. They have no need to look upon this firmament, to know through reading your word. For they always see your face, and read there without the syllables of time your eternal will. They read, they choose, they love. They are always reading . . . . the changelessness of your counsel.

True, St. Augustine emphasizes the fateful gap between the two levels of being ("the celestial" and "the earthly"), by pointing to the existence of a fundamental ontological differentiation between "angels" and "mortals" as far as their approach to the cosmic book is concerned: angels do not need to read this book at all, as they have direct access to the book's author, this being actually the hallmark of their superiority, whereas humans find in this book their *only* source of meaning (apart from the Scripture) during their earthly journey. Paradoxically, St. Augustine's fragment, for all the restrictions it imposes, points at the same time to the only way of (as well as the supreme purpose for) reducing the ontological difference: for it is precisely within this ontological interval that human beings are able to discover themselves and their world genuinely *by comparison* to, and by meditation on, the celestial "archetypes," and by finding out the likeness relationship connecting the earthly and the celestial. As Jesse Gellrich has noted, this Augustinian fragment "illustrates the value of meditating on their similitude, and his procedure corresponds perfectly with the broad exhortation of the fathers of the church who instructed mediaeval readers to clarify and explain the mysterious purpose of the divine Word within the revealed words, such as the Bible and the Book of nature" (Gellrich 1985: 29).

Almost needless to say, the fact that Christianity is a "religion of the Book" contributed greatly to the emergence and then flourishing of the speculations on the *liber mundi* throughout the Middle Ages and later.[6] It was the central (cultural, intellectual, religious, and social) role that the Bible[7] played within Christianity that made this topic not only immediately comprehensible, but also appealing to a remarkably wide audience. This huge prestige of the Bible, as *the* Book, had something important to say about the emergence (and then success) of a representation of the world in the shape of a book: "In its simplest form, the idea of the Book begins in mediaeval readings of the Bible" (ibid.: 32). Within the medieval *Weltanschauung*, the Bible played the role of a universal divine "prototype" of all possible human knowledge, and it was perceived as the model *par excellence* of every single form of writing, be it religious or profane. The Bible fascinated and enchanted the medieval minds to such an extent that eventually it came to be seen as providing some *a priori* "interpretative pattern" by means of which the whole natural and social world was to be perceived, understood, and explained. Even the inner psychological world of the individual came at some point to be seen as a book.[8] In other words, the sheer fact of the "centrality" of the Bible as the supreme sacred text in Christianity marked in a deep and serious way almost all the medieval conceptions about the natural world and the place of the human beings within it, about human society, human knowledge and the shape it should take, the functioning of the human mind, the "meaning of life," and what the ultimate aims of the human intellectual effort should be.

On the other hand—and in addition to the Christian prestige of the Bible itself (as a "revealed" or "divinely inspired" text)—the book had already become, at the time when Christianity emerged, a "cultural product" generally considered as the most important means for preserving, conveying, and enhancing human knowledge. It was regarded as one of the most significant "human inventions," with tremendously beneficial effects on the state of affairs in the field of the sciences and the arts: within a conveniently limited space it was always possible to store an enormous amount of information, and, what was more, that information could be conveyed to an audience belonging not only to other cultural spaces, but also to other epochs. (The fabulous prestige that the Library of Alexandria enjoyed over the centuries would be a sufficient, if anecdotal, proof of that.) Finally, the book was an "object" governed by some strict constructing and functioning rules, and therefore an autonomous and self-sufficient entity, a fine and precise device whose functionality and usefulness could be easily assured, controlled, and even enhanced. As such, by the time Christianity made its debut, the book had come to have all the theological, historical, technical, and symbolical premises to become a fully convenient and highly expressive metaphor to be successfully employed within the medieval cultural universe. A metaphor like this, especially within a cultural and religious context like the Judeo-Christian one, in which the idea of the book had acquired so privileged a theological status, had all the chances to become one of the dominant topics employed, for centuries to come, in the theological, philosophical, literary, scientific, devotional, and ethical discourses.[9]

Above all, it was precisely the use of such a topic that made it possible for the medieval man to see the surrounding natural word as a most meaningful thing. As Taylor remarked, in the medieval worldview,

> Nature, the realm revealed by our senses, is only half-real, but it suggests a further reality which lies beyond itself. It is a system of symbols, and we ascend to truth by learning to pass from the symbols to the non-sensuous realities symbolized. Christian thought was dominated by this view of nature from St. Augustine to St. Thomas, and it has never really outgrown it. (Taylor 1963: 41–42)

An important consequence of all this is the fact that, within such a context, the study of nature belongs decisively to the field of the theological disciplines, and there must necessarily be a certain religious sense in any "scientific" approach to the natural word. Nature is not to be studied for its own sake, nor for our pragmatic interests, but rather only as a means of learning more about God. For, in the last analysis, from a strictly theological standpoint, there is only one serious reason enabling the medieval man to do research on nature: "The true reason for seeking information about Nature is that given by St. Paul, that the invisible things of God have been made known from the beginning by the things which are visible" (ibid.: 45).

On the other hand, between nature and Scripture there is a privileged relationship. Not only is God directly involved in making both of these texts, by Creation and Revelation, respectively, but the book of nature might well serve as a prolegomenon to any serious study of the teachings of Scripture. Given the extreme difficulty of properly grasping what the Scriptures say, spending some time with the "reading" of nature, before starting to read the Scriptures, is highly recommended by the medieval authors:

> Nature, rightly understood, becomes a key to the divine hieroglyphics of Scripture. This is the only reason why Nature has an interest for the mind. In its own right, Nature would not concern the intellect at all, for the proper and adequate object of the intellect is not the symbols but the God whom they partially disclose. (Ibid.: 44)

Medieval Philosophy and the Topic of the Liber Mundi

In philosophy the notion of *liber mundi* or *liber creaturarum* had its promoters, too. A great number of important medieval philosophers may well be considered as belonging to this way of thinking inaugurated by St. Paul and St. Augustine: Johannes Scotus Eriugena, Guilelmus of Auvergne, Raymundus Lullus, St. Bonaventure, Raymond Sebond, and others. It is not the object of this chapter to study in detail how each of these thinkers made use of the topic of the book of the world, how they employed it in their writings, and how they enlarged some of its implications in doing so. Nevertheless, a brief look at some of their ideas would be sufficient to give us the sense in which *liber mundi* was indeed a serious source of inspiration for a good part of the medieval philosophy.

St. Bonaventure (1221–74) is one of the important medieval thinkers who systematically employed this topic, developed it, and threw a new light on it. According to St. Bonaventure, if we look carefully at the world around (*natura* or *creatura*), we will soon be able to discover within it something important about the nature and the ways of manifestation of God himself as creator of this world. In his treatise *Itinerarium mentis in Deum*, St

Bonaventure sees the knowledge of *creatura* as the first stage of an "ascending" epistemic process through which the human mind approaches God.[10] And this first stage (called *theologia symbolis*) presupposes a consideration of the sensible world as a system of signs (*vestigia*) revealing God. In a fragment faithfully echoing the Pauline language used in the text quoted earlier in this chapter, Bonaventure says: "We may behold God in the mirror of visible things, not only by considering creatures as vestiges of God, but also by seeing Him in them; for He is present in them by His essence, His power, and His presence" (Sed quoniam circa speculum sensibilium non solum contingit contemplari Deum per ipsa tanquam per vestigia, verum etiam in ipsis, in quantum est in eis per essentiam, potentiam et praesentiam) (Bonaventure 1998: 50–51). The things we come across in the world should not be taken in themselves, simply as "natural phenomena" with no significance beyond their sheer physical appearances, but they should always be considered in what they signify since, as far as we are concerned, they play the role of "reminders" of our divine author: "Haec autem omnia sunt vestigia, in quibus speculari possumus Deum nostrum" (ibid.: 54). Bonaventure took over from St. Augustine the notion of *Vestigia Trinitatis*, and integrated it within his own system of thought. According to him, if we discipline our thought and use it properly, we can see in nature the reflection of the Trinity itself: "If, therefore, all knowable things must generate a likeness of themselves, they manifestly proclaim that in them, as in mirrors, can be seen the eternal generation of the Word, the Image, and the Son, eternally emanating from God the Father" (Si ergo omnia cognoscibilia habent sui speciem generare, manifeste proclamant, quod in illis tanquam in speculis videri potest aeterna generatio Verbi, Imaginis et Filii a Deo Patre aeternaliter emanantis) (ibid.: 56–57).

Raymond Sebonde (d. 1436), to take another example, wrote a massive volume entitled *Theologia naturalis seu liber creaturarum*. In the prologue to this work, Sebonde attempts to offer the basis of a "science of the book of creatures." This is a book that every Christian must know in order to be able to defend the faith and, if necessary, even to die for its sake. He argues that it is only such a science that makes possible the unmistakable knowledge of the whole Catholic faith and the proof of its truth (et per istam scientiam tota fides catholica infallibiliter cognoscitur et probatur esse vera). This science is a complete and self-sufficient one, as it does not need any other complementary sciences or books. For the only two books God gave us are the book of nature and the book of Scriptures: "duo sunt libri dati nobis a Deo, sicut liber Universitatis creaturarum seu liber naturae, et alius est liber sacrae scripturae" (Sebonde 1966: 36–38). Like Bonaventure before him, Raymond Sebonde believed that even mentions of the doctrine of the Trinity could be easily found in "the book of creatures."[11]

Finally, although Sir Thomas Browne (1605–82) was a "modern man," living well into the modern era, I have chosen to discuss here his dealing with the topic of *liber mundi* since he offers an interesting synthetic view of this notion, and of how it was received in some circles toward the end of the Middle Ages and at the dawn of the modern era. His *Religio medici* contains an ample and sophisticated exposition of some of the theological, philosophical, and scientific implications that the employment of the *liber mundi* topic came to have for a seventeenth-century man:

> there are two Books from whence I collect my Divinity; besides that written one of God, another of His servant Nature, that universal and publick Manuscript, that lies expans'd unto the Eyes of all; those that never saw him in the one, have discover'd Him in the other. This was the Scripture and Theology of the Heathens: the natural motions of the Sun made them more admire Him than its supernatural station did the Children of Israel; the ordinary effects of Nature wrought more admiration in them than in the other all His Miracles. Surely the Heathens knew better how to joyn and read these mystical Letters than we Christians who cast a more careless Eye on these common Hieroglyphicks, and disdain to suck Divinity from the flowers of Nature. (Browne [in Boethius, Thomas à Kempis, Thomas Browne] 1943: 337)

The interesting thing about a passage like this is that, apart from the usual (traditional) considerations on the relationship between "the two books," it also reveals a new, then emerging "epistemic attitude" toward nature, and—more than that—it is implied that this attitude should be considered a serious and equally valid alternative to strictly theological knowledge. This new epistemic approach consisted in trying to know the essence of nature (the "Creature") in a more genuine way: namely, in the way in which the ancients did, or at least in the way Browne thought the ancients did. To the medieval implications, Browne added new overtones. To me, this fragment seems extremely symptomatic as it succeeds, under the guise of a rhetorical *tour de force*, in putting "face to face," within the same page or paragraph, as it were, two radically different attitudes to the natural world: the medieval one, sophisticatedly theological and highly symbolic, and the modern one, marked by a drive to "grasp" nature as it is in itself and for itself.

Considering the whole medieval system of representations, speculations, and doctrines clustered around the idea of *liber mundi*, it is fair to say now that in this tradition of thinking the knowledge of the natural world, of God's *Creatura*, had a certain soteriological dimension: what the medieval man sought in most cases in his encounter with the world was to gain a knowledge allowing him to break the veil of deceiving appearances, to understand what (or who) was hidden, to "save" his soul, and thus to secure his immortality. Let me also say that, in the long run, this particular type of connection between knowledge and faith (*id est*, the fact that knowledge of the world was seen as part of a religious experience), as a characteristic feature of the medieval worldview, might well be regarded as a premise for the outstanding scientific developments to take place later in Europe. In other words, the intensely religious/soteriological character of the medieval starting point might have conferred a certain strength and depth on the otherwise secular "drive to knowledge" subsequently characterizing the European scientific mind. This is not to say, however, that this is the only root of the modern drive toward knowledge as a form of essential human experience. In fact, there were medieval thinkers (Roger Bacon, to take only one example) who advocated a certain "reading" of the world for its own sake, without necessarily looking for its author within it, and no one can deny that such thinkers played an important role in announcing, and indirectly configuring, the modern *Weltanschauung*. All I want to say here is that the intense soteriological overtones that often accompanied accounts of the medieval "readings of the world" might have later some influence on the emergence of a modern (secular) "religion" of knowledge: "knowledge for its own sake," knowledge as a supreme, self-sufficient, and total experience.

In conclusion, *liber mundi* is a significant text of the things themselves and is the writing of a nonhuman author. "Learning to read the signs of that Book was a process not of 'inventing' or 'creating' *sententia* for the 'sentences' in the Bible or nature, but of coming to comprehend a writing" that was, as it were, objective (Gellrich 1985: 34). Since this writing is not a human product at all, but belongs to the things themselves and points to something beyond the things themselves, there arises the necessity of searching for its proper "author," for the ultimate source of this writing. Such a compelling necessity was felt and dealt with by all those who have been concerned with the problems of writing and authorship. Jacques Derrida (1976: 18), for instance, shows how writing transcends itself in search of its own "eternal" author. And what the medieval philosophy clustered around *liber creaturarum* did was precisely to address these issues in a wonderfully sophisticated and fruitful manner.

Everything Is a Book

As a "master metaphor," *liber mundi* is without a doubt present not only in mysticism, theology, and philosophy, but it is manifest in other cultural forms of the medieval life too. Given the "centrality" of the Bible in the medieval universe referred to earlier in this chapter, and the profound consequences this fact had on shaping and modeling the medieval life, in all of its forms, *liber mundi* ended up being received as a total metaphor, the highly condensed expression of the medieval civilization.[12]

Poetry, for example, was a privileged space where the topic could be exploited to the maximum and considered in all its facets. Ernest Robert Curtius proved this impressively in his *European Literature and the Latin Middle Ages* (Curtius 1979), and so did Jesse Gellrich in *The Idea of the Book in the Middle Ages* (Gellrich 1985), to give only a couple of examples. Their contribution to the study of the history of this topic in the Middle Ages is difficult to overestimate, and the present research is very much indebted to what these authors (and others, besides them) did.

Anyone studying the presence of the *liber mundi* in the medieval poetry cannot overlook Alan of Lille's contribution, as in it the topic of *liber mundi* undoubtedly reached its cultural maturity and one of the finest literary expressions:

> omnis mundi creatura
> quasi liber, et pictura
> nobis est, et speculum.
> Nostrae vitae, nostrae mortis,
> Nostrae status, nostrae sortis.
> Fidele signaculum. (Alan of Lille in Dreves 1909, 1:288)

It is probably worth noting how, in a passage like this, thanks especially to the formal aspects of the poem (sonority, rhythm, alliteration, and so forth), Alan of Lille succeeds in conveying to his readers the sense of existential ambiguity, subtle melancholy, and delicate uneasiness that seeing everything as a book, or as in a mirror, brings about. For, in spite of all the lofty metaphysics this topic presupposed, the poet felt that, ultimately, there was a sense in which to see something "as in a mirror" was to admit its ontological precariousness and uncertainty. Which is to say, yes, maybe these things are something in the eyes of God, but *hic et nunc* they are nothing more than mere letters and reflections coming out of an empty and cold mirror.

On the other hand, of course, Alan grasps here, in a most artful and elegant manner, almost all the fundamental metaphysical implications of the metaphor we have been dealing with in this chapter:

> Alan's most quoted verse reflects the sense that the whole of creation is a harmonious totality and a symbolic construction of things and words, a book and a mirror, whose alphabet can be deciphered, whose arcane signs can be distinguished and classified, and whose secret allegorical images can be revealed as a faithful representation (*fidele signaculum*) of our condition. (Mazzotta 1993: 17)

Another important medieval writer who artfully inserted this topic into the texture of his poetry was Dante Alighieri (1265–1321). In his book *Dante's Vision and the Circle of Knowledge* (ibid.), Giuseppe Mazzotta places Dante in Western literature's long tradition of using this metaphor and shows how Dante developed and enriched the use of the topic. Mazzotta refers to this marvelous fragment from *Divina Commedia*:

> Nel suo profondo vidi che s'interna
> legato con amore in un volume
> ciò che per l'universo si squaderna:
> sustanze e accidenti e lor costume
> quasi conflati insieme, per tal modo
> che ciò ch'io dico è un semplice lume (33.85–90)

> (I saw how it contains within its depths
> all things bound in a single book by love
> of which creation is the scattered leaves:
> how substance, accident, and their relation
> were fused in such a way that what I now
> describe is but a glimmer of that Light.) (Dante 1984: 392–93)

Mazzotta finds canto 33 of *Paradiso* in the *Divina Commedia* highly indicative of both what *liber mundi* means philosophically and theologically, on the one hand, and of the encyclopedic tendencies of the Middle Ages, on the other. As we saw earlier, the *liber mundi* topic was inextricably connected throughout the Middle Ages to a certain canonical form of organizing, administering, and transmitting all the knowledge then available: *encyclopedia*.

Encyclopedia is a holistic form of writing, one that tended to cover all subject matters and all topics of all disciplines. Just as the author of an encyclopedia aspired, by definition, to "grasp" and "embody" in it the entire corpus of knowledge about the world available at a given moment, so those who employed the idea of *liber mundi* had similar aspirations: to use an ingenious device by means of which to encapsulate the entirety of the world, and "translate" it, ideally, into one single ideogram. At the heart of both approaches lies one and the same "drive to completeness," one and the same dream of synthesizing everything into a conveniently limited device. And what Mazzotta finds in Dante is precisely this sense of universality and holism of knowledge: "At the end of the poem, the pilgrim's vision of the whole cosmos as a volume whose leaves are scattered through the layers of the material world . . . merely confirms both Dante's notion that creation is a book and his imaginative impulse of conflating and reconstructing into a unity the rich, unfolding variety of creation" (Mazzotta 1993: 18).

By way of conclusion, it would be fair to say that, from a broader perspective, the whole system of medieval speculations clustered around *liber mundi* reflected in fact some more profound religious and metaphysical suppositions on which the medieval culture was based. As has been noted, the medieval worldview did seriously imply the belief in an ordering and organizing principle as an earthly imitation or "shadow" of the heavenly order.[13] And it is precisely "the belief in a revealed theological-symbolic universe [that] is the premise making possible the representation of the totality and unity of knowledge" (ibid.: 5). All these notions of "unity," "totality," and "synthesis" of knowledge are constant and essential characteristics of medieval learning. Hence a general scholarly tendency that made itself visible all through the Middle Ages is "the commonplace attempt to gather all strands of learning together into an enormous Text, an encyclopedia or summa, that would mirror the historical and transcendental orders just as the Book of God's Word (the Bible) was a speculum of the Book of his Work (nature)" (Gellrich 1985: 18). As such, the idea of the book most conveniently represented the central principle organizing and structuring all knowledge about the world; by paraphrasing Thomas of Celano's words, this book would eventually be a book in which the total was contained (*liber in quo totum continetur*).

There is a wonderful story told about St. Francis de Assisi who, allegedly, collected and carefully saved every single piece of parchment he came across during his travels. To him, the "letters themselves were intrinsically sacred" (ibid.: 35). For he supposedly justified his doing so with this saying: "litterae sunt ex quibus componitur gloriosissimum domini Dei nomen" (Letters are the things from which the most glorious name of God is composed) (ibid.: 35). It is true, then, that—as Thomas Singer has excellently put it—the "metaphor always has and always will tend to take on a life of its own and ask to be understood literally" (Singer 1989: 69).

GEORGE BERKELEY'S "UNIVERSAL LANGUAGE OF NATURE"

In Search of a Tradition

Interestingly enough, the few major twentieth-century thinkers to recognize the presence of the topic of the book of nature in George Berkeley's thought were not English-speaking philosophers, but rather two French philosophers. First, in his influential *L'Intuition philosophique* (1911), Henri Bergson, in an attempt to explain Berkeley's philosophical system, came at a given moment to make the following remark: "It seems to me that Berkeley considers matter as a *thin transparent film* situated between man and God [comme une *mince pellicule transparente* située entre l'homme et Dieu]. Matter remains transparent as long as the philosophers are not concerned with it, and thus God is immediately manifest." This is why, Bergson believes, the most appropriate way of understanding Berkeley's philosophy is to consider the material world as being a "language that God speaks to us" [une langue que Dieu nous parle]. This would lead us, in Bergson's view, to grasp the essence of Berkeley's immaterialism properly. In contrast, Bergson says, the "materialist" philosophies, by emphasizing each syllable, as it were, and stating it as an independent entity, "divert us from the meaning" and "prevent us from following the divine word" (Bergson 1959: 1356). About one decade later, in 1922, Étienne Gilson would talk about a relationship that might be established between Berkeley's immaterialist philosophy and a certain way of thinking characterizing the Platonism of the Middle Ages. More precisely, Gilson saw a possible connection between Berkeley's notion of "optic language" and the philosophy of another Irishman, Johannes Scotus Erigena: "We would not betray Scotus Erigena's thought in saying that for him [Scotus], just as for Berkeley, Nature is the language that its Author is speaking to us [la nature est le langage que nous parle Son Auteur]. Let us dedicate this connection to Taine's memory: Berkeley and Erigena were both Irishmen" (Gilson 1944: 214).

Whether or not Berkeley was indebted for his employment of the topic of *liber mundi* precisely to his being (Anglo-)Irish, it is quite difficult to know. What can be shown more easily instead is that he made an impressively extensive use of this topic, turning it into a central argument in his philosophical system. And this is in fact one of the most remarkable things about George Berkeley's case: it renders his philosophy not only original in its eighteenth-century intellectual context, but also strikingly complex when considered in itself.

Starting with his first important philosophical work, namely *An Essay towards a New Theory of Vision*, published in 1709, Berkeley employed the notion of the world as a text. In this work he proposes a theory according to which the things we see in the world around us are in fact *signs*:

> These signs are constant and universal, their connexion with tangible ideas has been learnt at our first entrance in the world; and ever since, almost every moment of our lives, it has been occurring to our thoughts, and fastening and striking deeper on our minds. (Berkeley 1948–57, 1:229)

These signs are what we immediately experience when we encounter the world outside us. Even if, for strategic reasons,[14] Berkeley did not, in this first writing, overtly deny the existence of matter as such, he nevertheless considered the external word completely mind-dependent, and accessible to us only in the shape of these signs. In light of the subsequent developments of Berkeley's immaterialist philosophy, we cannot experience anything other than such immaterial signs, our cognitive faculties being unable to grasp anything of the nature of matter. Berkeley undertakes a rigorous analysis of the notion of its existence and is eventually compelled to conclude that matter does not exist as such since, in order for something to exist, we have to have some form of perception of it, which is not the case with matter. What we do perceive—properly speaking—is a succession of signs, a system of symbols, based on which, through habit and repetition, we can get a certain degree of understanding of the world around us. In other words, we humans are fated to live among symbols always, and to end up turning our lives into a form of everyday hermeneutics. Still, one cannot help asking this question: what are the principles on which such a peculiar system of thought is based?

A satisfactory answer to this question is possibly to be found in an essay Berkeley published many years later, in the shape of an explanatory and apologetic addendum to his earlier work on vision, and titled, quite significantly for the purpose of the present discussion: *The Theory of Vision; or, Visual Language shewing the immediate Presence and Providence of a Deity— Vindicated and Explained* (1733).[15] This addendum, by making much more explicit what was initially insufficiently clear or somewhat ambiguously stated, is extremely useful for understanding the principles on which Berkeley based his theory of the "visual language."

As the title clearly implies, Berkeley conceived of this "visual language" as being in immediate relationship with the "presence and providence" of God. This means that through this "language" God makes himself known to those who are able to understand such a language, and, moreover, that nature does not have a high value as such, but only insofar as it signifies something about God. It would be a sign of complete blindness on our side if we would simply stop in front of the phenomenal level of nature and take it as what nature is all about. In Berkeley, nature is more than what appears to our senses; nature is a metaphor for things higher than itself. More specifically, in smooth continuation with an entire tradition of theological thinking, some elements of which we examined earlier, the structure of this metaphor is such that it necessarily places God at the heart of the whole system of things. As William J. Mills pertinently put it, "To view the earth as a book is necessarily to view it theocentrically" (Mills 1982: 238). Given this fact, given that—within such a system of thought—nature can never tell us anything significant about itself, God is, and must be, the only source of meaning, the ultimate source of explanation for everything we see happening around us. Actually, in Berkeley, seeing is a very important thing, as it is our chief cognitive faculty: "*Vision is the Language of the Author of Nature*, from thence deducing theorems and solutions of phenomena, and explaining the nature of visible things and the visive faculty" (Berkeley 1948–57, 1:264) Or, even more explicitly, as Berkeley was to put it later on:

> the phenomena of nature, which strike on the senses and are understood by the mind, form not only a magnificent spectacle, but also a most coherent, entertaining, and instructive Discourse; and to effect this, they are conducted, adjusted, and ranged by the greatest wisdom. The language or Discourse is studied with different attention, and interpreted with different degrees of skill. (Berkeley 1948–57, 5:121 [*Siris*])

And this is exactly the fundamental supposition based on which all the medieval speculations around the topic of the *liber naturae/mundi* were developed, as has been shown in some detail in the first section of this chapter. There is a sense in which Berkeley's notion of the "visual language" faithfully reflects Johannes Scotus Erigena's insight "There is nothing, in visible and corporeal things, that does not signify something incorporeal and invisible" (Gilson 1955: 120). In his turn, Erigena based his approach on St. Paul's

Epistles, on St. Augustine, and on the doctrine of Jesus Christ's Incarnation, as well as on a markedly Platonic way of thinking. Then, Erigena's insights on the visible-invisible dialectics grew more and more popular over the centuries, with the long-term result that the notion eventually became widespread that the natural world (*natura*) was, to use the famous phase, "like a book written with God's own finger" (*quasi liber scriptus digito Dei*).

The World as a Divine Language: How It Works and for Whom

Returning now to Berkeley's works, we can see clearly how, once he appropriated the traditional insight of the world as a divine text, and placed himself within the framework delineated by this tradition, he further developed his own notion of a "visual language"—that is, a language of things, not of words, some sort of reified discourse—by following in detail the rules, laws, and principles based on which any human language (or, as he calls it, "artificial language") works.[16] For example, in the same addendum to his early writing on vision, Berkeley says:

> A great number of arbitrary signs, various and opposite, do constitute a language. If such arbitrary connexion be instituted by men, it is an artificial language; if by the Author of Nature, it is a natural language. Infinitely various are the modifications of light and sound, whence they are each capable of supplying an endless variety of signs, and, accordingly, have been each employed to form languages; the one by the arbitrary appointment of mankind, the other by that of God Himself. A connexion established by the Author of Nature, in the ordinary course of things, may surely be called natural; as that made by men will be named artificial. (Berkeley 1948–57, 2:265 [*The Theory of Vision*])

Let us note, at this stage, the special emphasis Berkeley always places on the importance of God as author of the world's discourse. Just as in the metaphysics underlying the medieval use of the *liber mundi* topic God is revealing himself through each individual letter of the world's book, so in Berkeley God has a crucial role to play within the cosmic scheme of things: God is by no means a remote entity, vaguely associated with the world, but rather he is immediately present in every element, in every single syllable, of the world's text as the only source of its meaning. God speaks the "language of nature," and we are his attentive audience. God is the supreme guarantor of the grammar of the world as he instituted the rules according to which the signs are combined and connected with each other; thanks to his continual care and attentiveness, the meaningful cosmos is prevented from turning into a meaningless chaos.

Indeed, there is a certain sense in which Berkeley's God is even more actively and immediately present than was the medieval God who "wrote" the *liber mundi*: Berkeley's God speaks through every single thing we see around, whereas in the medieval context of *liber mundi* we are, as it were, reminded of God as its author, the sensible things pointing to God as their creator. This is probably one of the significant differences between Berkeley and those medieval authors who saw God as the author of the book of nature: properly speaking, in Berkeley the "world is not, as it was for the mediaevals, the *book* of God, since written words have only an indirect connection with their creator. Rather, it is the *speech* of God, so many immediate expressions of, and testaments to, His presence with us" (Cooper 1996: 264). Of course, both Berkeley's "visual language" and the medieval *liber mundi* essentially belong to the same tradition of thought, operating within the same framework of metaphysical and theological presuppositions about the origin, meaning, and ultimate ontological makeup of the world. According to these presuppositions the world as we see it is just a system of signs, riddles, and symbols, and it is only through them that we learn something about the author of this world, about God himself, who is behind all these; nevertheless, we come in Berkeley across a certain shift of emphasis, with the result that God is given an even more prominent role than in the medieval universe, he is seen now as more directly and immediately present in the world. It is only for reasons of simplicity that I am talking in this chapter about Berkeley's use of *liber mundi*—*lingua mundi* would have been a more appropriate term to use in the case of Berkeley. Somehow as a compromise solution between the strictly medieval view of the world as an already written book and Berkeley's world as a language that God is constantly speaking to us, Branka Arsić, in her book on Berkeley, speaks at some point of the world as a living text, of God's world as a "work in progress." Thus, the world is not so much a "final product," in which no change can be made, as an unfolding process, a living thing. The book of nature

> has its rhythm, which is the rhythm of words and sentences, the rhythm of the succession of different milieus—the succession of ocean and land, city and desert, plants and animals. . . . Rhythms, therefore, are the blank space between words or lines. Everything unfolds as if God has to think over what to write next in his work in progress, in his infinite novel that we call the world. (Arsić 2003: 66)

In a way, the book of the world is not yet finished, it is not yet printed and bound, but it is a book in the making. In writing his book, God uses an ever-changing style, a style marked by spontaneity and freedom: "God does not care at all about 'the style' of the book he writes. His visual writing is a flood of words, and this flood is what we call the course of things" (ibid.: 109).

On the other hand, just as in the case of the medieval philosopher, for Berkeley studying "this world" is essentially a theological enterprise, and should be accomplished with the carefulness and purity of mind that an appropriate practice of theology requires. As he says:

> it is the searching after, and endeavoring to understand those signs instituted by the Author of Nature, that ought to be the employment of the natural philosopher, and not the pretending to explain things by corporeal causes; which doctrine seems to have too much estranged the minds of men from that active principle, that supreme and wise spirit, *in whom we live, move, and have our being*. (Berkeley 1948–57: 2:69 [*Principles*])

The last (italicized) phrase is, in fact, a quotation from the Bible (Acts 17.28),[17] and is one of the biblical sayings most frequently quoted by Berkeley throughout his works. The notion of God is absolutely central to the immaterialist scheme of things. Immaterialism is definitely a God-centered philosophy, in which God is the beginning and the end of everything. In its turn, this central position that God occupies in Berkeley's thought determines the way in which he sees the mission of philosophy itself as a discipline in charge of making sense of the world we live in: to him philosophy is not simply an academic discipline among many others, but above all philosophy is some form of "religious exercise" (*askesis*), and, as such, should have a privileged status among the humanistic disciplines. The primary aim of philosophy consists, as Berkeley says in his *Three Dialogues between Hylas and Philonous* in providing us with "the sublime notion of a God, and the comfortable expectation of immortality" (Berkeley 1948–57, 2:168). At the beginnings of a modern age in which almost all the stable truths of old were shaken and the theological certainties mercilessly questioned, in which theology and theological ways of thinking lost their prestige and social functions, Berkeley saw philosophy as a serious and credible replacement for theology. In his view, philosophy should have a definite apologetic and soteriological function, and it should be first of all considered in terms of disseminating and making clearer the Christian doctrine, and of pointing to "paths of salvation," of helping people find their ways in this world, and more importantly their ways out of it. He would happily agree with the Augustinian dictum: *una vera philosophia—Christiana philosophia.* And it is particularly this attitude of his toward what philosophy should be that, once more, points to a strong relationship between his own way of thinking and a certain medieval consideration of philosophy as somehow subordinate, as playing the role of "helper" of theology (*ancilla theologiae*). But more about that will be said in chapter 5 of this book, a chapter dedicated specifically to Berkeley's place in the history of Christian apologetics.

As we just saw, Berkeley believed that it is "endeavoring to understand those signs instituted by the Author of Nature, that ought to be the employment of the natural philosopher." The philosopher is, as it were, a "professional reader" of the cosmic text, one who has the superior ability and competence, along with the social recognition, to read and interpret the *liber mundi* for others, and more often than not this is not a very easy thing to do. Throughout his writings Berkeley gives ample and sophisticated explanations of the way the "discourse" of the world is constituted, what lies behind what we see in the first instance, how precisely the "reading" of the world should take place, and which are the best rules one has to follow when undertaking such an enterprise. In *The Principles of Human Knowledge* (1710), for example, he says:

> the connexion of ideas does not imply the relation of cause and effect, but only of a mark or sign with the thing signified. The fire which I see is not the cause of the pain I suffer upon my approaching it, but the mark that forewarns me of it. In like manner, the noise that I hear is not the effect of this or that motion or collision of the ambient bodies, but the sign thereof. (Ibid., 2:69)

Then, a crucial passage occurs in which Berkeley openly proposes a "methodological shift" from an explanation based on "causal" relationships between two given entities to one based on a relationship of "signifying" between those entities. He would say, for instance, that fire is not the cause of the pain, but rather a sign of the pain. Moreover, he considers that such a shift cannot but have hugely beneficial effects on the progress of knowledge and mark out our better understanding of the world around:

> the reason why ideas are formed into machines, that is, artificial and regular combinations, is the same with that for combining letters into words. . . .

Hence it is evident, that those things which under the notion of a cause co-operating or concurring to the production of effects, are altogether inexplicable, and run us into great absurdities, may be very naturally explained, and have a proper and obvious use assigned them, when they are considered only as marks or signs for our information. (Ibid., 2:69)

In a similar manner, in *Alciphron; or, The Minute Philosopher* (1732), namely in the fourth dialogue, Berkeley talks of the arbitrary, "non-necessary" character of the relationship between *signum* ("sensible signs") and *signatum* ("the things they stand for"). Just as between the particular way in which, for instance, the word "tree" sounds, on the one hand, and the form of a real tree, on the other, there is no resemblance or necessary connection, so is there no essential relationship, but simply an arbitrary one, between a certain configuration of shapes, colors, and movements we see at a given moment and the real thing they "signify." Besides, within the same dialogue, some important hints are given as to what is the ultimate purpose of the reading of the world:

God speaks to men by the intervention and use of arbitrary, outward, sensible signs, having no resemblance or necessary connexion with the things they stand for and suggest; . . . by innumerable combinations of these signs, an endless variety of things is discovered and made known to us; . . . we are thereby instructed or informed in their different natures; . . . we are taught and admonished what to shun, and what to pursue; and we are directed how to regulate our motions, and how to act with respect to things distant from us, as well in time and place. (Ibid., 3:149)

Our approach to the language of nature must first of all be a pragmatic one: we are users of the language called "world" because we have various necessities, needs, and practical interests in this world-language. Our interactions with the world are deeply marked by the practical needs that we need to address. The better and closer our "reading" of the world is, the happier and smoother our passing through the world will be. As a comprehensive conclusion of this part of the dialogue, Berkeley says:

Upon the whole, it seems the proper objects of sight are light and colours, with their several shades and degrees; all which, being infinitely diversified and combined, form a language wonderfully adapted to suggest and exhibit to us the distances, figures, situations, dimensions, and various qualities of tangible objects: not by similitude, nor yet by inference of necessary connexion, but by the arbitrary imposition of Providence, just as words suggest the things signified by them. (Ibid., 3:154)

In other words, just as there are puns and other tricks in the language proper, so in the language of nature are there such tricky signs as visual illusions. "These tricky signs show . . . that there is no necessary connection in either language between sign and thing signified" (Berman 1994: 139).

Le Grand Livre de la Nature *and the World as a Machine*

In his postulating God as an immediate "linguistic" presence, as one who is uninterruptedly speaking to us through the sensible things we come across, Berkeley was rather eccentric and somehow "outdated" in his own time. For, although the topic of the "great Book of Nature"—by virtue of its historical prestige and intrinsic suggestiveness, and thanks to the "guaranteed" rhetorical effects one would obtain through its employment—continued to be used to a large extent throughout the eighteenth century (and later, of course), sometime during the seventeenth century, a new, more successful, metaphor began to be increasingly employed in the scientific, philosophical, literary, and even political discourses: the world as a machine.[18] This change is in itself symptomatic of the new theoretical needs and interests of the epoch. For, as William Mills excellently put it, the choice of "one metaphor rather than another is highly indicative of the needs and aspirations of that society. The chosen metaphor is exploited for all its implications, around which a systematic world vision is elaborated" (Mills 1982: 238). In opting for a certain prevailing metaphor rather than for another, a culture betrays something deep and significant about its *Weltanschauung*. The machine metaphors (body as a machine, earth as a machine had been used long before, in a tradition that might be traced back to Girolamo Cardano and Leonardo da Vinci[19] or even earlier, but in the seventeenth century, within the context of the "mechanical" ways of explanation enthusiastically proposed by the "new philosophy," they gradually gained widespread popularity and unprecedented success. To the extent that, in sharp contrast with George Berkeley's philosophizing on the "visual language" that God is speaking to us, most of the promoters of the "new philosophy" (Locke, Descartes, Gassendi, and so on) became increasingly fascinated with a vision of the world as a precise and wonderful machine, as a mechanism that the philosophers have a duty to deconstruct and explain away.

One of the results of this vision of nature is that all human knowledge and philosophy in particular should serve to find the functioning rules and principles of this divine, most interesting machine that endlessly amazes and delights us. And one of the most consequential things about using the machine metaphor—especially when compared to the use of the book metaphor—is that the emphasis is placed not so much on God as the maker of this machinery (he is increasingly seen as a "retired engineer," and his "omniscience and omnipotence are now to be demonstrated only by His total abstinence from intervention in the world" [ibid.: 247]) as on discovering, describing, and enjoying the machine itself. Actually, these modern minds were so fascinated with the "constitution," "movements," principles, "predictability," and "inner parts" of this marvelous machine that they failed to care, and philosophize, about its "origin."

Of course, people continued to use the topic of the book of nature, but they saw in it less as the ultimate "model of the universe" and more as a convenient rhetorical device. Let us take only one example: René Descartes's case. It is true, at the very beginning of his *Discourse on Method* we come immediately across the famous Cartesian confession: "I resolved to seek no other knowledge than that which I might find within myself, or perhaps in the great book of nature" (Descartes 1956: 6). Nevertheless, this metaphor seems to play for him the role of a rather rhetorical device. Given the precise autobiographical context within which he places this confession, it is reasonable to suppose that what he implies by this statement is the fact that he prefers the empirical study of nature to the bookishness and book-worshipping character of, in his view, the Scholastic ways of thinking. That his mind was in a serious way attached to the idea of "the world as a machine" is proved by the repeated appeals to the mechanistic metaphor in, for example, *Principia philosophiae*. Here he says: "I have described the Earth and the whole visible universe in the manner of a machine" or: "The only difference I can see between machines and natural objects is that the workings of machines are mostly carried out by apparatus large enough to be readily perceptible by the senses (as is required to make their manufacture humanly possible), whereas natural processes almost always depend on parts so small that they utterly elude our senses". (Descartes 1954: 229, 236 [*Principia philosophiae* 4.188, 203]). And many other similar passages can be found throughout the Cartesian works.

Let me also say that, in choosing to use the metaphor of the world as a discourse rather than the machine metaphor, Berkeley was fully aware of the completely different metaphysical implications that the use of each of the two metaphors could have. By passionately advocating the world as a divine text, he endeavored to warn against, and rule out, the deistic implications that, thought he, the alternative choice might have brought about:

Some philosophers, being convinced of the wisdom and power of the Creator, from the make and contrivance of organized bodies and orderly system
of the world, did nevertheless imagine that he left this system with all its parts
and contents well adjusted and put in motion, as an artist leaves a clock, to
go thenceforward of itself for a certain period. But this Visual Language
proves, not a Creator merely, but a provident Governor, actually and inti-
mately present, and attentive to all our interests and motions, who . . .
designs throughout the whole course of our lives, informing, admonishing,
and directing incessantly, in a most evident and sensible manner. (Berkeley
1948–57, 3:160 [*Crito Speaks*])

Berkeley's "Pragmatism"

Finally, setting aside the distinction book-speech I mentioned above, there
is a sense in which Berkeley's metaphor of the "universal language of nature" brings something new in the history of the *liber naturae* topic. This
novelty is about one of the purposes of reading and understanding the cosmic discourse. More precisely, Berkeley talks at some point about a "universal language of the Author of Nature" whereby

we are instructed how to regulate our actions in order to attain those things
that are necessary to the preservation and well-being of our bodies, as also
to avoid whatever may be hurtful and destructive of them. It is by their
information that we are principally guided in all the transactions and concerns of life. And the manner wherein they signify and mark unto us the
objects which are at a distance is the same with that of languages and signs
of human appointment, which do not suggest the things signified by any
likeness or identity of nature, but only by an habitual connexion that experience has made us to observe between them. (Berkeley 1948–57: 1:231 [*An
Essay*])

The underlying supposition behind such a passage is, then, the idea that our
interests in understanding the "universal language of the Author of nature"
are above all practical interests, derived from necessities of our everyday life,
from the various practical needs we have to address in the course of our
earthly journey. The most immediate thing one can attain by grasping the
meaning of the "language of nature" is, in Berkeley's view, the "preservation and well-being" of one's body, and avoiding "whatever may be hurtful
and destructive" to it. As it were, some "letters" or "words" or "sentences"
of this visible language may cause injuries and troubles to its users, and have
therefore to be carefully avoided.

This is undoubtedly a significant change in the use of this metaphor within the European tradition. In a traditional Christian context, the book of nature had been always regarded as a prolegomenon to a better understanding of what the Bible says: the book of natue helped people realize what God's message was about as far as the natural world was concerned. Accordingly, considering the *liber naturae* in itself would have been for a medieval man the most incomprehensible thing to do. The two books (nature and scripture) were always considered together, and they were referred to as such. For instance, as Ernest Robert Curtius notes, for "the preacher the book of nature must figure with the Bible as a source of material" (Curtius 1979, 320). Reading the "revealed book" (the Bible) and reading the book of nature were performed with the understanding that these were complementary practices, and not at all alternatives. "Those who knew how to read this book [of nature] were able to understand the allegories hidden in the scriptures, where, beneath references to simple earthly things (plants, stones, animals), symbolic meanings lay" (Eco 1995, 15). There is an intimate connection between nature and scripture, as both are texts in whose making God is immediately involved. Therefore, reading the book of nature had a very clear soteriological and somehow "other-worldly" dimension: it was not for the sake of "this world" that one had to endeavor to understand the cosmic discourse, but for the sake of one's soul's fate once arrived in "the world after." A proper Christian life means to know how to grasp in the book of the world the truths revealed by the sacred doctrines. For instance, in his famous *Imitatio Christi* Thomas à Kempis says: "If thine heart were right, then every creature should be to thee a mirror of life and a book of holy doctrine" (Si rectum cor tuum esset, tunc omnis creatura speculum vitae et liber sacrae doctrinae esset) (Kempis [in Boethius, Thomas à Kempis, Thomas Browne] 1943, 175). Nature as such, along with our practical dealings and concerns with it, does not deserve any theoretical interest on our side; it is only the superior necessity of "getting rid" of this world that makes us have a temporary involvement in its affairs.

In addition to all this, Berkeley's attitude toward his "language of nature" brings into play a remarkably pragmatic attitude. Although Berkeley was a genuinely religious person, and an ardent apologist of the Christian faith, when he approached the natural world he did not look into it only for "paths to salvation," but he also tried to accommodate its conditions, rules, and requirements. In other words, his approach to the "external world" is also one of utility, efficiency, and well-being, and his religiosity is of a slightly different kind from that of the medieval believer. It is true, ontologically speaking, nature is still a text, a sophisticated system of signs, just as in the medieval tradition, but the real reason why one has to read this book differs from the reason a medieval man felt he had to do it.

This is not to say that the pragmatic attitude is the only one we might have to the surrounding world. Berkeley's world also displays a "great beauty," orderliness, and harmony. This is precisely because this world is God's epiphany. Moreover, in *Alciphron,* when talking about the tremendous benefits that the acceptance of the idea of God might have upon our understanding of the world, Crito shows that only in a world created by God there is place for beauty and orderliness:

> In a system of spirits, subordinate to the will, and the direction of the Father of spirits, governing them by laws and conducting them by methods suitable to wise and good ends, there will be great beauty. But in an incoherent fortuitous system, governed by chance, or in a blind system, governed by fate, or in a system where Providence doth not preside, how can beauty be, which cannot be without order, which cannot be without design? (Berkeley 1948–57, 3:129–30)

This being said, Berkeley's "pragmatism" should be seen not as an apology for our "using" of the world, but—on the contrary—as a wise means through which we can integrate ourselves, as smoothly as possible, in this beautiful world. Despite all his pragmatic attitudes, there is also sometimes a clear element of ecology in Berkeley's approach to nature. True, according to him, we have to accommodate ourselves to this world, and to satisfy our needs, but in doing so we have to take good care not to inflict any harm in it: "living reasonably while we are here upon earth, proportioning our esteem to the value of things, and so using this world as not to abuse it" (Ibid.:178).

Concluding Remarks

By way of conclusion, it should be clear enough by now that for George Berkeley the world is a text or, more precisely, a discourse (a "universal language") in an explicit and fundamental way. When Frederick Copleston comes to talk about Berkeley's philosophy, in his monumental *History of Philosophy,* he overtly recognizes that, for the Irish Bishop, "the whole system of Nature is a system of signs, a visual divine language, speaking to our minds of God" (Copleston 1993–94, 5:248). In contrast to other promoters of the "new philosophy," for whom the topic of *le grand livre de la nature* plays primarily rhetorical functions, for Berkeley "the language of nature" actually means that God is speaking to us by the means of the world, or, in his own words, "the great Mover and Author of Nature constantly explaineth Himself to the eyes of men. . . . In consequence, . . . you have as much reason to think the Universal Agent or God speaks to your eyes, as you can have for thinking any particular person speaks to your ears" (Berkeley 1948–57, 3:157 [*Alciphron*]). Thus, a far-reaching consequence of Berkeley's philosophy should be that, as the result of an appropriate and unprejudiced dealing with the world around, we must have the feeling, or the insight, that our life is ultimately an uninterrupted conversation with God: "In fact our understanding of what is the case amounts, for Berkeley, to knowing what God wishes us to do: correct description of the natural world is to engage in conversation with God who guides us" (Clark 1998: 24).

Of course, some of the medieval implications of the topic are not manifest in Berkeley's thought anymore, but the main metaphysical suppositions on which the use of the topic of the *liber naturae* was based are clearly reasserted in his philosophy. For Berkeley's explicit manner of postulating *liber naturae* implies: a) the perception of God as a divine author who has "spoken" the world; b) the perception of "this world" as a discourse, or text, or language—a meaningful whole and a coherent system of signs; c) the existence of a precise author/subject relationship between God and the world; and d) the existence of a "reader" who consciously and constantly endeavors to transcend the "sign" (*signum*) to the "signified thing" (*signatum*). Even if he brought about some changes and additions to the topic, he placed himself within the same theological and metaphysical framework as the medieval authors.

Moreover, it is worth noting that there is a certain sense in which, given his denial of the existence of matter, Berkeley is even more radical than any other author, medieval or modern, who had written on this topic before him. This radicalism comes from the fact that it belongs to the nature of any book, language, or discourse—the discourse of nature included—to resort to some material support, however lesser or insignificant, in order to make itself visible/readable: paper, ink, and so forth. Of course, if confronted with such a criticism, Berkeley would, based on the principles of his immaterialism, probably show that there is nothing inconsistent in supposing a text without a material support: a piece of paper, for example, is not matter as such, but only an idea, and that, similarly, in order for the world to be a discourse it does not need to be a material world. Nevertheless, in order for a sign to signify it has to make use of something that is not a sign itself: which is problematic when, as in Berkeley's philosophy, everything is a sign. It is true that, by saying that this world is God's speech, Berkeley reduces to a minimum the need for a material support of the sign: a spoken word, or a speech, needs comparatively less material than a book does. Nevertheless, if we take the metaphor literally, even God's speech, in order to make itself heard, needs—as in the case of any other sound—the physical vibration of "something."

This is another consequence of Berkeley's uncompromising immaterialism and should be considered, I think, in immediate connection to what I would like to call metaphorically the angelism underlying his whole system: just as in the world of angels there is absolutely no need for material entities, bodies, corporal substances, and the like, and nevertheless such a world works and remains coherent in its own way, so in Berkeley's world there is no need for matter and material substances, for bodies and corporeal things. Theologically, an angelic world can be represented in the absence of matter. For instance, angels can, according to the traditional view, perfectly communicate with each other, and uninterruptedly praise God without their having to be involved in the world of matter at all. They sing, and speak, and, in so doing, they use a language, but the language they use does not suppose any material support at all. In a fashion somehow similar to that of the angelic world, Berkeley's "visual language" seems to make sense, in its own way, in the absence of the realm of matter.

Finally, I would like to say a few words about the necessity of placing Berkeley in the tradition of the book of nature. There have been numerous studies published over the last decades dealing with Berkeley's "optic language." Nevertheless, the general tendency in the contemporary Berkeley scholarship, as far as this topic is concerned, is to isolate completely Berkeley's dealing with the "optic language" from the long tradition of the book of nature, cuttin it off from all the theology presupposed by this tradition. The "optic language" is most often considered as "Berkeley's argument for a divine visual language" and is discussed almost exclusively in terms of formal consistency, logical coherence, and so on, ignoring the long and complex tradition of thought behind Berkeley's approach. To take only one example, a recent article titled "Is Berkeley's World a Divine Language?" by James P. Danaher and published in *Modern Theology* (Danaher 2002), deals precisely with Berkeley's "visual language," but without making any reference, however vague or allusive, to the theological tradition of the book of nature, a tradition that certainly inspired and nourished Berkeley's notion of the world as a "discourse" of God. Berkeley's "visual language" is considered either in itself, as an argument for his immaterialism, or in connection to Locke's "semantic atomism," Saussure's "structuralism," Aristotle's doctrine of the "active intellect," or even Winston Churchill's speeches during World War II (ibid.). Nevertheless, there is no mention at all of the medieval tradition of the *liber mundi*. To write a paper with such a title, and, moreover, to publish it in an important theological journal, and, nevertheless, to avoid systematically any mention of the tremendously important theological implications of the notion of "divine language" is quite remarkable.

4.   *George Berkeley and the Alchemical Tradition*

In chapter 2 of this book George Berkeley's last published work, *Siris*, has been dealt with almost exclusively from the vantage point of the literary procedures and rhetorical techniques by means of which this writing was produced. In other words, in chapter 2 I considered *Siris* from a formal angle, from the perspective of how it is written, without paying too much attention to what *Siris* is about. In the present chapter I will deal with *Siris*'s content. The central idea of this chapter is that in *Siris* Berkeley comes to employ and make extensive use of one of the most ancient (if controversial) "spiritual techniques" and speculative ways of thought: alchemy. I will discuss Berkeley's arguments and notions in *Siris* by constant reference to alchemical topics, writings, and authors. It is the objective of the present chapter to show that, apart from its being under the strong influence of the Platonic tradition—though in close connection with it—Berkeley's thought, as it reveals itself in *Siris*, seems to have been also marked by some of the intellectual inclinations, spiritual concerns, and mind-sets characterizing the alchemical tradition.

THE SEARCH FOR THE *ELIXIR VITAE*

Siris: *A Peculiar Philosophical Writing*

In Berkeley's lifetime the controversial *Siris* (1744) became one of his very few "best-sellers." Nevertheless, despite its being "the most immediately influential of all Berkeley's books, with five editions in Dublin and London within the year," *Siris* does not in general interest researchers today, being "most frequently ignored by modern Berkeley scholars" (Walmsley 1990: 142). Most of today's presentations of (or introductions to) Berkeley's philosophy simply neglect to say anything about *Siris*. If they do, it is only in the context of the curiosities of Berkeley's biography. It is as if *Siris* were one of those regrettable pieces, scribbled sometimes by great men who get old and decrepit, when their poor minds produce nothing other than embarrassingly incomprehensible things, which—out of respect for their greatness of yore—we should pass over in silence. As a matter of fact, this work brought Berkeley trouble from the very beginning. Upon its publication, for all its immediate success, it tended to amuse the sober-minded scholarly circles of Berkeley's day, making many of his learned contemporaries laugh at him.[1] It was seen by many as just another of the Bishop's oddities, something an intellectually serious person should not buy or read in public. Then, with the passing of time, this work has embarrassed many adepts of Berkeley's philosophy, and caused some heated disputes among his commentators.[2] *Siris* is indeed a peculiar piece of writing: it is a fascinating and puzzling book, a book about everything in the world, a writing within which medical knowledge is curiously mixed with metaphysical speculations, alchemy is brought dangerously close to some of the findings of modern science, and the so-called "natural philosophy" is dealt with in often surprising proximity with ancient esoteric doctrines and exotic ways of thinking. As Horace Walpole quipped: "The book contains every subject from tar-water to the Trinity" (quoted in ibid.: 144). In short, with this writing, George Berkeley places himself in a tradition of thought that the modern "scientific spirit" cannot but reject in the strongest terms. Thinking alchemically and, in general, esoterically about nature was at that time a luxurious philosophical oddity that, of all the promoters of the modern scientific spirit, only Isaac Newton could afford.

The question is, of course: Why did Berkeley choose to write such an odd book? What were his intentions when writing this piece? What precisely made Berkeley embark on such a nonmodern way of philosophizing and thinking about nature? What triggered, in biographical terms, this intellectual adventure? Very briefly, to use Berkeley's own words, he embarked on writing this piece with the intention

> to communicate to the public the salutary virtues of tar-water; to which I thought myself indispensably obliged by the duty every man owes to mankind. And, as effects are linked with their causes, my thoughts on this low but useful theme led me to farther enquiries, and those on to others, remote perhaps and speculative, but, I hope, not altogether useless or unentertaining. (Berkeley 1948–57, 5:31 [*Siris*])

For Berkeley, these curative virtues are impressive and countless. He offered a detailed list of numerous individual cases in which this medicine had been successful, as well as the innumerable illnesses that could be cured using the

wonder medicine. It proved to work with excellent results against all sorts
of illnesses, of the most diverse nature: not only against various temporary
afflictions, but also against more serious diseases; it had beneficial effects not
only for the health of the body, but also for the well-being of the mind and
the powers of the intellect. As a matter of fact, in a private letter written
about the same time, George Berkeley even comes to confess that he thinks
tar-water may be a panacea:

> I freely own that I suspect tar-water is a panacea. I may be mistaken, but it
> is worth trial: for the chance of so great and general a benefit, I am willing
> to stand the ridicule of proposing it. . . . And if God hath given us so great
> a blessing, and made a medicine so cheap and plenty as tar to be withal so
> universal in its effects, to ease the miseries of human life, shall men be ridi-
> culed or bantered out of its use, especially when they run no risk in the trial?
> (Ibid.: 175)

As in the case of his "Bermuda project" some two decades earlier (a case
that I will discuss in detail in chapter 6), Berkeley was again ready to "stand
the ridicule" of proposing something that, although deemed absurd or crazy
by the majority's opinion, he believed would have tremendously beneficial
effects on his neighbors' well-being, either in spiritual terms (in the case of
the Bermuda project) or simply in bodily terms (in the case of tar-water).
When such a major thing as easing the "miseries of human life" is at stake,
thought Berkeley, the ridicule one might have to suffer as a result of this is
indeed a very low price to pay. For someone whose "sole end of all his
projects, and the business of his life" was the "charity to men's souls and
bodies" (Berkeley's wife quoted in Luce 1949: 182) "standing the ridicule"
of proposing a panacea must have been relatively unimportant. On the
other hand, apart from his touching readiness to stand the ridicule, what
makes his enterprise even more remarkable is the fact that it is not a very
common thing among modern academic, mainstream thinkers to deal with
such a magic medicine, or panacea, as that proposed by Bishop Berkeley.
There is, of course, the above-mentioned exception of Isaac Newton, who
became very interested in the alchemical tradition too, but he did not go as
far as to propose panaceas. Hence the numerous misunderstandings to
which Berkeley's proposal of tar-water as a panacea has given rise over the
centuries.

To put it very briefly, the story in *Siris* goes like this: against the background of the terrible famine in Ireland in the early 1740s, of the subsequent
epidemic, and, more importantly, of the lack of professional physicians in

his diocese, Berkeley (at that time Bishop of Cloyne) felt that he had to do something about this situation and "ease the miseries" of his neighbors' lives. During his stay in America in the late 1720s and early1730s he had learned that tar-water was successfully used there as a medicine. He later received further confirmation that tar-water was used as a medicine in other parts of the world too. Berkeley thus decided to recommend tar-water as a cure for the sick in his diocese. In order to make his case, he talked extensively of the various cases in which tar-water had worked well, explained its mode of preparation (by mixing pine tar with water, then allowing the mixture to settle, and finally draining off the clear fluid that resulted), and gave details about the best dosage to be used for the various kinds of maladies. The largest portion of the book, however, is dedicated to explaining why tar-water had these curative qualities. For this purpose, Berkeley employed the ancient topic of the "Great Chain of Being": tar-water has these amazing medicinal effects precisely because it is located at the very end of a cosmic chain connecting the lowest forms of existence (vegetal existence, in this case) to the highest (God). Based on some botanical observations about the role of sunlight in plant physiology, Berkeley concluded that tar was nothing other than "condensed light." Then he significantly enlarged the discussion by placing it within a sophisticated Platonic framework of thinking in which the sun was a visible symbol of God, thus pointing to tar as a gift that God himself generously sent us. Thus, he embarked on an ample historical journey in search for those esoteric (theosophical, alchemical, Hermetic) doctrines and authors who endorsed his own views on tar-water, the Great Chain of Being, and the cosmos as a divine epiphany. The book ends in this theological and speculative vein. (Needless to say, *Siris* is much more complex than I briefly outlined here.)

To today's readers what seems especially outdated is the "scientific" information described in Berkeley's *Siris*, and the modalities of its producing, exposing, and testing. Although "he studied the best chemistry and physics of his day" (ibid.: 205), Berkeley did no more, from our retrospective point of view, than summarize and (re)deliver the markedly deductive and speculative statements of ancient, medieval, or early modern science.[3] As one modern editor of Berkeley's *Siris* rightly noted, to "read Berkeley's scientific sections is humiliating, for here one of our ablest and most learned minds is writing things which the most mediocre student of to-day knows to be wrong" (Jessop 1953: 7). In short, as a "scientific approach," in the modern, generally received sense of the phrase, Berkeley's *Siris* is to be considered, either totally or partially, a failure.

Nevertheless, there is another, deeper aspect of this work that requires, I think, more particular attention and a more appropriate contextualization than it receives today. For, in some way, considered in its spirit and within the broader context of the history of ideas, Berkeley's specific dealing with tar-water as a panacea, as well as the whole historical and metaphysical argumentation he quite impressively employed for that purpose, could prove to be more significant and, theoretically, more fascinating than many of the sober, more rigorous medical writings of the eighteenth century. Of course, his approach to tar-water will not satisfy the modern scientific mind. But his being "right" or "wrong" is of little import in this context. I believe that George Berkeley's considerations in *Siris*, if we are to make some (deeper) sense of them and not simply rule them out as outdated, are not to be judged by standards imposed by the subsequent developments in physics, chemistry, and biology. If thus judged, this realization is all that we gain from reading *Siris*.

It is one of the central ideas of this chapter that, in proposing his panacea, Berkeley was in fact placing himself in a long (especially alchemical) tradition of the search for the *elixir vitae*, for some "magic tincture" or medicine that would cure all illnesses and supply the "patient" with a number of outstanding attributes: perfect health, well being, moral and intellectual betterment. From the standpoint of the alchemical way of thinking, George Berkeley's puzzling approach was not a "novelty" or an oddity at all; rather it could be regarded as a late, even if somehow "alienated," version of a powerful and widespread tradition. This explains many of the misunderstandings related to the reception of Berkeley's *Siris*. Even if it failed as a scientific or medical work (in today's sense of the word), it succeeded as a comprehensive and bold intellectual attempt at improving the "human condition" and proposing, or dreaming of, a "better life" for his neighbors. Berkeley's curious proposal of his panacea betrays a marked idealistic/utopian propensity toward human integrity and self-improvement. On the other hand, as far as today's reception of *Siris* is concerned, it is one thing to dismiss Berkeley's tar-water panacea as ancient medicine, but quite another thing—and a presumptuous one—to dismiss the whole alchemical cast of thought to which Berkeley's proposals belong. Certainly, it ill becomes people today—who make very large and sometimes utopian claims about the potential benefits of genetic engineering—to scoff at the idea of "transmuting" nature for our benefit. Berkeley openly placed his philosophizing in *Siris* within an alchemical framework of thinking, and in order to understand what this writing is about we certainly have to leave it there. Taking it out of this framework, and judging it by other standards, would only be a recipe for misunderstanding. By thinking alchemically in *Siris* Berkeley simply invites us, not necessarily to do the same, but at least to (empathically) look at the alchemy as the proper place where his writing is to be considered and thought of.

I will in the following discuss in some detail the alchemical notion of *lapis philosophorum*, its significance, complexity and especially symbolism, and the relationships it bears especially with some elements of the traditional Christian *Weltanschauung*. Given the fact that the alchemist's *lapis* is equated in this chapter with Berkeley's tar-water, it is hoped that a detailed discussion of the *lapis philosophorum* will also cast a better light on—and bring forth a better understanding of—Berkeley's bold speculations on tar-water, its curative virtues, and the broader spiritual consequences deriving from its existence.

The Lapis Philosophorum *as a Universal Medicine*

Within the medieval alchemical traditions one of the most important functions of the "philosophers' stone" was to stand for a universal medicine, for some miraculous substance (the so-called *elixir vitae*) capable of healing all imaginable bodily illnesses, as well as conferring upon man a constant perfect health and a prosperous, long—or rather "prolonged"—life. As Eric John Holmyard has put it, the "Stone was also sometimes known as the Elixir or Tincture, and was credited not only with the power of transmuting but with that of prolonging human life indefinitely" (Holmyard 1990: 15). The area of applicability of the *lapis* was not at all limited to the mineral world, to transmuting metals and nonorganic substances into substances of a superior quality, but rather it supposedly worked with good results within the organic realm as well. Paracelsus, for example, starts out one of his alchemical tracts in this vein:

> Having first invoked the name of the Lord Jesus Christ our Saviour, we will enterprize this Work; wherein we shall not only teach to change any inferiour Metal into better, as Iron into Copper, this into Silver, and that into Gold, & c., but also to help all infirmities, whose cure to the opinionated and presumptuous Physicians, doth seem impossible: But that which is greater, to preserve, and keep mortal men to a long, sound, and Perfect Age. (Paracelsus 1975 B)

As a matter of fact, within the Latin alchemical literature one can quite often encounter this equivalence between the stone as a transmuting substance

and as a medicine: *lapis philosophorum seu medicina universalis*. Most importantly, such equivalence is not some accidental feature, but it seems to be
central to every system of alchemical thought/practice—in any case, it is
one of the factors that make possible the survival and development of alchemy, as well as the popularity it has widely enjoyed over the centuries.[4]
There are sophisticated symbols and hardly intelligible terminology involved in alchemy, and it is quite frequent that, when coming across an
alchemical text, one has to decipher some Hermetic and highly ambiguous
manners of saying things, but, in spite of all the obstacles of understanding
and impossibility of obtaining a unique homogeneous interpretation, this
single fact is relatively unambiguous and clearly supported by bibliographical
evidence:[5] the special role played in the alchemical literature by the *lapis*
considered as a medicine, as *elixir vitae*, whatever the (differing) names under
which this is known: Red Tincture, *pharmakon athanasias*, *pharmakon zoes*,
aurum potabile, and the like. For example, in *Theatrum chemicum britannicum*
(1652), in one of the poems there is a mention of

> the Golden Oyle called *Aurum potabile*,
> A medicine most mervelous to preserve Mans health,
> And of Transmutation the greatest can bee. (Ashmole 1968: 422)

Why this equivalence? How is it possible for the alchemists to arrive at this
equation between the agent of transmutation and the panacea? The explanation lies, I suppose, in the fact that, in realizing their *magisterium*, the alchemists are, in the first instance, somehow self-oriented: all the outward
things they seems to work upon, and which seem to suffer so radical a transformation (*transmutatio*) through their approach, play as a matter of fact only
the role of a *visible*, "solidified" metaphor for the inner transformation occurring within the alchemists themselves. In other words, a successful process of *transmutatio* presupposes the accomplishment of some state of perfect
ontological transparency between the inner spiritual world of the alchemist
(*artifex*) and the natural world around, as—according to the alchemical
teachings—the *lapis* seems to be an empirical object belonging to the physical world and, at the same time, an ultimate abstract principle on which life
itself is based: "Verum est quod ista res [lapis philosophorum] sit ea que
magis in te fixa a deo creatur, et ubicumque fueris, semper tecum inseparata
manet, et omnis a deo creatus, a quo hec res separatur, morietur" (Morienus
1974: 26). Granted, there is a certain amount of ambiguity implied here, but
this is an ambiguity making possible the constant and fruitful interplay between the "inside" and the "outside" of the alchemical work. The outside

appears as richness, good health, prolonged life, and so on, all of which are accompanied, on the inside, by moral transformation, spiritual purity, and even sainthood. Dealing with this dialectical relationship between the inward transmutation and the outer one Crisciani and Gagnon speak of

> les indications assez fréquentes, même si parfois seulement allusives, sur la connexion nécessaire entre transmutation extérieure et intérieure, cette dernière consistant dans l'augmentation de puissance des valeurs spirituelles dans l'âme de l'artisan (*artifex*), comme aussi la fréquente interchangeabilité des buts sotériologiques prévus par certains courants alchimiques (correspondant à des sommets de perfection en différentes séeries hiérarchiques: or, santé, longue vie, renouvellement spirituel). (Crisciani and Gagnon 1980: 50)

And it is particularly this fact that, in a sense, makes alchemy a "spiritual technique," rather than simply a practical, profit-oriented craft. On the other hand, and in the long term, this explains sufficiently why alchemy enjoyed so long an interest among several psychoanalysts in the twentieth century. Carl Gustav Jung, with his writings on alchemy—especially his *Psychology and Alchemy* (Jung 1953, 12)—is the most widely known of them.

According to such a line of thought, the external, visible effects of the *magisterium* (serenity, spectacular longevity, perfect health) are only the "social signs" of a successful inner transformation; they are the inevitable (and pleasant) consequences of a deep and complex, sometimes painstaking, "inward transmutation" successfully performed. As a direct consequence of this fact, as has been noted, the "European alchemical literature overflows with delightful legends of adepts who attained magical longevity by virtue of their chemical accomplishments. The successful practitioner was typically revered as an ancient man whose physical well being, in addition to his wealth, marked outwardly the nobility of spirit derived from inward transmutation" (Stavenhagen 1974: 66) This is why the myth of longevity is, in most cases, related in some way or other to the arcane world of alchemy, if not openly derived from it.

Although the search for (not to say obsession with) a panacea is manifest in practically all alchemical traditions, it is within the Islamic alchemy that the *elixir vitae*, in the shape of a "real," concrete pharmaceutical product, played a quite outstanding role. Here alchemy was practiced most often by professional physicians, and some special relationships between alchemy and medicine were established. Such brilliant personalities as Jabir Ibn Haiyan (721–815), al-Razi (866–925), or Avicenna (980–1036) were known as physicians and alchemists at the same time. Indeed, it happened sometimes that the medical art itself was considered first and foremost as a form of alchemy, as the alchemical "products" were constantly been used with good results in curing various illnesses. Razi, for example, explicitly states, "if the elixir is unsuitable to transform lead into gold or glass into rubies, it may quite possibly serve as a medicine" (Federman 1969: 71). In such a case, the medical function of the "philosophers' stone" is exclusive and fundamental. Also, following Razi's ideas, Avicenna saw in the philosopher's stone a medicine,

> a medication of universal efficacy, the cure-all, the panacea. It was he who . . . started off the medieval adepts, who saw in the elixir the way to eternal health and everlasting youth. Though the line that leads from Avicenna to Paracelsus passes through the brains of ever so many monks, physicians, madmen and quacks, the idea is the same. It is the idea of the grand arcanum that cures all ills. (Ibid.: 73)

In general, as several historians have noted,[6] Islamic alchemy had a marked "empirical" character, with a special emphasis on its (re)sources in the natural world, as well as on its would-be applicability to the sphere of everyday life (in medicine, technology, and so on). Islamic alchemy was above all a practical enterprise, usually leaving little room, if any, for abstract speculations or esoteric developments.

The Lapis Philosophorum *as a Symbol of Salvation*

Christian alchemy, instead, came to acquire a strong esoteric and speculative dimension. Of course, the Islamic "medical" component was to a great extent transmitted to the Christian world along with the alchemy itself (sometime in the twelfth to thirteenth centuries). But, in addition to all the practical and technical considerations, the Christian alchemists supplied their *magisterium* with a high degree of metaphysical and theological sophistication, as well as with a complex system of ethical and mystical speculations. Under the new Christian circumstances, alchemy turned out to be not only a simply medical technique but also a sophisticated "soteriological art," with its main component (*opus magnum*) playing the role of a metaphor for the Christian's efforts to acquire "eternal salvation": "In Christian Europe, the Great Work, already reflecting a spiritual significance, often took on a profoundly soteriological character. Here, the stages of the Work, from the initial chaos of matter stripped of its basic qualities to the triumphant success of the last stage were regarded as a metaphorical process mirroring the struggle of the human soul toward salvation" (Kren 1990: viii).

Let us have a closer look at some of the phases of this process. First of all, there were the ethical, religious and "existential" requirements the alchemists had to meet before properly starting their approach. In other words, performing the alchemical art presupposed a careful and detailed *praeparatio* on the side of the alchemist, not only in terms of getting a specific knowledge and technical instruction, but also in terms of personal morality, self-discipline, and even liturgical *katharsis*: "The adept has to be morally worthy; his magisterium only witnesses the degree of refinement in virtue he has personally attained. Nobility of birth, ascetic faith, piety, and humility were still the fundamental requisites, failing which the magic elixir would certainly elude the seeker after knowledge" (Stavenhagen 1974: 66–67). Why so? Because, to put it briefly, at the very heart of their approach, the alchemists would come across the "fingerprints" of the creator himself: to transmute elements, to produce miraculous, life-prolonging substances meant deciphering the ultimate codes on which the material universe was based. As such, the alchemist had to be prepared (purified, initiated) for this special enterprise as it would be at this point that, thanks to the distinctiveness and superiority of his art, the alchemist would meet God—of course not *facie ad faciem*, but through the numerous *vestigia* he has left in every single item of this world. Thus, as has been rightly noted, alchemy comes very close to the "doctrine of signatures," a doctrine—professed, among others, by Paracelsus[7]—according to which, for our better guidance, God left in the natural world various signs whose relationship to what they signified was self-evident: "Signatures were natural symbols that bore a real resemblance to what they signified" (Harrison 2006: 20). Peter Harrison (1998, 2006) shows in detail how "the doctrine of signatures" brings alchemy remarkably close to the whole tradition of the book of nature; as he points out, Paracelsus is one of the thinkers in whose philosophy the two coexist most harmoniously.

This encounter of the alchemist with God in the deep heart of nature obviously requires a special ethical preparation and a serious spiritual/theological training on the alchemist's side. As Paracelsus says,

> This ART was by our Lord God the Supreme Creator, ingraven as it were in a book in the body of Metals, from the beginning of the Creation, that we might diligently learn from them. . . . Therefore, when any man desireth thoroughly and perfectly to learn this Art from its true foundation, it will be necessary that he learn the same from the Master thereof, to wit, from God, who hath created all things, and onely knoweth what Nature and Propriety he himself hath placed in every Creature. (Paracelsus 1975: B–B1)

One of the most important guiding principles in Christian alchemy was that expressed by the formula *tam ethice quam physice*: the alchemist's involvement in his *operatio* was explicitly regarded not only as an empirical approach toward the physical world, but also as a way of accomplishing spiritual (ethical) values pursued *ad majorem Dei gloriam*. The medieval Christian alchemist has to be considered some sort of priest or ascetic, rather than simply a secular scholar.[8] For Paracelsus, being able to perform the "royal art" was, in fact, not so much matter of scholastic instruction, but some consequence of a long series of *exercitia spiritualia* under the guidance of God himself:

> We will therefore take him [God] to be our Master, Operator, and Leader into this most true Art. We will therefore imitate him alone, and through him learn and attain to the knowledge of that Nature, which he himself with his own finger hath engraven and inscribed in the bodies of these Metals. (Ibid.: B1)

Eventually, as a result of this complex preparatory process, the alchemists are in a position to hope that they will be considered chosen (*electi*), that they will receive the *donum Dei*—that is, the special divine gift enabling them to perform the *opus magnum*. There is a sense in which the alchemists must be deeply modest persons, with an acute awareness of the partial, provisional—somehow uncertain—role that they have to play within the complex alchemical process. In other words, the alchemists have to be seriously aware that many of the things occurring during the *operatio* are out of their control, and that ultimately the "secrets of alchemy are never merely to be found out by human labour, but by 'bi teaching or revelacion' and the Stone is to be obtained by grace, rather than reading." The revelation was the key factor here: "alchemy depended ultimately on divine revelation. There is a notion of alchemical 'election,' just as there is a religious one." (Roberts 1994: 79). Such a fact is clearly and repeatedly affirmed by the alchemical texts themselves. In some of these texts one can encounter the very term *donum Dei*, used in connection with the success of the alchemical approach:

> No one will be able to perform or accomplish this thing [the Great Work] which you have so long sought or attain it by means of any knowledge unless it be through affection and gentle humility, a perfect and true love. For this is something which God gives into the sure keeping of his elected servants until such time as he may prepare one to whom it may be handed on from among his secrets. Thus it is only the gift of God, who chooses among his humble and obedient servants those to whom he reveals it. (Morienus 1974: 11)[9]

The next stage of this process consisted of considering the entire alchemical process from a purely symbolical point of view. And the most appropriate religious framework within which such a symbolism could take some concrete forms was that offered by the Christian theology. Indeed, it was the Christian doctrine, with all its complex and already matured soteriology, Christology, *sacramenta*, and ethics, that became at that moment something like a perfect home to the newly adopted alchemy. C. G. Jung shows in details how, for example, the holy *sacramentum*, as it is described by St. Ambrose, is highly compatible with the alchemical "inner transmutation": "St. Ambrose called the transformed [transsubstantiated] bread *medicina*. It is the *pharmakon athanasias*, the drug of immortality, which, in the act of communion, reveals its characteristic effect in and on the believer—the effect of uniting the body with the soul. This takes the form of a healing of the soul (*et sanabitur anima mea*) and a *reformatio* of the body (*et mirabilius reformasti*)" (Jung 1953, 12: 297–98). In a way, from its very outset, alchemy contained a set of features that could be easily interpreted in a Christian manner: "Images of death and resurrection, which for later alchemists prefigured the dissolution of the prime matter and its reconstitution into the glorious Stone, were central to Christian doctrine. . . . In the eighth century Stephanos of Alexandria used the transformation of metals as an analogy for the transformation of the soul. Later alchemists too thought of metals being redeemed from their 'sins'" (Roberts 1994: 78). Once projected (explicitly and systematically) onto the Christian theological background, all the sophisticated symbols, figures, scenarios, and devices of the traditional alchemy could live, so to speak, *una vita nuova* and enjoy a degree of sophistication, dissemination, and, eventually, popularity never known before.

As a result of this complex process, throughout the Christian literature on this subject the alchemical process came to be considered symbolically: "The base matter . . . was man, corrupted by sin; the elixir was the cleansing power of the holy spirit; and so on. Consequently, the ultimate attainable by the Great Work was an *imitatio*, an approach to perfection as symbolized by alchemical gold" (Stavenhagen 1974: 66). As a result, the *elixir vitae* (*lapis philosophorum*) comes to be considered not only a panacea (*medicina universalis*), as it used to be in the Hellenistic or Islamic alchemy, but also a strong metaphor for salvation itself, and constantly seen as a *speculum* of any human perfection. This is why, eventually, within the mainstream of the Christian alchemical tradition, the *elixir vitae* was regarded primarily not only as a means of curing people's bodily illnesses, but also of saving their souls. As it were, producing the *elixir* was a way of searching for an "eternal," sanctified life, rather than simply of obtaining a worldly medicine. Alchemy was not about "making gold" (*crysopoiesis*) anymore, but about making people feel "saved," or at least spiritually elevated.

It was the above-mentioned notion of "inward transmutation" that played a central role within this form of alchemy, giving birth to what is usually called "mystical alchemy." This is an interesting notion, as it describes in detail the entire alchemical apparatus and the successive operations required by the performance of the alchemical *magisterium*, but does not necessarily imply their actual occurrence. The *operatio* was now seen as a purely inner process occurring within the alchemist's mind, without supposing the real existence of the alchemical substances, laboratory, devices, and so on.[10] To put it simply, "mystical alchemy"

> gradually developed into a devotional system where the mundane transmutation of metals became merely symbolic of the transformation of sinful man into a perfect being through prayer and submission to the will of God. . . .
> in some of the mystical treatises it is clear that the authors are not concerned with material substances but are employing the language of exoteric alchemy for the sole purpose of expressing theological, philosophical, or mystical beliefs and aspirations. (Holmyard 1990: 15–16)

As a result, based on the profound knowledge and assimilation of the Christian theology, there have been established a set of fundamental symbolic equivalencies: "philosophers' stone" = Jesus Christ, "prime matter" = sinful and corrupted man to be saved through the *magisterium*, "alchemical gold" = state of salvation.

The most important and spectacular of all these symbolical equivalencies was by far the *lapis*-Christ parallel. Once this paralleling took place, the "marriage" between alchemy and Christianity was complete: the main figure in Christianity, Jesus Christ himself, came to be associated with the most important notion of any alchemical system, the *lapis philosophorum*. Moreover, this parallel was not a circumstantial one or merely some rhetorical device: it was essentially based on fundamental similitudes and common patterns of thinking. For example, the very sacrifice of Jesus Christ, along with his resurrection (the central points of the Christian doctrine), were to be rigorously mirrored within the alchemical process: "the death of our Lord Jesus Christ and His resurrection in a glorified body was to the alchemist to be compared to the death of the metals and their rebirth as the glorious stone" (Taylor 1951: 152–53). In the English alchemical poetry, to take only a random example, one could find such convincing evidence of the Christ-*lapis* parallel as this one offered by the poem of John Donne (1527–1608): "For these three daies become a minerall; / Hee was all gold when he lay downe, but rose / All tincture" (Donne 1952: 28).

The Christ-*lapis* parallel plays a quite prominent role in C. G. Jung's fascinating book *Psychology and Alchemy* (Jung 1953). Jung was one of the main modern promoters (or rediscoverers) of this interpretation. As for contemporary alchemical commentaries, the parallel enjoys a broad acceptance among important experts on medieval Christian alchemy. Claudia Kren's and Lee Stavenhagen's considerations on the subject are quoted above. Chiara Crisciani and Claude Gagnon, to take another example, offer a synthetic and finely systematized image of the *lapis philosophorum* in view of its mystical association with Jesus Christ. Their view is that the stone

> est presque la déification du projet de salut, au point que dans de nombreux textes de l'alchimie latine il est présenté comme l'analogue du Christ. Le *lapis* est aussi le lieu où s'apaisent les hiérarchies (il est unique, indépendant, sans généalogie); il ne rentre pas dans les hiérarchies et les efface. La fonction du *lapis* apparît claire si l'on observe le langage qu'il produit: il est sans nom et par conséquent il peut prendre touts les noms possibles: il supporte toute prédication parce qu'aucune le referme dans une définition univoque; il est le seul possible prédicat de soi-même dans une tautologie représentative de son être universel et particulier à la fois, étant parole de Dieu incarnée. (Crisciani and Gagnon 1980: 50)

"THE GREAT CHAIN OF BEING"

Preliminary Remarks

The notion that Berkeley's speculations in *Siris* could be placed within the alchemical tradition of thinking is supported not only by the equation of the *lapis philosophorum* with tar-water, but also by other arguments. That there might be an alchemical "reading" of Berkeley's *Siris* has been noted, even if with some embarrassment and regret, by some of Berkeley's modern commentators,[11] and A. D. Ritchie announced the notion in 1954 in a lecture at the British Academy on Berkeley's *Siris* (Ritchie 1954). Unfortunately, Ritchie barely did more in his lecture than point to a possible alchemical reading of Berkeley's *Siris*. He did not delve deeply into the argument and did not fully develop the consequences of his insight.

I would like to deal in this section with another important argument supporting the notion of the presence of alchemical thinking in Berkeley's *Siris*. This argument is based upon the idea of the Great Chain of Being, resorted to by both Berkeley and the alchemists. Both in *Siris* and in the alchemical works, what actually makes possible the existence, power, and efficacy of the panacea is the special relationship it bears to the rest of the creation, or, in other words, its particular place and function within the Great Chain of Being. George Berkeley shares with the alchemists the same fundamental belief in the special virtues that a certain link within the chain ("vegetable tar" and "philosophers' stone," respectively) comes to acquire, condense, and manifest.

The topic of the Great Chain of Being is one of the oldest and most prestigious metaphysical and cosmological notions employed throughout the history of European philosophy. As Arthur Lovejoy has put it, the topic of the Great Chain of Being is about a "conception of the plan and structure of the world" which, from remote antiquity to the eighteenth century, "many philosophers, most men of science, and, indeed, most educated men" accepted "without question." Structurally speaking, the universe is, according to this theory of the Great Chain of Being,

> composed of an immense, or . . . of an infinite, number of links ranging in hierarchical order from the meagerest kind of existents, which barely escape non-existence, through "every possible" grade up to the *ens perfectissimum*—or . . . to the highest possible kind of creature, between which and the Absolute Being the disparity was assumed to be infinite—every one of them differing from that immediately above and that immediately below it by the "least possible" degree of difference. (Lovejoy 1964: 59)

Based, originally, on a set of religious and mythical suppositions, the notion that everything existing "in Heaven and on Earth" is in some way unified, linked together, and interconnected, fit, so to speak, perfectly into man's primordial need for understanding the world and its workings. According to this principle, there is nothing chaotic or arbitrary in the universe; everything is orderly and in its appointed place; everything has a role to play within the whole, and the whole could not exist (or, anyway, could not work properly) if even the smallest part were incapacitated. As an epistemological consequence of the theory of the Great Chain of Being, the world becomes essentially comprehensible. Not that we are, in a mysterious way, in a position to know instantly everything about the world, but the Great Chain of Being enables us to know how to gain knowledge of the world.

For one of the major merits of this theory comes from the fact that it offers an explanation of how it is that our knowledge of the world is possible, and how precisely this knowledge is structured, produced, and can be increased. From an acquaintance with those links which are immediately accessible, we can safely infer knowledge about the remoter links; based on what we are given in our immediate encounters with the world, we can make statements and predictions and propose hypotheses about things that are, by virtue of their own nature, far away from us, if not simply out of our reach. The result is that, according to the theory of the Great Chain of Being, there is orderliness, hierarchy, interconnection, harmony, meaning, and beauty in the world, and—what is equally important—our mind has the capacity of grasping them.

The Great Chain of Being in Alchemy

It is precisely this notion of the Great Chain of Being that the alchemists made use of and upon which they built up and developed their cosmological speculations. The idea of "the harmony and unity of the universe, 'One is All, and All is One', led to the belief that the universal spirit could somehow be pressed into service . . . by concentrating it, so to speak, in a particular piece of matter—the philosophers' stone" (Holmyard 1990: 23). In fact, this fundamental principle postulating the unity of the world, in the particular form of an unseen cosmic chain penetrating and interconnecting everything, as well as conferring upon it a certain identity, homogeneity, and continuity, could be recognized even in what is believed to be the very first and most important alchemical writing, namely *Tabula Smaragdina*, a short Hermetic text attributed to the mythical founder of alchemy, Hermes Trismegistus:

> True it is, without falsehood, certain and most true. That which is above is like to which is below, and that which is below is like to that which is above, to accomplish the miracles of one thing. And as all things were by the contemplation of one, so all things arose from one thing by a single act of adaptation. (Quoted in Holmyard 1990: 97)

All the subsequent developments, however sophisticated, the exotic speculations and countless refinements of the alchemical theories throughout the centuries echoed this original principle. Any definition of alchemy today must take seriously into account the theory of the Great Chain of Being as one of its fundamental ingredients. Claudia Kren, for example, when trying to offer a synthetic description of alchemy, says:

By almost universal agreement, alchemy in Western Europe was one of the products of a Hellenistic culture—Hermetic and neoplatonic—where the universe was a unified cosmos with all parts interrelated in a web of hierarchical correspondences and with all aspects in some way animate and active. This complex of semi-religious notions was joined by an influential theory which held that the elemental forms of matter were convertible one into another. (Kren 1990: viii)

This notion of a chain unifying everything in alchemy was not only a matter of historical coincidence, a theoretical device that just happened to be employed by the alchemical authors in their discourse, and without which the alchemy would have remained more or less the same. The notion of the "unity of the world" belongs structurally and functionally to the alchemical way of thinking. It was not, so to speak, an accident, but a substance. As has been noted, the "unity of matter" was one of the two "*a priori* postulates upon which the deductive reasoning of alchemy was mainly based" (Read 1947: 4) (the other one being the existence of the transmuting agent). In the absence of a theory firmly postulating the unity and homogeneity of the world, the alchemists would have lost one of the main metaphysical and cosmological premises enabling them to believe in the very possibility of transmutation and, by way of consequence, in the existence and efficacy of their panacea. For from the notion of the unity of matter they derived another assumption, namely that of the "philosophers' stone,"

> the medicine of the base metals, would act also as a medicine of man; hence, in the form of the Elixir Vitae or Red Tincture, the stone was depicted as an agent for curing all human ills and conferring longevity. Herein may perhaps be perceived a Greek influence, emanating from the Platonic conception that nothing exist that is not good and from Aristotle's dictum that nature strives always towards perfection. (Ibid.: 4)

The Great Chain of Being in Siris

It is in a strikingly similar manner that Berkeley sought to explain in *Siris* how it is that such a thing as his panacea was possible.[12] This is one of the most remarkable things about *Siris* and, certainly, one of the most important arguments for placing it in the alchemical tradition. As a philosopher, Berkeley did not find it sufficient simply to propose his "medicine" and list its magic virtues and qualities without looking into what was behind it. He felt he had to look for, and offer, a philosophical explanation of how his panacea was ontologically possible. A panacea is not a thing like any other; if it exists (and Berkeley thought it did), then there must be some deeper reasons accounting for its existence and for its magic powers. So that, after describing in detail the mode in which tar-water is to be prepared, after listing the various forms of illness and medical case histories in which this medicine proved to be successful, and after inquiring into the chemical properties of the vegetable tar, Berkeley proceeds in *Siris* to propose the theory of the Great Chain of Being as making his panacea ontologically possible. In perfect consistency with a long tradition, Berkeley sees the Great Chain of Being as the theory that there "runs a chain throughout the whole system of beings. In this chain one link drags another. The meanest things are connected with the highest" (Berkeley 1948–57, 5:140 [*Siris*]).[13]

For that purpose he undertakes a detailed historical "journey" in search of those, ancient or modern, "past masters" (philosophers, poets, scientists, alchemists, physicians, and so forth) supporting, in some way or other, his own ideas regarding the Great Chain of Being. Berkeley's approach in *Siris* is deeply interdisciplinary, highly speculative, and of an impressive theoretical openness and generosity. *Siris* (this title is based on the Greek word for "chain") thus becomes the mirror-book of the Great Chain of Being. In its effort to reflect the scale of nature, the book turns itself into a chain of complex speculations pertaining to different scholarly fields which are progressively born out of one another: biology, chemistry, physics, and so on. In other words, there is also a "great chain of knowledge" charged with explaining how the Great Chain of Being works. As has been remarked, medicine "leads Berkeley to botany, botany to chemistry, chemistry to metaphysics, and *Siris* finally comes to rest on the nature of God" (Walmsley 1990: 144). Berkeley traces the topic of the Great Chain of Being to the most ancient of its sources and promoters, to the mythical views professed in ancient Egypt, or to the cosmological and metaphysical speculations of the early Greek (pre-Socratic) philosophers, not to mention the repeated appeals he makes to Plato, Aristotle, Plotinus, or to the Renaissance Platonists. He sympathetically summarizes the ancient doctrines, at the same time always bearing in mind, and frequently alluding to, his own tenets to be strengthened and supported by the dictums, fragments, and beliefs of the celebrated figures of the past. I have already talked, in chapter 2, about the specific rhetorical procedures and methods through which Berkeley placed himself in the tradition of philosophy as palimpsest, and about the broader historical and metaphysical presupposition behind this way of thinking. In a way, as I remarked in that chapter, *Siris* has a distinct character of "intertextuality": Berkeley's own words are constantly echoed by those of the others, just as the other authors' words are mirrored in his own wording. Their voices are mixed in a most harmonious way, and the result is a body of knowledge of a symphonic nature:

> If we may trust the Hermaic writings, the Egyptians thought all things did partake of life. . . . from all the various tones, actions, and passions of the universe, they supposed one symphony, one animal act and life to result. . . . It is a doctrine among other speculations contained in the Hermaic writings that all things are One. And it is not improbable that Orpheus, Parmenides, and others among the Greeks, might have derived their notion of *to hen*, THE ONE, from Egypt. Though that subtle metaphysician Parmenides, in his doctrine of *hen hestos*, seems to have added something of his own. . . . one and the same Mind is the universal principle of order and harmony throughout the world, containing and connecting all its parts, and giving unity to the system. (Berkeley 1948–57: 5:128–34 [*Siris*])

This is reminiscent of a process of alchemical transformation, within which primary elements are successively combined with one another, resulting in more and more complicated substances. Furthermore, some of the notions that Berkeley borrows in this work from the ancient philosophers (the world as a symphony, the fundamental metaphysical unity behind the multiplicity of the visible things) are closely related to a theme he had already touched on in his earlier philosophical works: namely, the world as a coherent system of signs and the cosmos as a divine epiphany. Once again, in *Siris* Berkeley seems to have pushed to the ultimate ideas to which he had only vaguely alluded in his earlier writings.

Berkeley comes to use the phrase "Chain or Scale of beings" in its proper, traditional sense. He quotes Jamblichus's fragment asserting the "world to be one animal," an animal whose parts

> however distant each from other, are nevertheless related and connected by one common nature. . . . there is no chasm in nature, but a Chain or Scale of beings rising by gentle uninterrupted gradations from the lowest to the highest, each nature being informed and perfected by the participation of a higher. As air becomes igneous, so the purest fire becomes animal, and the animal soul becomes intellectual: . . . each lower nature being, according to those philosophers, as it were a receptacle or subject for the next above it to reside and act in. (Ibid.: 129)

What is interesting at this point is that, for Berkeley, this chain is not only of a cosmic nature, animating, unifying, and interrelating the outside world, but it is also a chain unifying our own minds, and conferring upon them orderliness, unity, and identity. This "chain" thus functions as an "inner chain" connecting and interrelating our mental faculties and making them work properly. As a faithful mirror of the cosmos, the human mind reproduces for itself, on a much smaller scale, the Great Chain of Being. The human mind is of such a nature that it reflects the hidden, complex architecture of the universe:

> By experiments of sense we become acquainted with the lower faculties of the soul; and from them, whether by a gradual evolution or ascent, we arrive at the highest. Sense supplies images to memory. These become subjects for fancy to work upon. Reason considers and judges of the imaginations. And these acts of reason become new objects to the understanding. In this scale, each lower faculty is a step that leads to one above it. (Ibid.: 140)

And it is precisely through this inner chain that, in Berkeley's view, we have access to divinity. He believes, in an Augustinian manner, that the divine is precisely what we discover at the end of the "inner ascension": "the uppermost naturally leads to the Deity, which is . . . the object of intellectual knowledge" (ibid.: 140). Consequently, this "dual chain," manifesting itself both in the cosmic realm and in ourselves, points to the ancient Hermetic analogy between macrocosm and microcosm, an analogy that plays a fundamental role within any alchemical tradition:

> As the Platonists held the intellect to be lodged in soul, and soul in aether; so it passeth for a doctrine of Trismegistus . . . , that mind is clothed by soul, and soul by spirit. Therefore, as the animal spirit of man, being subtle and luminous, is the immediate tegument of the human soul, or that wherein and whereby she acts; even so the spirit of the world, that active fiery ethereal substance of light, that permeates and animates the whole system, is supposed to clothe the soul, which clothes the mind of the universe. (Ibid.: 91)

Then, keeping in mind that "luminous spirit lodged and detained in the native balsam of pines and firs" (ibid.: 105), tar emerges as a secretion of the vegetal realm coming to play a special role within the cosmic chain. Just as the *lapis philosophorum* condenses the noblest qualities of the cosmic chain, and carries within, in a concentrated form, its magic powers, so tar encapsulates and makes manifest the most powerful medicine that nature could offer. A. D. Ritchie even says that the choice of tar is, in itself, another alchemical "trace" in *Siris*: "It was one of the alchemical doctrines that the 'essence' of plants is to be found in aromatic or sweet-smelling constituents, especially when these are volatile and can be concentrated by distillation" (Ritchie: 1954: 50). Nevertheless, there are authors who believe that Berkeley's choice of the "vegetable tar" is quite circumstantial.[14]

But how is it that tar proves to be so important a link within the cosmic chain? What precisely makes tar play such an important role? What are the inner workings of nature that make tar such a special substance?

At some point in his historical (as well as cosmological) "journey," Berkeley came to talk about "a certain pure heat or fire, which had something divine in it, by the participation whereof men became allied to the gods." This fire is not at all what we commonly designate by the word, it is not any ordinary, "worldly" fire, but rather has a definite metaphysical significance as something that was the object of philosophical speculations from the ancient Greeks to the Renaissance Platonists. This fire is, in Berkeley's own words, the

> purest and most excellent fire, that is heaven, saith Ficinus. And again, the hidden fire that everyone exerts itself, he calls celestial. He represents fire as most powerful and active, dividing all things, abhorring all composition or mixture with other bodies. . . . This is the general source of life, spirit, and strength, and therefore of health to all animals. . . . The same spirit, imprisoned in food and medicines, is conveyed into the stomach, the bowels, the lacteals, circulated and secreted by the several ducts, and distributed throughout the system. (Berkeley 1948–57, 5: 104 [*Siris*])

And it is precisely the tar that, in Berkeley's opinion, best serves as "a vehicle to this spirit" (ibid.: 106). In a manner clearly reminding us of the alchemical speculations on the *lapis philosophorum*, and of its complex religious symbolism (for example, the powerful symbolic relationship between gold and the sun), Berkeley sees the vegetable tar as having a special "affinity" with the solar light, which is to say, with "the general source of life," as it grasps and concentrates light, disseminating and conveying to the animal body its regenerating powers: "light attracted, secreted, and detained in tar . . . is not a violent and sudden medicine . . . but a safe and mild alterative, which penetrates the whole system, opens, heals, and strengthens, the remote vessels, alters and propels their contents, and enters the minutest capillaries." (ibid.: 68). As a result, by virtue of the special relationship it bears with the metaphysical substratum of the world (that is, the celestial fire), tar, once properly prepared and consumed in appropriate doses, necessarily brings in us a fundamental "restoration." In other words, thanks specifically to this characteristic of the tar, our bodies are healthily and harmoniously linked anew to the whole of the cosmic chain. Consistent with a long tradition of medical thinking, Berkeley saw health as a restoration of a lost equilibrium between bodily components and as an appropriate insertion of the human body into the workings of nature. Tar does not add anything new, or extraneous, to what already exists in the body but rather simply helps it find its lost equilibrium. Tar does not address some fundamental ontological lack but rather removes an accidental disfunctionality, for example, an unnatural change of rhythm or the preeminence of one humor over others. As such, health is not the absence of an illness (illness does not have a positive existence). It is state of well-being of the body. In light of Berkeley's speculations about tar-water and its working in the human body, it can be safely said that, for him, health is not so much a physiological state as an ontological one. Through an appropriate infusion of tar-water, we become who we really are, or more precisely what we ontologically should be, in terms of bodily integrity, the ideal balance between humors and, especially, in terms of our appropriate situation in the cosmos and on the "Scale of Being." As in the case of traditional alchemy, where the philosophers' stone worked to assist the base materials to fulfill their inner potential, in Berkeley's *Siris*, tar-water helps our bodies better pursue their natural drives toward a state of well-being.

Most importantly, for Berkeley tar functions as a special link within the cosmic chain due particularly to its peculiar capacity to retain, store, and transform light: "This balsam . . . abides the action of the sun, and, attracting the sunbeams, is thereby exalted and enriched, so as to become a most noble medicine: such is the last product of a tree, perfectly matured by time and sun" (ibid.: 44). In other words, to put it in alchemical terminology, tar has the capacity to "transmute" light into life successfully. I consider the passage where Berkeley talks about tar as "a vehicle" to the spirit of life as the climax of the entire book: It is in this passage that we see how the divine wisdom, so generously cast upon the things of this world, suffers some dramatic cosmic metamorphosis and becomes something that has the capacity of restoring what in this world has become unwise, ugly, or ill. With tar the cosmic circle closes up, the world is reunited with God, and God manifests his infinite generosity and wisdom. It is this symbolism of light and fire, the dream of our "restoration" and of a redeeming "renewal" of our bodies, the notion of a smooth and harmonious reintegration of the human within the cosmic realm that, once again, strengthens the relationship between Berkeley and the alchemical tradition.

ALCHEMY AS "PERENNIAL WISDOM"

Alchemy Revisited

Even though the alchemists strongly believed that what they were doing was "science"[15]—that is, a determined, honest attempt at understanding nature—today alchemy appears dramatically "outdated"; it belongs to the history of science, rather than to science proper. Nevertheless, however outdated alchemy might seem to some today, it is about a need for transcendence, about a drive toward human perfection and moral improvement, which certainly confers upon it a noble mark of authenticity. As Jung put it, there are "very modern problems in alchemy, though they lie outside the province of chemistry" (Jung 1953: 267). Alchemy is, of course, "wrong," but this does not makes it less interesting as a cultural, historical, and philosophical phenomenon. Based on the arguments and bibliographical and historical evidence brought forth above, I believe that some broader, more far-reaching considerations on alchemy can also be made.

First of all, in a certain sense, the alchemists could be said to have been the first "ecologists" as they heartily cared about the state of the material world around, and tried as it were to "heal" it. In their approaches to the natural world, the alchemists were led by an ideal of perfection, by a certain standard of "sanity" and well-being by which they considered the materials on which they acted: "In alchemy imperfect metals, often considered as ill, were helped to perfection and an ideal internal balance by the medicine of the elixir. Alchemy teaches 'the restoral (*restituere*) of all fallen and infirm bodies and how to bring them back to a true balance (*temperamentum*) and the best of health'" (Roberts 1994: 37). Considering some components of nature "ill," making them work for their own benefit, and searching for medicines to cure them, betrays indeed a very ecological attitude. And it is precisely this vivid sense of tenderness and attentiveness toward the surrounding world that, from our retrospective point of view, makes alchemy so curiously interesting. In their enterprises the alchemists were consistently driven by a set of considerations that could be rightly seen as "environmental" in a serious way. They held a generous view of the natural world and conceived it as driven by a perpetual quest for equilibrium, perfection, and "salvation." For them, everything in nature tended toward a superior state, a state of purity and optimum equilibrium. And gold symbolized this perfection most appropriately. As one anonymous English alchemical writer said: "I must tel you, that nature alwaies intendeth and striveth to the perfection of Gold" (quoted in Read 1947: 6).

On the other hand, it is true that the alchemists' relationship to their immediate physical environment (*natura*) were marked by a certain form of anthropomorphosis. As it is proven by numerous pieces of evidence, the alchemists did not consider nature in terms of a radical ontological *alteritas*, as something completely different from the human world, but rather they saw nature as being constituted, structured, and made operational somehow in human terms. For example, when talking about the relationships between chemical elements to be combined they used terms that ordinarily describe human relationships. And this was definitely a way of humanizing nature: "To give to the combination of the two substances to make a third the name or symbol of 'a marriage and birth' was to fit the phenomenon into his world and so to make sense of it. He would then act on the principle that the phenomenon *was* a marriage and birth" (Taylor 1951: 158). But this antropomorphization of *natura* did not mean that alchemists were using (much less abusing) the natural world for their own benefit. For this process of humanization was in general regarded only as a first step of a more complex soteriological enterprise in which both *natura* and *anthropon* were considered in terms of divine scenarios (sacrifice, redemption, rebirth), scenarios in which nature and man were on an equal footing, and eventually overcome. As I showed above when I discussed the theology of the *lapis*-Christ analogy, Jesus Christ emerged into the alchemists' world to save both man and nature, to overcome them and eventually give them a new meaning. As such, in view of these grand scenarios of salvation and transfiguration, a subordination of nature by man did not make any sense.

Secondly, and as a consecquence of this anthropomorphosis, alchemy presuposses a unified conception of nature, man, and God. This is a direct corollary of the conception of the Great Chain of Being, on which the whole of alchemy was based, and which we followed in some detail earlier in this chapter. As a theory stating that everything "on Earth and in Heaven" is tightly interconnected and governed by a perfect harmony, this conception had also a number of epistemological implications, the most important being that the entire knowledge of reality is unified and homogeneous, that there is only one *scientia mundi* making possible and explaining every particular science, every piece of "local knowledge," and guaranteeing its validity. As such, the alchemists' knowledge is, strictly speaking, not something specialized, belonging, say, to "natural science," or to "theology," but it is a knowledge that, in an ambitiously comprehensive way, encompasses all specialized discourses, at the same time transcending them and placing them into a larger context dominated by scenarios of cosmic restoration, redemption, and eternal salvation.

Finally, however outdated or even frivolous it might seem today, alchemy ultimately betrays a serious need for transcendence, a drive toward human perfection and moral betterment, which makes it, to some extent, perennial. True, alchemy is utopian, but so are the most fundamental drives of the human mind. Alchemy is a project that transcends history, and so are our most essential dreams: "l'alchimie se désigne immémorialement: art royal et sacerdotal. Elle n'a pas d'histoire, son histoire étant celle de la vie, de la mort, de la résurrection de l'univers en chaque homme" (Robert Marteau quoted in Crisciani and Gagnon 1980: 23). Beyond any sophisticated practicalities involved, beyond the numerous arcane technicalities one encounters when reading an alchemical text, alchemy may ultimately be seen as a discourse about the eternal human quest for a conciliation between the many (often divergent) forms of being in history. There is a sense in which the human being becomes dissatisfied with pursuing, in an exclusive fashion, such divergent specialized projects as science, religion, philosophy, and practical life, and comes to dream about pursuing only one single superproject, something able to unify and give a superior meaning to all these fragmented practices. It is a dream of meaningful life and redemption, a utopia of inclusion, totality, and totalizing experiences. In this way, the alchemist, as one whose main objective is to propose precisely this synthesis of science, religion, philosophy, and practical life, comes to be seen as an exemplary person. As has been remarked, the alchemist's approaches to life acquire a paradigmatic character: "Il y a dans l'alchimie une représentation du Moi qui est exactement et précisément l'image d'une certaine façon de connaître et de travailler que nous avons subconsciemment mais pas moins rationnellement écartée. Cette façon n'est qu'une interférence et cette interférence n'est audible que dans l'histoire" (ibid.: 79). In its strict details, an alchemical approach might be wrong and even seem "funny," especially if judged in the light of modern science, but—considered in its spirit, and in a broader cultural and epistemic context—it proves to be a quite impressive attempt at offering a complex and integrated image of the human condition. There is something generous, far-reaching, and positively utopian about the alchemists's enterprises. For (and this is very important) what the

alchemists—through all their writings, speculations, and curious undertakings—did was nothing other than attempt to offer a bold and refreshing
synthesis of science, religion, and philosophy. They based their approach
on the supposition that there always has to be a harmony, a good balance,
between the objectives of science, man's need for understanding the world
in which he found himself, on the one hand, and man's need for transcending himself, that is, his religious drive, on the other hand. Leading a good
life means precisely striving to keep this balance. As one scholar rightly said,

> Alchemy has suffered the misfortune of being classed as a science from a
> modern point of view. . . . Scientific it certainly was when it first reached
> the West sometime late in the twelfth century, but in a thoroughly medieval
> sense, in which nothing, science least of all, could be separated from ethics,
> morals, and religion. For if science could not substantiate man's claim on
> immortality, what use was it? (Stavenhagen 1974: 66)

As such, the most important thing about reading an alchemical text today is
not to take it by the letter, but to read between the lines. If taken literally,
any alchemical text is certainly "wrong." One cannot turn base metals into
gold, or produce a panacea. But if we read the alchemists' work between
the lines we have a chance to come across the wonderful richness of alchemy and its perennial significance: that is, a never-ending quest for moral
transformation, inward transmutation, and self-transcendence. Ultimately,
alchemy is about breaking boundaries and challenging the habits of ortho-
doxies, no matter their names.

Berkeley's Use of Alchemy

I hope that it has become clear by now that, in *Siris*, Berkeley uses extensively alchemical notions and ideas.[16] But even without going too deeply
into the archeology of the notions and arguments he uses, Berkeley's alchemical allegiances are evident at the textual and terminological levels as
he abundantly quotes not only such late alchemists (or early chemists) as
Paracelsus, Homberg, Van Helmont, and others, but also celebrated figures
of the alchemical tradition, such as Hermes Trismegistus and the Renaissance Platonists, who openly placed themselves within the tradition of alchemy.

More than that, what is amazing is the fact that Berkeley seems to have
literally believed in the possibility of "alchemical transmutation," of transforming base metals into gold. Interestingly, he did so by placing the transmutation within the proper theoretical and historical framework that the

alchemists themselves used. Thus, at a given point in his demonstration in *Siris*, Berkeley brought forward in support of his idea that "bodies attract and fix the light" the results of what obviously was a transmuting experiment performed by a French alchemist, Homberg:

> Of this there cannot be a better proof than the experiment of Monsieur Homberg, who made gold of mercury by introducing light into its pores. . . . By this junction of light and mercury both bodies became fixed, and produced a third different from either, to wit, real gold. . . . This seems to have been not altogether unknown to former philosophers; Marsilius Ficinus . . . and others likewise before him, regarding mercury as the mother, and sulphur as the father of metals; and Plato himself, in his *Timaeus*, describing gold to be a dense fluid with a shining yellow light, which well suits a composition of light and mercury. (Berkeley 1948–57, 5:97–98 [*Siris*])

However puzzling Berkeley's belief in the possibility of making gold out of base metals might appear to today's reader, it has nevertheless the merit of pointing to Berkeley's commitment to a worldview whose fundamental tenets and metaphysical suppositions functioned also as the theoretical justification for what the alchemists were doing.

Yet, alchemy was not primarily about making gold. Some modern scholars of alchemy are even inclined to believe that the gold-making side of alchemy was actually a form of disguise, something behind which they pursued their real interests, which were philosophical and spiritual in essence.[17] Indeed, what Berkeley took from alchemy was the medical, cosmological, and metaphysical components, primarily a belief in the existence of an ontologically privileged substance through which our bodies can be "healed" and restored to a state of perfect health. More than that, there is a sense in which Berkeley went beyond strict medical technicalities, and shared with the alchemists some important spiritual affinities: the belief in a supreme principle of order (the Great Chain of Being) by virtue of which everything "in Heaven and on Earth" is secretly united and interconnected; the belief in the possibility of a cosmic restoration, either at a macro- or microlevel; the conception of the world as a symphony in which every single detail is meaningful and has its own role to play; the felt need for transcendence, moral betterment, and intellectual growth; and, more generally, the notion of a divine-cosmic story in which humans are characters with a role to play. He also took from alchemy the "ecologist" dimension, the view that, as he says in *Alciphron*, throughout our earthly journey we should always endeavor to "live reasonably," to take care not to harm the surrounding world in any way, "proportioning our esteem to the value of things, and so using this world as not to abuse it" (Berkeley 1948–57, 3:178). Berkeley took from the alchemical tradition the emphasis on the necessity for tenderness and care that we should always display in our dealing with God's world. Berkeley's conviction that God is permanently speaking to us has now acquired a higher degree of specificity. As it were, the message that *Siris* sends might read: if we are attentive enough to the world around—that is, to what God is telling us—we will learn more than simply how to deal in general with this world; we will learn specific arts and techniques through which this world will be kept in order, and our passage through it made smoother and healthier.

On the other hand, Berkeley's case, a case in which the "medical science" in the traditional, Hermetic sense coexisted with a number of features of modern philosophical discourse, demonstrates how difficult it is to postulate some radical and unbridgeable gap between the traditional (medieval) and the modern. After a life dedicated primarily to promoting such fundamental ideals of European philosophical modernity as the constant appeal to experience, common sense, and critical, rational argumentation, we see in *Siris* a Berkeley who is "quitting science for venerable metaphysics, where he all but blends his own original philosophy with the theosophical theories of ancient Greece and the yet more ancient Middle East" (Jessop 1953: 7).[18] As I showed in detail in a previous chapter, in *Siris* Berkeley openly gives up all the antiauthoritative and antischolastic rhetoric of his early years (a rhetoric characterizing, in fact, the whole school of *nouvelle philosophie*) and embarks on a way of thinking at the heart of which lies authorial humbleness, philosophical modesty, and a method of thinking based on repeated appeal to past authorities. This is undoubtedly a very interesting step on Berkeley's part, and should probably be considered by commentators otherwise than with embarrassment, regret, or retrospective apologies. Berkeley took this step at a time when he had reached his full intellectual and existential maturity, after a life full of scholarly, literary, and public accomplishments, at a time when he had become rich in experience, in knowledge, and wisdom. That is why, I believe, such a step was a deeply symbolic gesture on the part of the philosopher, betraying a fundamental shift in his conception of philosophy: a shift from philosophy considered as an "individualist," tradition-breaking approach toward a more traditional conception of philosophy, toward philosophy as a spiritual technique and a way of recovering an immemorial wisdom. *Siris*, as a "chain" of cosmological, physical, chemical, and medical speculations, is undoubtedly about things or facts of the external world but as an alchemical approach is behind all these concerns; there is a need for overcoming, or reconciling, the fragile, limited "human condition" with a cosmic-divine narrative. Berkeley's philosophy in *Siris* is a philosophy that is no longer "pure"; it seriously overlaps with such other fields as religion, mysticism, theology, poetry, theosophy, alchemy, and others, and has concerns that, unfortunately, are not the concerns of philosophy anymore.

5.   Philosophy as Apologetics

God plays a central role in Berkeley's immaterialism, as he is the supreme perceiver of the world, which means that it is only thanks to him that things exist in the fullest sense of the word. Yet, God cannot remain an abstraction and nothing else. Gods does not exist only in metaphysics, but also in history: there are always concrete modalities through which God pervades people's lives, conferring upon them meaning, and through which people worship God, seek to approach him, and make him part of their lives. Hence the practical necessity of religion. Berkeley was not content with simply postulating God as the supreme author of the world; he also did a great deal of philosophizing on religion, on its forms of manifestation and importance in people's lives.

In this context, what follows is an attempt at considering George Berkeley's thought from the standpoint of the Christian apologetic tradition. My objective here is to show that one of the roots of Berkeley's thought could be found precisely in this tradition.[1] The chapter has two main sections. The first one is dedicated to delineating the broader theoretical framework within which the discussion of Berkeley's apologetics is to be placed, and then looks at the special relationship that theism bears, in Berkeley's system, to his immaterialism. The second section deals with *Alciphron* as an apologetic writing, in an attempt to place this book in the tradition of Christian apologetics.

FIGHTING AGAINST ATHEISM[2]

In Search of a Framework: The Relationship between Philosophy and Religion

It is almost a truism to say that, historically, philosophy has overlapped with religion and theology. Yet, not only in a historical sense do many philosophical traditions seem to emerge from certain developments occurring in the sphere of mythology and religion (or religious thought), but there is also a structural sense in which philosophy is sometimes related to the religious. In this structural sense, there is something in the nature of a philosophical exercise itself that has at bottom a certain religious character; in some way or other, explicitly or implicitly, much of philosophy has aimed at providing "ultimate explanations," which at the same time is one of the distinctive marks of any mature religion. And it is precisely this situation that gives birth sometimes to a certain rivalry between philosophers and theologians, to a certain competition for an audience. Surely, religion and philosophy differ—sometimes to a significant extent—in the specific ways in which they explain the nature of God, his creation of the world, the role of man within the world, and his relations to God, but the fact remains that religion and philosophy both address the same issues, the same need we feel to make sense of our existence in this world, and each of them tends to assert itself over the other. As Frederick Copleston has remarked,

> It seems evident . . . that as far as doctrines and theories are concerned, philosophies can overlap with religions. Both may provide frameworks for life-orientation and doctrines about God and man's relation to him. And for this reason it is understandable if some theologians are inclined to look on metaphysical systems as rivals to divine revelation and as offering an *ersatz* religion. (Copleston 1974: 5)

To put it differently, just as some of the important philosophical questions are also problems with which theologians are concerned (even if they look at them from a different angle), so some of the theological problems happen to be common currency in certain areas of philosophy. It is probably this fundamental "impurity" of philosophy, in the sense of its being sometimes "contaminated" by certain religious aspirations and claims of "ultimate explanations," that confers upon it the tremendous cultural prestige it has enjoyed over the centuries; and it still enjoys a certain "superiority of principle" over other humanistic disciplines. That the value, or quality, of philosophy proves to be below one's expectations is not relevant in this case: what is relevant is that philosophy, by its mere existence, is an expression of man's fundamental need for self-understanding, and for understanding the world within which he finds himself. Again, as Copleston says,

> philosophical systems have in the past been inspired by a felt need which can properly be described as religious. Moreover, whether the philosopher is or is not the proper person to meet the need, the need has hardly vanished. . . .

> This need is based on man himself, on man as existing in a historical situation
> in which . . . he has to act in view of ends or goals. Hence it seems to me
> untrue to say that the idea of a religious promise or religious *a priori* is out-
> moded. (Ibid.: 8)

Needless to say, the fact that philosophy and religion address similar fundamental questions does not mean at all that the answers, or solutions, they
will bring forth are the same. Sometimes they might have something in
common, just as sometimes they might differ radically. Theism, deism, atheism, agnosticism, various forms of religious/cultural relativism, and skepticism are all particular manners (each with its own principles, suppositions,
and methods) of addressing the same set of interrogations, at which both
philosophy and religion ultimately arrive. But it is not my intention here to
deal in detail with the complex and multifaceted interdisciplinary situation
resulting from the overlapping of philosophy and religion, however fascinating its investigation might be. What I am mainly concerned with is only
to delineate, even if in a sketchy manner, the theoretical framework within
which a discussion of George Berkeley's apologetic philosophy is to be
placed. This is why I will in the following focus on only a few aspects of
theistic (Christian) philosophy.

One of the first things that a Christian philosopher—*qua* philosopher—
has to do is undoubtedly to attain a proper rapport between faith and understanding. To put it very schematically, just as faith without understanding
would rule him out as a philosopher, so understanding without faith would
rule him out as a Christian. As a consequence, a Christian philosopher will
look, whether knowingly or unknowingly, for the most harmonious possible relationship between faith and understanding. Of course, even within a
nonreligious context, faith and understanding are not completely independent from each other: a complex dialectics and a subtle interdependence
between the two terms are always at work here. Any intellectual exercise
presupposes "faith" in a certain set of (logical, methodological, and other)
axioms, rules, and principles, just as any act of faith has a certain "understanding" behind it, completely "blind faith" being an impossibility. But it
is in precisely the sphere of religious philosophy that this dialectical relationship between faith and understanding reaches its highest degree of complexity. St. Anselm expressed the fact most poignantly in his *Proslogion*: "I do not
seek to understand that I may believe, but I believe in order to understand.
For this also I believe—that unless I believed I should not understand" (Anselm 1962: 6–7). In Anselm's view, the act of faith must necessarily buttress

any attempt at understanding the divine and discussing it; without the existence of faith such attempts would be not only a *hubris* (unforgivable arrogance) in ethical/spiritual terms, but they would also be completely fruitless in strictly epistemic terms. Not that St. Anselm initiated this debate, or "invented" the problem (the issue had been present in Christianity from its beginning, and Augustine, for example, dedicated a great deal of thinking to it), but it was Anselm who most acutely realized the crucial importance that the relationship between faith and understanding might have for the idea of a specifically Christian philosophy. As a matter of fact, as Copleston has rightly noted, once the process through which faith seeks self-understanding has made its debut, the emergence of a coherent system of Christian metaphysical thought is, in a way, unavoidable: "the process of faith seeking understanding of itself must lead at some point or other to what can reasonably be described as metaphysical reflection" (Copleston 1974: 53). The notion of *fides quaerens intellectum* will become one of the distinctive marks of Christian theism, defining it as a distinctive form of philosophizing. Of course, within such a context, philosophy had what we would call today an "instrumental value": it was not in general pursued "for its own sake," as it seems to be today, but rather all its undertakings, approaches, and "discoveries" were overtly put into the service of that supreme end: "the faith seeking understanding of itself." If we prefer, we might say that philosophy was "subordinated" to religion—that is, to an end alien to philosophy itself. But, I suppose, this language belongs to our own anachronisms, to our own projections onto the past, rather than to what medieval thinkers themselves thought of what they were doing. When one reads medieval philosophical texts one never feels any frustration that a "subordination," or "enslavement," of philosophy should normally bring forth. On the contrary, one of the most common notes of these texts seems to be a certain gladness of mind, intellectual enjoyment, and visionary delight on the part of their authors. They simply tend to take what this form of "subordinated" philosophizing might bring to them as the supreme good one can ever attain in one's lifetime: "Since I conceive of the understanding to which we can attain in this life as a middle term between faith and the [beatific] vision, I judge that, the more anyone attains to it, the closer he comes to the vision to which we all aspire" (Anselm 1962: 178 [*Cur Deus homo*]).

Although faith has to support understanding, it nevertheless does not interfere with the intellect's specific approaches. Anselm explains that what he aims at in the *Monologion* is to explain things in such a way that nothing from Scripture should be urged on the authority of Scripture itself, but that whatever the conclusion of independent investigation should declare to be true, should, in an unadorned style, with common proofs and with a single argument, be briefly enforced by the cogency of reason, and plainly expounded in the light of truth. (Ibid.: 35)

This is possible thanks to the fact that one of the fundamental principles upon which theism is based is that truth does not result from any human imposition, interpretation, negotiation, etc., but truth is the Truth, one of God's names. Truth is what both faith and understanding incessantly look for, each in its own way. "The order of faith" and the "order of understanding" are only different modalities of approaching one and the same thing. Truth, in this theological acceptance, is precisely what makes possible various "truths," in philosophy, in science, or even in everyday life; at the same time, it is what confers upon one's faith certitude and firmness. That being said, one of the consequences of this view is that, within such a system of thought, it would be practically impossible for a mind to arrive at something contrary to what faith asserts, as long as that mind has been well instructed and conducted, and the faith has been a "right" faith. The existence of Truth is the supreme "principle of order" conferring upon the believer's life meaning, integrity, and direction. As Stephen Clark expressively remarked with regard to the case of Christian theism,

> Christian theists acknowledge that there is a Truth wider than our conception of It, which demands our worshipful attention; that Its nature is such that It needs no further explanation; that It is such that we can reasonably think we might find out about It; that It is One, and therefore immaterial; that It must actually and entirely be what, intermittently, we are—that is, conscious; that it contains the standards for each finite being; that there must somewhere be something that is at once completely human and completely God. (Clark 1998: viii–ix)[3]

One of the most ironic things about the relationship between theism and atheism, as it has been remarked, is that atheism is massively dependent on theism. This dependence is in terms of vocabulary,[4] arguments, historical contexts, and "techniques of persuasion," but atheism is also dependent in a deeper and more serious sense: its existence depends upon what occurs in the sphere of theistic thinking. Michael Buckley, in his monumental *At the Origins of Modern Atheism*, undertakes a systematic study of atheism in light of its "necessary" dependence on theistic thinking: "If the emergent atheism simply reveals dialectically the internal contradiction which was lodged within the content of theism itself, then the understanding of atheism is possible only through the understanding of its generating matrix, theism. One issues from the other; one cannot make sense unless the other does" (Buckley 1987: 16). Just as the word itself "atheism" derives from "theism," so the reality that the word signifies derives historically from certain developments that occurred in the field of theistic philosophy. As a result, any investigation of the history of atheism, in its various shapes, should take as its starting point a thorough study of the tradition of theistic philosophy:

> Any attention to the origins of atheism in the West must attend as much—if not more—to the theism of the theologians and the philosophers as to the atheism of their adversaries. Atheism must be seen not as a collation of ideas which happened to arise in Western thought but as a transition whose meaning is spelled out by the process and whose existence is accounted for in terms of the ideas which preceded it. (Ibid.)

If Buckley considers atheism dependent on theism in terms of vocabulary, historical contexts, and influences, and so forth, Stephen Clark takes a step further and considers this dependence in a structural sense: atheistic thinking would not even be able to formulate itself, and make itself intelligible, in the absence of those principles of intelligibility postulated and advocated by theism. As a result, in the process of contesting the theistic worldview, the atheist is actually confirming the doctrine he opposes:

> even atheists, as long as they are rational ones, rely on Christian axioms, on theorems that would not be true if Christian theism—or something very like it—weren't. . . . If rational discourse is only possible in a God-directed universe, it follows that rational atheists must actually rely upon the truth of theism even to argue against it: this is not to say that atheists are incapable of rational thought, but only that—perhaps forgivably—they miss the implication of their own practice. (Clark 1998: viii)

To Stephen Clark a theistic philosophy seems to be "the safest option" (ibid.: 134), and his ultimate idea is that, given our particular ontological makeup, and the type of relationships we can establish with each other, with the world, and with our past, the best thing we can do—here and now—is to resort to faith philosophically, to ground our intellectual pursuits in faith, and to live on faith.[5]

The Philosopher's Mission

The first two editions (1713 and 1725) of George Berkeley's *Three Dialogues between Hylas and Philonous* bore the following long subtitle: *The design of which is plainly to demonstrate the reality and perfection of human knowledge, the incorporeal nature of the soul, and the immediate providence of a Deity: in opposition to Sceptics and Atheists. Also to open a method for rendering the Sciences more easy, useful and compendious.* When Berkeley published the third edition (1734) of the *Dialogues*, he shortened this subtitle, and left only this phrase: "In opposition to Sceptics and Atheists." Yet, even in its shortened form, the subtitle makes it clear that Berkeley took as his supreme mission in the *Dialogues* (which, one might say, is a "translation" of the *Principles* into a more accessible and agreeable language, aiming at a larger and more diverse audience) to fight and silence what he saw then as the increasingly influential groups of atheists, sceptics, and freethinkers, and in so doing he took his immaterialist philosophy as his main weapon. He knowingly "subordinated" his philosophical enterprise to a nonphilosophical end, but he seemed particularly happy in doing so.

It should be emphasized at this stage that Berkeley's notion of philosophy as a form of modern apologetics lies at the heart of his thinking. In other words, his intention was not, among other things, to silence the atheists with the arguments provided by his philosophy, but this was precisely his main intention, and he did everything in his power to accomplish it. Most importantly, he deliberately designed his immaterialist philosophy as a means of countering what the atheists and freethinkers were saying, and if one overlooks this fact there is a chance that one will seriously misrepresent the essence of Berkeley's immaterialist philosophy. True, from a formal, more abstract point of view, his immaterialist arguments might be seen as interesting and original in themselves, but what Berkeley wanted to accomplish through his immaterialism was not to exhibit philosophical inventiveness or some shocking originality of thinking, but, first of all, to offer a metaphysically sound basis for a specifically Christian philosophy, which would in turn offer the basis for a Christian ethics, as well as for an entire Christian way of living, which would result in a spiritually and morally healthier human society, into a happier and nobler humanity. Above all, he was interested in making philosophy useful for others, helping them live meaningful lives, and saving their souls in eternity. But in order to accomplish all these ends he felt he had to shake decisively the philosophical foundations of atheism and skepticism by silencing those modern philosophers

(Hobbes, Collins, Spinoza, Gassendi) whom he saw as offering philosophical arguments in their favor. In the absence of a sound philosophical basis, thought he, both atheism and skepticism would collapse immediately, the public would lose any serious interests in them and would stop not only agreeing with their (wrong) doctrines, but also following their immoralist ethics. Berkeley represented the intellectual public sphere as a "marketplace of ideas," some public space hosting philosophical debates, where philosophers are supposed to bring forth their theories and arguments, engage in logical and rhetorical battles, and defeat one another according to the powers of their minds or the rightness of the opinions they defend. More importantly, at the end of the battle, the winners in the battle gain the right of claiming that their theories are the only true ones, and will remain so in the future, and that the persuaded public have from now on to live their lives according to the ethical principles accompanying (or derived from) the the winning theories.

In the introduction to the *Three Dialogues between Hylas and Philonous* Berkeley expresses what he considered to be the main objective of writing this book: namely, an "utter destruction of atheism and scepticism." He specifically believes that this will take place simply as a logical consequence of his new philosophical principles' being accepted by the public:

> If the principles, which I here endeavour to propagate, are admitted for true; the consequences which, I think, evidently flow from thence, are, that *atheism* and *scepticism* will be utterly destroyed, many intricate points made plain, great difficulties solved, several useless parts of science retrenched, speculation referred to practice, and men reduced from paradoxes to common sense. (Berkeley 1948–57, 2:168)

It was his ardent hope that, as a result of a proper public assimilation and dissemination of his philosophy, not only would such intellectual diseases as skepticism and atheism disappear, but many of the current problems, theoretical difficulties, and puzzles in the sciences would be solved forever, as it were, as long as commonsense would triumph over paradoxes. The "paradox" was for Berkeley one of the most obvious symptoms of a serious intellectual illness. In this context, as he saw it, his immaterialism had a certain therapeutic value. His philosophy was intended to be, above all, a medicine for curing the harmful effects that the atheist and skeptical philosophies had had on people's minds. He says in *Alciphron,* in Crito's formulation: "as bodily distempers are cured by physic, those of the mind are cured by philosophy" (ibid., 3:139). This manner of seeing philosophy in terms of medical metaphors has a long history behind it, with Buddha, Socrates, and Plato at the beginning, and with a long list of brilliant representatives following thereafter.

Then, in the same introduction to the *Dialogues* a crucial passage occurs in which Berkeley confesses his philosophical creed that "the sublime notion of a God, and the comfortable expectation of immortality, do naturally arise from a close and methodical application of thought" (ibid., 2:168). In a manner that definitely places him in the tradition of theistic Christian philosophy I discussed very briefly above, Berkeley comes to see the contemplation of God as a natural end of all the mind's pursuits: if well and carefully conducted ("a close and methodical application of thought"), the human mind cannot but arrive at the sphere of the divine, enjoying the infinitely delightful prospects of immortality and eternal peace. The divine is the place where the mind can fulfill all its potentialities and finally find its rest. There is in us, according to this line of thought, a set of fundamental natural inclinations that should make us always direct our desires, intellectual interests, and actions toward what is divine, eternal, and unchanging: "Among all these things . . . those only are the true objects of enjoyment which we have spoken of as eternal and unchangeable" (Augustine 1877: 18). (If, in reality, the situation is different and we find ourselves sometimes desiring perishable or insignificant things, this happens—we will be advised—only because we are temporarily alienated from our true mission in this world.) At the same time, all these considerations about our innate inclinations toward searching for what is changeless and eternal come very close to the issue of Platonism, which I discussed earlier in this book.

Either God or Matter

It was Berkeley's most profound conviction that the best way in which he could serve the cause of theism was to deny the existence of matter and of the material world. As has been remarked, this was one of his earliest philosophical insights: even "as a teenager, Berkeley was already convinced that the notion of matter was incoherent, superfluous, at odds with common sense, and dangerous" (Cooper 1996: 260). At the beginning of his philosophical career, at the time when he was compiling his *Commonplace Book*, Berkeley observed: "Matter once allow'd. I defy any man to prove that God is not matter" (Berkeley 1948–57, 1:77). For the young Berkeley, God and matter were two absolutes: one cannot have both at the same time; the option for the former means nothing other than the dismissal of the latter, and the other way around. In a certain sense, all he did after that, through all his writings, was an incessant and laborious attempt at confirming, again and again, that early intuition. In another chapter of this book (chapter 7) I will be trying to propose a look at Berkeley's immaterialism from the point of view of the Cathar doctrines about matter, and to show how Berkeley's intuition of the nonexistence of matter reflects at bottom a certain anxiety, on his side, of a Gnostic and Dualistic nature. But, for the time being, I only try to see how his immaterialism functions as a form of apologetic philosophy.

First of all, there is no need for matter. Not only is matter unintelligible—we cannot, properly speaking, say that we perceive matter—but there is no reason whatsoever for accepting matter even as a problematic notion, to accept matter as, say, some "hypothetical notion" we might provisionally employ for "the sake of the argument," as it were. For Berkeley, the acceptance of matter would bring us no theoretical benefits simply because there cannot be benefits, of any kind, that the acceptance of matter might bring about. Philosophically speaking, matter is unnecessary and superfluous. God is more than sufficient as a source of meaning and (causal) explanation: all things have their "roots" in God, and it is in God that we can easily find their ultimate cause and explanation. God is what makes every explanation possible, meaningful and—above all—God is what confers upon any explanation completeness. Having no reason for accepting the existence of matter, only one reasonable solution remains—its complete denial:

> it is evident that the being of a *spirit infinitely wise, good, and powerful* is abundantly sufficient to explain all the appearances of Nature. But as for the *inert senseless matter*, nothing that I perceive has any the least connection with it, or leads to the thoughts of it. And I would fain see anyone explain any the meanest phenomenon in Nature by it, or shew any manner of reason, though in the lowest rank of probability, that he can have for its existence; or even make any tolerable sense or meaning of that supposition. (Ibid., 2: 72 [*Principles* § 72])

Berkeley becomes concerned with the unhealthy effects that the acceptance of the existence of matter might have upon our minds, and upon the notions, theories, systems of interpretation we resort to in our attempts to make sense of the world we live in. Berkeley's fundamental thesis is that the acceptance of the existence of matter is not an innocent thing at all. Although superfluous, the belief that matter exists, once given a place within our worldviews, tends to corrupt the other views we hold, to contaminate our native common sense, and induce in us various pernicious notions and unhealthy theories. Chief among them is atheism. For Berkeley atheism is one of the likely consequences of the acceptance of matter. An atheist is someone who gets the (wrong) idea that the world he finds himself in is the only world, the only reality; he is, as it were, "blinded" by what he immediately encounters, and thus put in a position from which he cannot see anything beyond the cause of his blindness. And then he names this blinding world "matter." As Berkeley puts it, it is precisely upon the doctrine of matter or corporeal substance that "all the impious schemes of *atheism* and irreligion" have been raised.

> Nay so great a difficulty hath it been thought, to conceive matter produced out of nothing, that the most celebrated among the ancient philosophers . . . have thought matter to be uncreated and coeternal with him. . . . All their [the atheists'] monstrous systems have so visible and necessary a dependence on it, that when this corner-stone is once removed, the whole fabric cannot choose but fall to the ground; insomuch that it is no longer worth while, to bestow a particular consideration on the absurdities of every wretched sect of *atheists*. (Ibid., 2: 81 [*Principles* § 92])[6]

According to Berkeley, not only are the atheists wrong: what is worse in their case is that they mistake their intellectual disease for excellent health, and, as if this misfortune were not enough, they seek to propagate and widely disseminate their disease among others. Atheism has ingrained in itself a desire to "convert," to make proselytes. As has been observed, militant atheism "trades on exactly the same conviction as any proselytizing creed: that those who don't align themselves with Truth are lost, and must—for their own sake—be disabused of all their false conceptions, even if it kills them" (Clark 1998: 44).[7] As such, thinks Berkeley, atheists must by all means be stopped, and the harmful effects of their doctrines removed. But it is of no avail to fight just the effects of something; one must get to its cause. Thus, Berkeley concludes that the only solution lies in a systematic attempt at "healing" these sick people, the sickest of all—the atheists. And this is precisely what Berkeley tries to do by the means of all his philosophical writings. The fact that he decided to "translate" the philosophical substance contained in *The Principles* into a more accessible and friendly language in the *Three Dialogues between Hylas and Philonous* attests precisely to the determination that Berkeley invested in this project.

Berkeley was deeply "disturbed at the remoteness of the 'God of the philosophers' from the intimate God of simpler belief" (Cooper 1996: 260), and was seriously convinced that the solution for bridging this gap between the "two Gods" would consist in expelling the notion of matter out of the sphere of philosophy, arts, and science, eventually out of everyone's mind. For Berkeley, this would have as a result a replacement of—to use the famous Pascalian phrasing—*le Dieu des philosophes et des savants* with the true God of Religion, *le Dieu d'Abraham, d'Isaac, et de Jacob, le Dieu de Jésus-Christ.* God will be then venerated properly, and will be resorted to as our ultimate source of metaphysical and existential meaning, and, as a result, some *magna restauratio* will necessarily take place in all branches of knowledge, in all the sciences and arts, with tremendously beneficial effects upon the future state of affairs of mankind. As Berkeley famously puts it:

> Matter being expelled out of Nature, drags with it so many sceptical and impious notions, such an incredible number of disputes and puzzling questions, which have been thorns in the sides of the divines, as well as philosophers . . . ; that if the arguments we have produced against it, are not found equal to demonstration (as to me they evidently seem) yet I am sure all friends to knowledge, peace, and religion, have reasons to wish they were. (Berkeley 1948–57, 2: 82 [*Principles* § 96)[8]

FIGHTING AGAINST FREETHINKING

Alciphron

In 1732, more than twenty years after he published his first writings of speculative philosophy, by means of which he was trying to "utterly destroy atheism and skepticism," Berkeley published his longest work, in the shape of seven philosophical and apologetic dialogues. Its full title is: *Alciphron; or, The Minute Philosopher: In Seven Dialogues Containing An Apology for the Christian Religion, against Those Who Are Called Free-Thinkers.* From several points of view, *Alciphron* is significantly different from all Berkeley's previous writings (with perhaps the exception of the *Three Dialogues*). This difference is in terms of length, contents, types of argumentation, reliance upon past authorities, style, literary devices, and rhetorical techniques employed, and even in terms of the audience intended. The fact that his early philosophical writings had not enjoyed the public success that Berkeley had expected, or even some minimal form of acceptance among the wide public, had probably something to do with why *Alciphron* differs so much from them.

First of all, from a strictly literary point of view, *Alciphron* is almost unanimously recognized as one of the major accomplishments in the English language: "as a work of art it stands supreme in the whole body of our English literature of philosophy, and perhaps supreme also in our literature of religious apologetics" (Jessop 1950: 2). Certainly, Berkeley's writing had always been elegant and highly expressive, but with *Alciphron* the artistry and literary qualities of Berkeley's writing came to occupy a central position, functioning as a distinct means of persuasion and as an important weapon in his dispute with freethinkers and atheists; the emotions aroused in the reader by the artful writing in *Alciphron* are certainly of the greatest help in his anti-atheistic endeavors. Considering the artfulness of this writing, T. E. Jessop, one of *Alciphron*'s modern editors, placed Berkeley's *Alciphron* in a tradition of the dialogical form in philosophy whose history could be traced as far back as the Platonic dialogues. Indeed, when reading *Alciphron,* one cannot help thinking that Berkeley wrote this work bearing constantly in mind the Platonic art of the philosophical dialogue, with all that this means. As Jessop remarks:

> his model was clearly Plato, from whom he learned more than anyone else has done the art of writing philosophical dialogue. After his master, only he has produced dialogues that are at once good philosophy and eminent literature. Some of his passages read as though they were transcripts of a Socratic conversation in a new Attic tongue. Outside Plato there is nothing in this genre to compare *Alciphron* with, except Berkeley's own *Three Dialogues.* (Ibid.)

Both Crito and Euphranor, the two characters standing for Berkeley's own position in the confrontation (Crito's "knowledgeable, sarcastic, and witty interventions express one side of Berkeley's mind; Euphranor's simple sincerity expresses the other side" [ibid.: 15]), make abundant use of Socratic irony, merciless sarcasm, pretended ignorance, and other Socratic-Platonic techniques of puzzling and silencing opponents. (More will be said about this later on in the chapter.)

In the second place, *Alciphron* differs from Berkeley's other writings in the sense that it is conceived as an apologetic writing, and it has to follow the specific rules of the genre to which it belongs. Indeed, as has been remarked, in *Alciphron* "Christian beliefs are stated defensively, not in the order required by their own logic, but with a shape and emphasis devised to meet the contemporary objections of intellect and mood. The philosophy in it is subservient to that aim" (ibid.: 4).[9] Embarking on an apologetic line of thought changes one's discourse in the sense that it belongs to the very definition of "apologetic" to be, first of all, "the defence of a cause or party supposed to be of paramount importance to the speaker." "Apologetic" is different both from "polemic (which need not assume any previous attack by the opponent) and from merely epideictic or occasional orations" (Edwards et al. 1999: 1). Therefore, when writing *Alciphron* Berkeley was not simply supposed to formulate his philosophical position on such and such an issue, and then support it with arguments and various forms of evidence. The fundamental requirement that an apologist has to meet is to cope successfully with what his opponents claim against his position, to counter their claims by showing, as well as he can, that the counterarguments brought against the position he defends are flawed in some way or other: "apologetics address outsiders, and must deal with the views of their own group and others' misconceptions of them" (Price 1999: 106). Moreover, not only does he have to perform all these things, but he has to do so in such an elegant, persuasive, and compelling manner that the current opponent should mysteriously, as it were, become one day a supporter of the apologist's position. For an apologetic is not only about defending a given position, but it is also about gaining others (more and more others) for this position, persuading them to give up what they used to believe in, and believing in something new. Deep at the heart of the idea of apologetics lies, whether the apologist admits it or not, an invitation to conversion. As a result, what we should expect to find in *Alciphron* is not a systematic presentation of the Christian philosophy, but a refutation of what freethinkers then thought about Christianity, and—more importantly—an effort to convince them to adopt the religion.

In the third place, *Alciphron* is specifically and vigorously directed against a certain social and intellectual group, or "sect," increasingly influential in Berkeley's time, namely, the freethinkers: "The author's design being to consider the free-thinker in the various lights of atheist, libertine, enthusiast, scorner, critic, metaphysician, fatalist, and sceptic" (Berkeley 1948–57, 3:23). Of course, as we have seen above, in a way all Berkeley's philosophical writings were conceived as means of silencing the atheists, skeptics, and freethinkers. Yet, whereas in his previous writings he dealt with the theoretical principles on which he thought atheism was founded (the doctrine of matter, for example), and brought forth speculative arguments against these principles, in *Alciphron* Berkeley addresses freethinking as a (pathologic) social and cultural phenomenon:

> Free-thinking was rampant in drawing-rooms, coffee-houses and taverns, and there it was less decent than it was in books. To call that a cult of reason would be cant, and to stigmatize Berkeley's satire as overdrawn would be to

take our picture of the life of his day from its published documents. He rightly makes his characters . . . remind us that free-thinking as a social fact was to be found most in conversation. . . . He was dealing less with a theory . . . than with a fashionable attitude, one that regarded religious people, and most of all the clergy, as stupid, inelegant, and either sycophantic or tyrannical. (Jessop 1950: 6)

The necessity that Berkeley stringently felt of "healing" his neighbors' minds and morals, of immediately expelling the intellectual disease of free-thinking from society, requires that the emphasis in *Alciphron* be placed not so much on the would-be philosophical doctrines behind freethinking (although a great deal is dedicated to tracing their sources, in Spinoza, Hobbes, Gassendi, and Collins, and to pointing out their flaws) as on warning against, describing in detail, and combating the extremely pernicious effects that these doctrines might have on people's morals, on public and private morality, on civic life, and on the well-being of the community. Berkeley is particularly biting on this issue. The character Crito speaks: "If any man wishes to enslave his country, nothing is a fitter preparative than vice; and nothing leads to vice so surely as irreligion" (Berkeley 1948–57, 3:104); "all those who write either explicitly or by insinuation against the dignity, freedom, and immortality of the human soul, may so far forth be justly said to unhinge the principles of morality, and destroy the means of making men reasonably virtuous" (ibid.: 23).[10]

In a way, this was the wisest solution that Berkeley could arrive at. One of the reasons, from the Christian apologetic point of view, it is so difficult to counter and fight efficiently against atheism is that there are so many ambiguities about it. Atheism is multifacetious, ever-changing, and flexible; atheism is always in search of retreats or new targets, always in a process of redefinition, readjustment, and refurbishment. As Michael Buckley said,

The problem with atheism is that it is not a problem. It is a situation, an atmosphere, a confused history whose assertions can be identical in expression and positively contradictory in sense. The ambiguity which marks such terms as *god* and *atheism* can be discovered in almost every critical proposition about this situation. (Buckley 1987: 13–4)

Thus, realizing that the metaphysical argumentation against materialism, and disputes with atheists at an abstract level, might in fact be of no practical use (the fortune of his earlier writings might have convinced him sufficiently of that), Berkeley decided to change his modalities of expression, employ new types of argumentation and rhetorical tools, and resort to some novel, more efficient weaponry. First of all, he resorted to the old rhetorical trick of using some of the weapons used by his own opponents.

Approaching Freethinking à la *Voltaire*

One of the most interesting and refreshing things about *Alciphron* is probably the fact that the two characters standing for Christian apologists (Crito and Euphranor) make—in defending their Christian faith and refuting the claims advanced by the freethinkers—an extensive and impressive use of rhetorical tools traditionally attributed to the freethinkers themselves: devastating irony, caustic satire, arguments based on the *reductio ad absurdum*, sophisticated derision, fine humor, and so on and so forth. Obviously, *Alciphron* is not only that: it contains a great deal of theological, historical, ethical, and philosophical material, but—besides all these—there is in this book a distinct element of devastating irony, refined humor, and supremely artful satire systematically directed against freethinkers and their ideas. This makes Berkeley's freethinkers appear defeated with the weapons they themselves provided; as it were, in a purely *Voltairian* manner.[11]

It goes without saying that Berkeley used these rhetorical procedures deliberately and expected from their employment certain results in terms of asserting his own views more vigorously, persuading the audience of their truth, and gaining the audience's approval and support: "Like all satire, *Alciphron* is designed to encourage and direct our feelings of contempt and resentment" (Walmsley 1990: 115). Once he becomes caught up within the carefully woven narrative, the reader of Berkeley's book ceases to be an impartial and detached observer, but—thanks precisely to, again, the admirable artistry, refined rhetoric, and sophisticated techniques of persuasion Berkeley employs—he feels that he has to make a certain choice: namely, to side with the cause of Christian theism. All of Berkeley's rhetorical tricks and refined ironies are directed precisely to preparing this choice in his reader's minds. And, as a result, his reader will make this choice for the simple reason that, in the context delineated by *Alciphron*, siding with the freethinkers would simply go against his emotions and the feelings aroused in him by the internalization of the book. Of course, this is exactly what is supposed to happen, as satire (and *Alciphron* is an admirable satire) is a means of providing an "emotive constraint on the vicious man, playing upon his fears of rejection. But satire also appeals widely to public spirit, stirring our anger against those who threaten the *status quo*" (ibid.).

The two freethinkers in the dialogue are Alciphron and Lysicles. Both are, of course, fictitious characters, but most readers, on the publication of the book, were easily able to see in Alciphron a representation of the third Earl of Shaftesbury (1621–83) and in Lysicles a representation of Bernard Mandeville (1670–1733). (Many critics accused Berkeley of badly misrepresenting in *Alcipron* Shaftesbury's ethical theory, and Mandeville's theory that "private vices are public benefits.") The two freethinkers are portrayed only sketchily at the beginning, and as the dialogues progress, they are made to reveal themselves in their entirety. As Crito sees them, "they are both men of fashion, and would be agreeable enough, if they did not fancy themselves freethinkers. But this, to speak the truth, has given them a certain air and manner which a little too visibly declare they think themselves wiser than the rest of the world" (Berkeley 1948–57, 3:33). A first hint is thus dropped that what is called "free-thinking" is not positive and substantial, but it just happens that there are some eccentric people who decide to "fancy themselves" freethinkers. This is, in fact, one of the main rhetorical arguments that Berkeley uses against freethinking in the book: through derision and underevaluation of his opponents' position, he insinuates that freethinking is not a serious intellectual conviction, but some caprice, some cheap amusement on the freethinker's part, some temporary whim that will certainly pass after a while. The freethinker is not even a freethinker. Berkeley thus suggests that "free-thinking" is merely a word some people use in order to ennoble their eccentricity or desire to *épater le bourgeois*. The elder freethinker, Alciphron, "is above forty, and no stranger either to men or books." He is well traveled ("through the polite parts of Europe") and since his return from *le grand tour* "he hath lived in the amusements of the town, which being grown stale and tasteless to his palate, have flung him into a sort of splenetic indolence" (ibid.: 32). In a sense, Alciphron is depicted by Crito as an honest and commonsensical person, having become an atheist only as a result of a series of skeptical crises.[12] Due to the numerous prejudices that freethinkers are, according to Berkeley, particularly predisposed to, Alciphron was not able to overcome these crises and chose to "fancy himself a free-thinker." Lysicles is much more interesting a case, and Berkeley abundantly exercises his devastating irony when portraying him. "The young gentleman . . . is . . . one of lively parts and a general insight into letters, who, after having passed the forms of education and seen a little of the world, fell into an intimacy with men of pleasure and free-thinkers, I am afraid much to the damage of his constitution and his fortune" (ibid.).

Lysicles is cynical, stubborn, and sophistical; as Walmsley says, he "is a philosopher only so far as he may use reason to undermine those laws, human and divine, which threaten to rob him of his pleasure" (Walmsley 1990: 111). In fact, Crito exaggerates somewhat when remarking about Lysicles that he has a "general insight into letters": Lysicles himself confesses, later on in the course of the dialogues, that caught up as he was in the demanding practice of freethinking he could not find the time, in his university years, to "mind the books."[13] Otherwise, he finds the university perfectly entertaining, and does not have any reproach for it. Lysicles: "For my part, I find no fault with universities. All I know is that I had the spending three hundred pounds a year in one of them, and think it the cheerfulest time of my life. As for their books and style, I had no leisure to mind them" (Berkeley 1948–57, 3:197).[14]

One of the recurrent ideas in *Alciphron* is that there is a fundamental duplicity in the current behavior of freethinkers, and that the use of double standards is one of their favorite tricks. Not only are freethinkers destroyers of morality proper (as upholders, among other things, of the "private vices, publick benefits" theory), but, suggests Berkeley, by the way in which they behave in debates and intellectual confrontations, they break the fundamental rules and codes of any "ethics of knowledge": "To me it seems the minute philosophers, when they appeal to reason and common sense, mean only the sense of their own party" (ibid.: 243) In this way they prepare logical traps in which they themselves fall later. For example, as Crito notices, thanks to their compulsive desire to *épater le bourgeois*, freethinkers often come to place themselves in (to say the least) embarrassing situations of the following kind:

> When one of them has got a ring of disciples round him, his method is to exclaim against prejudice, and recommend thinking and reasoning, giving to understand that himself is a man of deep researches and close argument. . . . The same man, in other company, if he chance to be pressed with reason, shall laugh at logic, and assume the lazy supine airs of a fine gentleman, a wit, a *railleur*, to avoid the dryness of a regular and exact enquiry. This double face of the minute philosopher is of no small use to propagate and maintain his notions. (Ibid.: 158)

As Berkeley suggests throughout the dialogues, the freethinker is too much an actor to be an authentic and honest thinker. His behavior is dictated primarily by the imperative of pleasing, provoking, or wooing various audiences. The freethinker, as portrayed in *Alciphron*, does not feel any special need for self-coherence or intellectual honesty: "If Mahometanism were established by authority, I make no doubt those very free-thinkers, who at present applaud Turkish maxims and manners to that degree you'd think them ready to turn Turks, would then be the first to exclaim against them" (ibid.: 193). What they pursue is not the truth, but what happens to be fashionable at a given moment or seen as scandalous in conservative circles. Yes, they do make frequent references to common sense, experience, and nature—at some point Alciphron exclaims, "O nature! Thou art the fountain, original, and pattern of all that is good and wise" (ibid.: 62)—but it is obvious enough from the dialogues that as soon as the common sense, nature, and experience will infirm their claims, they will call any appeal to them "prejudice" and "obscurantism." Thanks to their lack of seriousness and intellectual honesty, to their duplicity, thirst for social success, and permanent eagerness to *épater le bourgeois*, Berkeley's freethinkers are very much like some of the ancient sophists, as Plato depicted them in his dialogues. The freethinkers' enjoyment is not a philosophical enjoyment, one derived from some deeper intellectual quest, but rather comes from the childish pleasure of doing things "for the sake of the game." This makes Euphranor advance, very ironically, the idea of a certain "resemblance between fox-hunters and free-thinkers; the former exerting their animal faculties in pursuit of game, as you gentlemen employ your intellectuals in the pursuit of truth. The kind of amusement is the same, although the object is different" (ibid.: 175). As a result, irresponsible as they are, the freethinkers are never prepared to accept the logical outcome of what they have been saying or assenting to in the course of a given conversation or intellectual debate.[15] If the definition of prejudice is to take as starting point what can only be attained through argumentation, and to refuse to accept what has been attained through argumentation, then the two freethinkers are simply caught in *flagrant délit* of gross prejudice:

> *Alciphron*: I have been drawn into some concessions you won't like.
> *Lysicles*: Let me know what they are.
> *Alciphron*: Why, that there is such a thing as a God, and that His existence is very certain.
> *Lysicles*: Bless me! How came you to entertain so wild a notion? (Ibid.: 162)

One of the supremely humorous scenes in *Alciphron* occurs when Crito openly accuses freethinking of bigotry. This is an instance where the use of the rhetorical technique of defeating an adversary with his own weapons becomes most evident. The accusation of bigotry is exactly the type of accusation that we expect the least to be brought against freethinkers.[16] To draw a contemporary comparison, it is as though a feminist activist were openly accused of *macho* attitudes. The accusation reads:

> it has been often remarked by observing men that there are no greater bigots than infidels. . . . I see a bigot wherever I see a man overbearing and positive without knowing why, laying the greatest stress on points of smallest moments, hasty to judge of the conscience, thoughts, and inward views of other men, impatient of reasoning against his own opinions . . . , and attached to mean authorities. (Ibid.: 283)

This peculiar bigotry and the freethinkers' histrionics, playfulness, and lack of any deeper intellectual commitment are, for Berkeley, precisely what undermine their approaches most. For instance, the freethinkers cannot succeed in proving God's nonexistence because, properly speaking, they have decided not to do so. All they mainly wish to do is to draw people's attention to them, by incessantly shocking those who happen to listen to them. As a result, their atheistic claims, if taken seriously, seem to the two Christian apologists so weakly supported by arguments and evidence that Crito simply exclaims: "I cannot help thinking there are points sufficiently plain, and clear, and full, whereon a man may ground a reasonable faith in Christ: but that the attacks of minute philosophers against this faith are grounded upon darkness, ignorance, and presumption" (ibid.: 280).

Let me mention in passing here that, behind Berkeley's humorous attack, there might be the serious point that, as has been said, "there are more difficulties than atheistical commentators . . . suppose in conceiving a truly godless universe in which it would still be reasonable to prefer one outcome to another" (Clark 1998: 14). Thus, the crucial existential advantage that the recognition of God's existence might confer upon the one who makes the theistic claim is that, in making this claim, he is thoroughly self-consistent. This line of thought must go like this: God exists, He is the Logos, the ultimate principle upon which human reason itself is based, and without which no meaningful utterance would ever be possible. Therefore, pushing the limit of the reasoning, the very fact that one is saying "God exists" is, in a certain way, a proof of God's existence. The possibility of a meaningful utterance is based, within a theistic framework of thinking, on the fact that there is a meaning (precisely because there is God). Of course, from a strictly logical point of view, this might be seen as circular, but the theist might well answer this objection by pointing to the fundamental circularity that generally characterizes our discourses. In close connection with this specific line of thinking, Stephen Clark points to the interesting fact that the "rules and axioms of free-thinkers are also taken upon trust, and are less acceptable than religious rules and axioms just because they claim that nothing should be taken upon trust" (Clark 1998: 130). Ironically, freethinkers, despite their declared war against prejudices of all kinds, and the things we take for granted, come to rely on various prejudices and take things for granted themselves:

> self-styled free-thinkers who spoke out against "religious prejudice" neces-
> sarily relied on prejudice themselves, while simultaneously denying them-
> selves the right to do so. Those who say there is no inner light at all, cannot
> coherently trust their own judgment; those who say that testimony and
> inherited opinion must all be abandoned condemn themselves to an incorri-
> gible ignorance. (Ibid.: 129)

This is, of course, too complex to be satisfactorily dealt with here, in a chapter not specifically dedicated to the problem of atheism. All I wish to point out is the larger context within which Berkeley's discussion of freethinking should be placed.

"The Holy Alliance"

One of the important means by which Crito and Euphranor constantly support their theistic claims consists in resorting to the tradition of wisdom, to sayings of various Oriental sages, ancient thinkers, and other authoritative figures, in order to validate their claims. This will be, in fact, Berkeley's main working method in *Siris*, but he uses this technique to a great extent in *Alciphron* too. If the arguments brought forth by Crito or Euphranor for accepting such and such an opinion, however strong they might be, are nevertheless deemed insufficiently compelling by their opponents, then a reference is made to some past venerated (and more authoritative) figures who held the same, or a similar, opinion. The supposition behind the use of such a technique is that—human reason being one and the same every-where and at all times—by accepting theism, one in fact accepts what is only natural for reason to accept, that, in other words, theism in nothing but the most reasonable philosophy, or the healthiest doctrine, of mankind, having been confirmed again and again over the centuries, not only in Europe, but also in China or Persia, not only by Christians, but also by heathens or Jews:

Reason is the same, and rightly applied will lead to the same conclusions, in all times and places. Socrates, two thousand years ago, seems to have reasoned himself into the same notion of a God which is entertained by the philosophers of our days, if you will allow that name to any who are not of your sect. And the remark of Confucius, that a man should guard in his youth against lust, in manhood against faction, and in old age against covetousness, is as current morality in Europe as in China. (Berkeley 1948–57, 3:58–59)

Not that we should accept unconditionally all that comes from authorities. This would be simply prejudice and laziness of mind. But the point of Berkeley's argument is that, in those cases in which, after we have been given reasonable arguments that a certain doctrine is true, and—more than that—had it endorsed by the wise men of the past, there is no reason left not to accept it.

Resorting to the wisdom of past centuries functions in *Alciphron* as another test that the notions advanced by the two freethinkers have to pass. The fact that these notions fail to pass this test is one more proof that the freethinkers are mistaken. Of course, this line of thought goes, there were already sufficient logical, philosophical, and metaphysical arguments against the freethinkers' theories, but Berkeley, through his mouthpieces Crito and Euphranor, wants us to see even more clearly not only that freethinking is unnatural to our reason, but, more importantly, that it has been so throughout mankind's history.

Let us see how this testing process works. Crito explains how the freethinkers have taken a course contrary

to all the great philosophers of former ages, who made it their endeavour to raise and refine human-kind, and remove it as far as possible from the brute; to moderate and subdue men's appetites; . . . and direct them to the noblest objects; to possess men's minds with a high sense of the Divinity . . . and the immortality of the soul. . . . But . . . our minute philosophers act the reverse of all other wise . . . men; it being their end . . . to erase the principles of all that is great and good . . . ; to unhinge all order of civil life, to undermine the foundations of morality, and . . . to bring us down to the maxims and way of thinking of the most uneducated and barbarous nations, and even to degrade human-kind to a level with the brute beasts. (Ibid.: 54)

In other words, the past is not dead, nor vanished, but it constantly comes into the present to give it shape, more coherence and self-understanding.

What has been significant and valuable in the past is now condensed, or embodied, in various forms; in our current dealings with the world, or in our dealings with ourselves, we cannot simply pass over these embodiments of the past. Just as one person has his own heritage of private memories, stories, and personal histories, a heritage that actually shapes his present life, conferring upon it coherence and identity, so a community—be it a village, a city, or a nation—has its own stories and historical memories that shape its present, and future, life. As it were, not only do we have to just "take into account" our past, but—more importantly—we have to know how to make the best use of it.

The use that Berkeley makes of the "wisdom of the Heathens," and of the other "past authorities" is in fact a feature that Berkeley shares with the entire Christian apologetic tradition. From its very beginning, Christian apologetics showed a marked tendency to appeal to, and make use of, non-Christian elements in order to support its own claims. These non-Christian elements were put together by the Christian theologians and made to work in harmony *ad majorem Dei gloriam*. Needless to say, what was overtly contrary to the principles of the Christian faith was left aside and refuted, following the advice of St. Justin Martyr: "Reason dictates that those who are truly pious and philosophers should honour and love only the truth, declining to follow the opinions of the ancients, if they are worthless" (Justin 1997: 23). But there were still enough elements of the classical Greek-Roman culture that the early Christian philosophers and apologists could safely take aboard and use in their interest.[17] And so they did: "The leading apologists [of the first Christian centuries] are almost unanimous in opting for a synthesis of Biblical faith with classical culture. They take over many of the characteristic theses of Ammonius Saccas, Plotinus, and Porphyry" (Dulles 1971: 71). Classical Greek philosophy was especially highly regarded by the early Christian authors, and they made every effort to take over its "healthy" part and to incorporate it into the doctrines of Christianity. Not only was Greek philosophy (particularly the Platonic tradition, as Aristotle was to become fashionable among Christians much later) seen as "in agreement" with some of the fundamental tenets of Christianity, but some of the early Christian authors also developed the consequential notion that it was particularly through their philosophy that the ancients prepared for Christ's coming. As it was commonly said, while the Jews of the Old Testament had Moses, the Greeks had Plato:

> With writers such as Justin Martyr, Clement of Alexandria, Origen, Eusebius of Caesarea, we find the notion of philosophy as the instrument by which

the Logos, which illuminates every man who comes in to the world, prepared the minds of the Gentiles for the gospel of Christ. The Jews were prepared by the Law and the prophets, the Gentiles by philosophy. The
Christian revelation was the fulfillment of both. (Copleston 1974: 25)

The early Christians saw Plato as, so to speak, a "Christian before Christ,"
a Christian who did not know that he was a Christian. For, this line of
thought goes, philosophy, at its best, cannot be but work in the service of
Logos; one cannot practice philosophy without being, at the same time, a
lover of the divine Wisdom, a worshipper of the true God. Jesus Christ
was revealed to the Jews personally, in flesh and blood, but to the Greeks
philosophically, as philosophical *logos*. In St. Justin Martyr's words: "not
only among the Greeks through Socrates were these things revealed by reason [*logos*], but also among the Barbarians were they revealed by logos personally, when He had taken shape, and become man, and was called Jesus
Christ" (Justin 1997: 26).

Not only did this borrowing from the ancients take place, but we can
even find in St. Augustine a sophisticated theory about the Christians'
"right" to incorporate what was valid in the past: in St. Augustine's own
words, it is a taking over "from those who have unlawful possession of it."
In this context, reading analogically the story of the Jews' flight from Egypt,
Augustine offers an excellent and powerful sample of Christian philosophizing about history, about deaths and births of civilizations, and about ways of
using the past:

> if those who are called philosophers, and especially the Platonists, have said
> aught that is true and in harmony with our faith, we are . . . to claim it for
> our own use from those who have unlawful possession of it. For, as the
> Egyptians had not only the idols and heavy burdens which the people of
> Israel hated and fled from, but also vessels and ornaments of gold and silver,
> . . . which the same people when going out of Egypt appropriated to them-
> selves, designing them for a better use . . . , in the same way all branches of
> heathen learning . . . contain also liberal instruction which is better adapted
> to the use of the truth, and some most excellent precepts of morality; and
> some truths in regard even to the worship of the One God are found among
> them. Now these are, so to speak, their gold and silver. . . . These . . . the
> Christian . . . ought to take away from them, and to devote to their proper
> use in preaching the gospel. (Augustine 1877, 75–76)

As we can see, the past was not dead at all for these authors, and they knew
how to make the best use of it.

In *Alciphron* Berkeley used all these techniques provided by traditional Christian apologetics for making a better use of the past, and showing that the truth of the Christian faith had been grasped long before Christ or after him, in those geographical regions where Christianity did not prevail, by all those who practiced an honest and unprejudiced way of thinking. Of course, in principle, the two freethinkers could have, in their turn, made exactly the same point, showing how criticisms have been brought against religion in all times and in different cultures, and how, historically, if not freethinkers proper, at least various dissidents and heretics have always followed in the footsteps of the founders of religions, always bothering and challenging them, and so on. But Berkeley, the God-puppeteer of the *Alciphron*, decided not to leave the two freethinkers room to do that.

The Argument of Utility

Since the "visual language argument" for God's existence that George Berkeley brings forth in *Alciphron* is the subject of another chapter in this book (chapter 3), I will in the following deal with only what might be called "the argument of utility" that Berkeley provides in this writing for God's existence. This argument is not a novelty. As I will show below, several other philosophers and theologians used it before Berkeley. But it contrasts boldly with the Christian apologetic context of the seventeenth and eighteenth centuries, in which the emphasis was in general put on the argument of design.

The two Christian apologists in *Alciphron*, after having brought a great deal of logical, philosophical, historical, and authoritative arguments and evidence in support of their claim that Christian theism is "the best option," arrive at a point where they decide to employ a series of pragmatic arguments for accepting the Christian faith. In other words, if the previous arguments are not to be considered compelling enough, then there still remains the possibility that one should accept Christianity for reasons of utility. Not that, for Berkeley, the philosophical and historical arguments would be weak or in some other way unsatisfactory; but he simply wants to show that there is an abundance of arguments, of diverse natures, for accepting Christian theism.

The "argument of utility" is based on the observation that, historically, Christianity has improved people's lives. The extremely beneficial effects that accepting Christianity has for centuries had on people's lives, morals, and well-being; the wonderful "works" that Christianity has constantly performed in terms of making people better, wiser, happier, more virtuous, and readier to help their neighbors; the social peace, general harmony, and public reconciliation that living by Christian standards always brings about; the entire "Christian civilization" that this religion established—all of these are undeniable proofs that this religion is the right choice, and that anyone, if he is a man of sense, has to accept it without reservation:

> one great mark of the truth of the Christianity is, in my mind, its tendency to do good, which seems the north star to conduct our judgment in moral matters, and in all things of a practic nature; moral and practical truths being ever connected with universal benefit. . . . the Christian religion, considered as a fountain of light and joy, and peace, as a source of faith, and hope, and charity . . . , must needs be a principle of happiness and virtue. (Berkeley 1948–57, 3:178)

In his "natural state," man is a rather gross, rude, and unpleasant creature. His reason is weak, and untrained, his feelings are elementary and brutal, and his opinions uncertain and shapeless. His aspirations are reduced to mere survival, meeting the elementary needs of life, and sheer absence of suffering. In this context, it is religion that helps him rise from this state of brutality and become a creature "in the image and likeness of God." Christian religion in particular, in those places in which it has come to prevail, has proven to be an invaluable means of civilizing people and bettering their lives. In order to illustrate this argument, Berkeley gives a number of concrete examples. One of them regards the formation of the English people under the guidance and stimulation of the Christian faith. He takes it as an "invincible proof" of the "power and excellency of the Christian religion" that, "without the help of those civil institutions and incentives to glory, it should be able to inspire a phlegmatic people with the noblest sentiments, and soften the manners of the northern boors into gentleness and humanity" (ibid.: 184–5). Berkeley is not saying that this was a miracle, but the note of enthusiasm of these and other passages implies that we could safely use here the term "miracle," at least in a metaphorical sense.

Fascinated as he was with the world of the South, which produced—among other good things—Greek and Roman classical antiquity, Berkeley thought that it was only thanks to the tremendous civilizing efforts that Christianity constantly made over the centuries that modern English culture was now able to raise itself to the same level of sophistication, refinement, and good taste as that of the ancient Greeks. Given the particular circumstances under which the northern peoples had to live their lives, they had to do through great effort what the ancient Greeks did simply by virtue of their natural inclinations. And, in this respect, the Christian religion has had its own role to play:

> what but religion could kindle and preserve a spirit towards learning in such a northern rough people? Greece produced men of active and subtle genius; and their natural curiosity was amused and excited by learned conversations, in their public walks and gardens and porticos. Our genius leads to amusements of a grosser kind: we breath a grosser and a colder air; and that curiosity which was general in the Athenians . . . is among our people of fashion treated like affectation. (Ibid.: 201)

Obviously, this is not a fact pertaining only to British history. Wherever and whenever Christianity has been accepted and left to guide people's lives, its practical effects have always been impressive. In times of crisis and uncertainty, the church has been the only stable ground, the only hope for those who sought certainty and hope. If there still was in Europe a sense of what classical antiquity meant, that was due mainly to the sustained efforts of Christianity to preserve the remains of classical culture. The transmission of the classical heritage to modern times was only possible through the important efforts made by the church. As Berkeley reminds us, Christian authors (and authorities) have always paid a special attention to the preservation and encouragement of classical learning:

> But who are they that encouraged and produced the restoration of arts and polite learning? What share had the minute philosophers in this affair? Matthias Corvinus King of Hungary, Alphonsus King of Naples, Cosmus de Medicis, Picus of Mirandola, . . . famous for learning themselves, and for encouraging it in others with a munificent liberality, were neither Turks, nor Gentiles, nor minute philosophers. Who was it that transplanted and revived the Greek language and authors, and with them all polite arts and literature, in the West? Was it not chiefly Bessarion a cardinal, Marcus Musurus an archbishop, Theodore Gaza a private clergyman? (Ibid.: 203)

Finally, we should not take the utility argument as being concerned only with social, historical, civilizational, and cultural aspects. In addition to this, there is also a deeper sense in which accepting the points of Christian theism would have significantly beneficial effects upon our inner lives. For being a Christian means not only performing certain social rites and observing a certain set of moral rules, but also a certain way of looking at, of understanding and making sense of the world in which one has found oneself. Christianity has left its mark not only on the world outside us, but also on the ultimate structure, makeup and workings of our inner world. Thanks to this, we are in a better position to understand the natural world outside us. For, in Berkeley's view, it is precisely by adopting a Christian theistic position that we are given a key to the ultimate beauty, harmony, and orderliness of this world:

> In a system of spirits, subordinate to the will, and the direction of the Father of spirits, governing them by laws and conducting them by methods suitable to wise and good ends, there will be great beauty. But in an incoherent fortuitous system, governed by chance, or in a blind system, governed by fate, or in a system where Providence doth not preside, how can beauty be, which cannot be without order, which cannot be without design? (Ibid.: 129–30)

It is worth observing that Berkeley's *pragmatism* in matters apologetic was not at all his own invention. In fact, in employing the argument of utility he was actually placing himself in a long tradition of Christian thinkers, theologians, and apologists who have in the past made a similar use of the utility argument. Pointing to the beneficial effects that accepting the Christian faith could have on one's social, moral, and intellectual life had been a method used by apologists since the beginning of Christianity. For example, in his *First Apology*, St. Justin Martyr explains how the idea of an all-knowing and all-seeing God makes Christians necessarily improve their morals and live better lives: "not only our deeds, but also our thoughts are open before God. And many, both men and women, who have been Christ's disciples from childhood, have preserved their purity at the age of sixty or seventy years. . . . what shall we say then of the countless multitude of those who have turned away from intemperance?" (Justin 1997: 32). In his turn, Origen draws a sharp contrast between the social behavior of various communities of Christians ("Churches of God") and the behavior of their (non-Christian) fellow-citizens. The Christian way of life definitely helps the former live a more decent and virtuous life than the latter do:

> The Church of God, say, at Athens is meek and quiet, since it desires to please God. But the assembly of the Athenians is riotous and in no way comparable to the Church of God there. . . . If the man who hears this has an open mind, and examines the facts with a desire to find the truth, he will be amazed at the one who both planned and had the power to carry into effect the establishment of the Churches of God in all places. (Origen 1953: 147)

Origen then observes how those Christians who are in positions of authority or charged with public responsibilities show, due to their virtuous private lives and their "improved" natures, a tendency to serve their communities better, and to be better rulers than the non-Christians: "compare the ruler of the Church in each city with the ruler of the citizens, and you will understand how . . . there is a superior progress towards the virtues surpassing the character of those who are councillors and rulers in the cities" (ibid.: 148). In short, leaving aside all other theological and philosophical considerations, there are numberless practical points of view from which adopting Christianity can be seen as the best, the safest, and most profitable solution.

The special role that the performance of miracles might play in inspiring people's faith and in converting them to Christianity might also be considered in connection with this line of pragmatic apologetics. In his *De civitate Dei* St. Augustine[18] talks of three "incredibilities" revealed by Jesus' life and the subsequent expansion of Christianity:

> It is incredible that Christ should have risen in His flesh and, with His flesh, have ascended into heaven; it is incredible that the world should have believed a thing so incredible; it is incredible that men so rude and lowly, so few and unaccomplished, should have convinced the world, including men of learning, of something so incredible and have convinced men so conclusively.[19]

St. Augustine does not explicitly say the rapid expansion of Christianity was a miracle, but he seems to suggest it.[20] As it were, everything was—by all common human standards—so incredible and beyond any reasonable expectation that only through the secret intervention of the divine might can we explain why Christianity spread the way it did.

Later on, the issue would be taken up by St. Thomas Aquinas, who would overtly consider the successful conversion of large communities of people a "miracle," a "sign" that God sent us as a means through which we could learn even more about the truth, rightness, and providentiality of the Christian religion. As St. Thomas puts it,

> This wonderful conversion of the world to the Christian faith is the clearest witness of the signs given in the past; so that they should be further repeated, since they appear most clearly in their effect. For it would be truly more wonderful than all signs if the world had been led by simple and humble men to believe such lofty truths, to accomplish such difficult actions, and to have such high hopes. Yet it is also a fact that, even in our own time, God does not cease to work miracles through his Saints and for the confirmation of the faith. (Aquinas 1955–56: 1.72–73 [*Summa contra gentiles*])

But all this discussion is, obviously, another story. The only reason why I have made these references to some of the figures of Christian apologetics is to point out the line of apologetic practice that predated Berkeley considerably, and to offer an intelligible historical framework within which to place Berkeley's pragmatic arguments for the Christian faith in his dialogue *Alciphron*.

6.   *George Berkeley's "Bermuda Project"*

The objective of this chapter is twofold. First, I will show that not only was Berkeley's philosophizing rooted in ancient and medieval traditions of thought, but also even when designing such a practical undertaking as the "Bermuda project" Berkeley was, in a serious way, under the modeling influence of the past. More precisely, this chapter offers a discussion of Berkeley's plan to build a theology college in the islands of Bermuda (the so-called Bermuda project) in terms of symbolic geography and utopian projections, and in light of some traditions and patterns of thought governing Western representations of the "happy islands," "earthly paradise," educational utopias, and *eschaton*. In the second place, I will point to a certain relationship that might be established between the substance of Berkeley's immaterialist philosophy and the utopian character of his Bermuda project.

Between "Earthly Paradise" and Educational Utopia

Berkeley's "Happy Island"

In 1725 George Berkeley published a paper titled—not particularly concisely—*A Proposal for the better Supplying of Churches in our Foreign Plantations, and for Converting the Savage Americans, to Christianity, By a College to be erected in the Summer Islands, otherwise called The Isles of Bermuda* (Berkeley 1948–57, 7:343–60). This title in fact describes almost the whole project. Prior to that, the philosopher, since about March 1722, had written several private letters to friends and acquaintances on the same topic, each of them offering enthusiastic descriptions of the Bermuda islands. The letter to Lord Percival, dated March 4, 1722 (ibid., 8:127–29), is of special interest, as in it Berkeley announces for the first time his intention to establish a theology and fine arts college in those remote islands, and—more importantly—to spend all the rest of his life there. ("It is now about ten months since I have determined with myself to spend the residue of my days in the Island of Bermuda,

where I trust in Providence I may be the mean instrument of doing good to
mankind" [ibid.: 127]).[1] Finally, there are those famous stanzas by Berkeley
dedicated to the project, confessing his lack of satisfaction, if not disappoint-
ment, with the Old World, and announcing that "Westward the Course of
Empire takes its Way" (ibid.: 7:373 [*Verses on America*]).

Despite the fact that he had never traveled to Bermuda (and, ironically,
he never would do so), Berkeley offered in both his letter to Percival mentioned above and his *Proposal* a very detailed description of the islands, of
their natural landscapes, beauties, resources, richness, and prosperity; he
gave various details about the happy inhabitants of these islands and about
their way of life, praising the purity of their morals and innocence of their
manners.[2] Berkeley's literary talent helps him portray the islands and the is-
landers magnificently, compensating for the absence of a direct familiarity
with them. Since the description itself is an excellent piece of writing and
plays a significant role in my argument, I will reproduce below some ex-
cerpts from it:

> The climate is by far the healthiest and most serene, and . . . the most fit for
> study. . . . There is the greatest abundance of all the necessary provisions for
> life, which is much to be considered in a place for education. . . . It is the
> securest spot in the universe, being environed round with rocks all but one
> narrow entrance, guarded by seven forts, which render it inaccessible. . . .
> The inhabitants have the greatest simplicity of manners, more innocence,
> honesty, and good nature, than any of our other planters. (Ibid.: 128 [*Letter
> to Percival*])

A place like this is always predestined to become the location for some great
deeds: it simply invites them. On the other hand, although the *Proposal* is
written some years after this letter, it still retains the same enthusiasm and
idealization. Berkeley used generously winged words to express this sense
of perfection and astonishment. Everything about those islands was as perfect as something could possibly be in this world:

> no Part of the World enjoys a purer Air, or a more temperate Climate, the
> great Ocean which environs them, at once moderating the Heat of the South
> Winds, and the Severity of the North-West. . . . the Air of Bermuda is per-
> petually fanned and kept cool by Sea-breezes, which render the Weather the
> most healthy and delightful that could be wished, being . . . of one equal
> Tenour almost throughout the whole Year, like the latter End of a fine May.
> (Ibid.: 7:351)

A crucial part of the description is that in which the numberless natural "beauties of Bermuda," of all kinds, are listed. The islands seem unusually full of wonders and blessings, abundantly supplied with natural resources as useful as they are beautiful. On the islands of Bermuda there is no need for hard work to produce the goods necessary for living: these goods are already there, ripe, fresh, and ready for consumption. They are in trees, on fields, in water, everywhere. In Bermuda, as it were, the whole of nature conspired to produce one of the most beautiful and happiest places in the universe. The fact that the island was a "chosen" place for unusual spiritual accomplishments was for Berkeley beyond any reasonable doubt. The only thing one can do is just to admire unreservedly what one encounters there:

> the summers refreshed with constant cool breezes, the winters as mild as our May, the sky as light and blue as a sapphire, the ever green pastures, the earth eternally crowned with fruits and flowers. The woods of cedars, palmettos, myrtles, oranges &c., always fresh and blooming. The beautiful situations and prospects of hills, vales, promontories, rocks, lakes and sinuses of the sea. The great variety, plenty, and perfection of fish, fowl, vegetables of all kinds, and . . . the must excellent butter, beef, veal, pork, and mutton. But above all, that uninterrupted health and alacrity of spirit, which is the result of the finest weather and gentlest climate in the world. (Ibid.: 8:128 [*Letter to Percival*])

Now, one of the first ideas that occurs to one when reading such a description is that the way in which Berkeley describes the islands of Bermuda is strikingly similar to the way the earthly paradise has traditionally been described and represented within the medieval *mirabilia*, in the medieval, Renaissance, and early modern travel literature, and various other "amazing" accounts of "happy islands." Exactly in the same fashion in which Berkeley depicted the Bermuda islands (the location for his future college of theology), generations of ancient and medieval authors before him had seen the earthy paradise: as marked by a sense of virginal perfection, overwhelmed by the enchanting beauty of nature, abundant in goods of all kind, well-protected from the outside world, a place closer to God than anywhere else on earth. One of the striking things about Berkeley's portrait of his islands is that behind his detailed description of them does not actually lie any actual documentation or "field research," but only the primordial fantasy, so to speak, of a wonderful, innocent, and uncorrupted world. In a way, Berkeley did not even need to go see the islands in order to be able to describe them: he apparently found them, with all their wonderful paradisical appearance, in the repertoire of his own inner intellectual world. On writing these texts, Berkeley seemed to be driven toward "idealization," or "sacralization," of something otherwise quite profane. He ends up attributing to a neutral group of Atlantic islands almost all the ennobling characteristics of the earthly paradise, as it had traditionally been imagined since Greco-Roman antiquity.[3]

First of all, it is the very notion of island that confers on the whole story a special character.[4] An island is not a place like any other; an island is a clearly privileged space, a space that—thanks to its isolation, remoteness, and difficult accessibility, to its mysteriousness and autonomy—has acquired a particular symbolic dignity from the very beginning of human culture.[5] The sophisticated interplay between water and land, the complex dialectics between these two primordial elements (*stoicheia*) gave birth eventually to a new, intermediary entity: the island. The island is more than land-and-water, as it acquires something that neither land nor water as such has: the capacity to provoke in us a greater fascination, curiosity, and awe. Indeed, islands always attract us because, among other things, islands cause in us a distinct feeling of the sublime: a sense of greatness and of danger at the same time. There is something at once powerful and fragile about an island: it offers protection, noble isolation, autonomy, but it also insinuates a sense of directionless floating and of lack of roots. Not that islands are closer to heaven, but they are certainly not so close to earth; they are detached from earth, which makes them better prepared for all kinds of heavenly adventures and extraordinary events. As Claude Kappler excellently put it, if there are "any places that have a special appeal for imagination it is islands. . . . an island is by its nature a place where marvels exist for their own sake outside the laws that generally prevail. . . . Ever since Greek antiquity, islands have been favorite places for the most astounding human and divine adventures" (quoted in Delumeau 1995: 98).[6] This makes islands have an impressive metaphorical value. Like mountains, for example, they are often present in several forms of the intellectual discourse: literary, poetic, theological, mythological, utopian, political, and so on. An island could be made to signify hope, survival, salvation, separation, freedom, heresy, regeneration, certitude, danger, rootlessness, independence, and so on. No wonder then that the earthly paradise itself has often come to be located somewhere on an island: "Dante . . . gave the earthly paradise the characteristics of an island, and in many medieval travel stories, especially Mandeville's, the kingdom of Prester John is located on an island. According to Mandeville, mysterious India is 'divided into isles on account of the great rivers which flow out of Paradise'" (ibid.).

The usual name under which the earthly paradise islands have been traditionally known is that of "happy island(s)." Why this particular name? Medieval scholars had their own way of explaining it. Pierre d'Ailly, for example, says that the "name 'Happy Isles' means that these islands contain all good things. It is the fruitfulness of the soil that makes people believe that paradise was located in these islands" (quoted in ibid.: 99). In fact, as Jean Delumeau has shown, this explanation was borrowed from Isidore of Seville, and it widely spread throughout the Middle Ages. In his *Etymologiae*, Isidore says: "The name 'Happy Isles' means that they produce all sorts of good things; that they enjoy a quasi-blessedness and have the advantage of happy abundance. By their very nature they give birth to precious trees and fruits. The slopes of the hills are naturally covered with vines. Instead of grass the soil for the most part yields crops and vegetables" (quoted in ibid.).

This repetition, in several cases, of the same explanation, emphasizing the same factors (abundance of goods, ideal climate, wonderful landscapes) certainly contributed to the strengthening of the tradition, and confirms that the happy island was not an isolated and marginal *topos* at all, but a deeply rooted and long lasting one. It was a topic onto which people projected their most ardent expectations, nostalgias, and fantasies, a topic that caused them to daydream, desire, and hope. If the heavenly paradise was still remote and inaccessible, the earthly one was perceived as being somewhere closer, at least close enough to allow them to turn it into a major topic of their narratives. This fascination that surrounded the happy islands in the Middle Ages played an essential part in the formation and dissemination of a complex symbolic geography, one which, as we will see later on in this chapter, would massively shape the conceptions and representations of the Western discoverers and travelers at the dawn of modern era:

> the Happy Islands stand in a Greco-Roman poetic tradition that is based on passages in Homer, Hesiod, and Plutarch. According to this tradition, beyond the towering Atlas there lie islands with enchanted gardens, a constant temperate climate, and fragrant breezes, where human beings have no need to work. In the Christian era Isidore of Seville gave this belief a new popularity by assigning it a place in his geography, which then exerted a lasting influence on Western culture. (Ibid.)

What is interesting at this stage is that Berkeley himself, in another private letter, uses the term openly: he came to talk about "that happy Island" with explicit reference to his Bermuda project (Berkeley 1948–57, 8:156). As is well known, he had an impressive classical training and was a lecturer in Greek and Latin. So it is reasonable to suppose that he knew something about this tradition of the *insula pomorum que fortunata vocatur* (the island of apples that is called the happy island), as Geoffrey of Monmouth (d. 1154) describes it in his *Vita Merlini*, as well as about the various ways in which the earthly paradise had been searched for, described, and eulogized in the European world ever since classical antiquity.

In consequence, based on the (imaginary) account that Berkeley gives of the islands of Bermuda, and on the various similar accounts by ancient, medieval, or early modern authors, of which some were referred to above, it can safely be suggested that Berkeley's representation of the location and settings of his future theology and arts college was deeply marked by a certain nostalgia for an earthly paradise. When writing down his educational project Berkeley, knowingly or unknowingly, placed himself in the middle of a long tradition of representations of the earthly paradise that in Europe (and not only in Europe) went back many centuries, gave birth to a sophisticated symbolic geography (in terms of people's cultural projections upon place, space, and distance), and eventually shaped to a significant extent their understanding of the real geography involved. In formulating his Bermuda project Berkeley used abundantly the repertoire provided by this symbolic geography. More than that, it was probably the religious substance of this nostalgia for an earthly paradise that gave him an extraordinary strength and determination to pursue his project for so many years, and overcome all the criticisms it encountered from the side of the more practical politicians and "technicians" of the day. It may also have been this nostalgia for the earthly paradise that made him so wonderfully enthusiastic[7] and, as we shall see below, particularly unrealistic about the situation of and problems with those islands (the poverty and immorality of the inhabitants, unstable climate, strong winds, and so forth).

To conclude, it would be fair enough to say that the "natural place" of Berkeley's Bermuda islands—with all their countless wonders and amazing resources and paradisical landscapes, with their perfect situation, the "gentlest climate in the world," "the securest spot in the universe"—is to be found not in the real world, but only on one of those "detailed maps from the end of the Middle Ages [which] still teaches" us that "there exist in the West paradisal islands 'that abound in all good things.' These islands combine most of the elements that make for an earthly paradise: pleasant warmth, perpetual spring, delicious and fragrant fruits" (Delumeau 1995:

100–2). Somewhere on the same (imaginary) map, Thomas More's island is to be found too. There, just as in Berkeley's Bermuda, the visitor is instantly welcomed by the same paradisical landscape, so rich in promises of unusual encounters: "all things begin by little and little to wax pleasant; the air soft, temperate, and gentle; the ground covered with green grass; less wilderness in the beasts" (More 1974: 17). Even if Berkeley's Bermuda islands cannot possibly exist in terms of actual geography, they certainly have an important role to play in the history of symbolic geography. Needless to say, it is not a very common thing for a philosopher, much less a promoter of the "new philosophy," to deal with such a "frivolous" and speculative subject as the earthly paradise. But this is perhaps what makes Berkeley so interesting: his being a truly uncommon philosopher.

Quite expectedly, the project eventually failed, Berkeley being much laughed at, and even considered mad, by some London wits of that time.[8] Nevertheless, as I will show below, despite its failure, this project is significant not only for what it shows about Berkeley's personality, but also about the deeper intellectual perspectives that nourished his intellectual life, his philosophy, and his ways of understanding the world, as well as about his rapport with the past. Just as the Platonic tradition, the alchemical way of thinking, or the tradition of the *liber mundi* deeply permeated Berkeley's metaphysics and, to different degrees, as we have seen in the previous chapters, left their mark on it, so it could be followed in some detail how various cultural and mythical representations of place and space, how various notions of symbolic geography had a distinct impact on his philosophy of history, his social and political philosophy, and on his intellectual world as a whole.

Berkeley's Utopia

Nostalgia for an earthly paradise, is only one of the facets of Berkeley's Bermuda project. The happy island is only the spatial framework within which something (important) would take place, the item of symbolic geography within which his project would be put into practice. There is another element of this project we have to deal with now: it is, namely, its utopian dimension. George Berkeley's project, far from being an isolated attempt, a personal and incomprehensible caprice, might well be coherently placed in the long tradition of the "educational utopias." Berkeley did not just dream about the paradisical islands of Bermuda. He needed this place precisely as a spatial framework, as an ideal setting, for his educational project. Since his main intention was to establish a college there, dedicated to learning and the cultivation of science, an investigation of the utopian tradition in Berkeley's Bermuda project will cast light on the entire affair. Let me mention at this stage that I am not the only one to use the term "utopia" in relation to Berkeley's Bermuda project. A hundred years ago, dealing with Berkeley's educational project, A. C. Fraser came to talk about Bermuda as "a region whose idyllic bliss poets had sung, and from which Christian civilisation might radiate over the Utopia of a New World, with its magnificent possibilities in the future history of the human race" (Fraser 1901, 4:343).

As Northrop Frye once put it, any utopia is ultimately a discourse about education. Even if it is not conceived as an educational project per se, any utopia aims in fact at changing people's lives by means of a radically new vision of education, learning, and *Bildung*. If not in their explicit purposes and statements, at least implicitly the utopian authors presuppose a consideration of education as a decisive factor in transforming (improving) their fellow humans. For, of course, it is much easier to educate people differently, to inculcate new ideas in people's minds when they are still at an early age, than to change them suddenly and forcedly, at a time when they are already mature and deeply rooted into certain ways of life and accustomed to certain ways of thinking. Indeed, in Frye's view, any utopia has a certain Platonic component, whether or not the utopian writers are Platonists themselves:

> And though not all utopia-writers are Platonists, nearly all of them make their utopias depend on education for their permanent establishment. It seems that the literary convention of an ideal state is really a by-product of a systematic view of education. That is, education, considered as a unified view of reality, grasps society by its intelligible rather than its actual form, and the utopia is a projection of the ability to see society, not as an aggregate of buildings and bodies, but as a structure of arts and sciences. (Frye 1965: 37–38)

In Thomas More's Utopia, for example, even if this is not primarily an educational utopia, learning and science play a central role in people's lives: "a great multitude of every sort of people, both men and women, go to hear lectures, some one and some another, as every man's nature is inclined" (More 1974: 65). In Utopia knowledge, education, and instruction are democratically accessible to all its inhabitants; in a way, learning is a form of entertainment here. The cultivation of arts and science and of expertise in one or more fields is so widespread among Utopians that Utopia is more advanced, scientifically, than any other place on earth:

But they be in the course of the stars and the movings of the heavenly
spheres very expert and cunning. They have also wittily excogitated and
devised instruments of divers fashions, wherein is exactly comprehended and
contained the movings and situations of the sun, the moon, and of all the
other stars which appear in their horizon. (Ibid.: 83)

In a rigorous sense, when compared to Plato's *Republic,* Berkeley's utopia
is only an incomplete, partial utopia. It is not a hard, but a soft *utopia,* so to
speak. More than the ambitious ideal state envisaged by Plato, Berkeley's
Bermuda resembles to some extent, for example, that *Bildungsprovinz* described in Herman Hesse's *Das Glasperlenspiel*: an ideal scholarly society,
dedicated to cultivating superior arts and science, located in some privileged
space, clearly separated from the corrupted and corrupting outside world,
and designed to embody, preserve, and convey the noblest values and virtues of mankind. The island thus becomes a spatial symbol of salvation and
regeneration through learning, science, and fine arts. Bermuda is "the world
of Mind—artificial, more orderly, more secure, but still in need of constant
supervision and study" (Hesse 1990: 100). Just like Hesse's Castalia, Berkeley's utopian island is projected as "the training ground and refuge for that
small band of men whose lives were to be consecrated to Mind and to
truth" (ibid.).

The notion of (utopian) separation from the outside (profane) world,[9]
of self-protection and inaccessibility is clearly expressed, several times, by
Berkeley: "The Group of Isles . . . walled round with Rocks, which render
them inaccessible to Pirates or Enemies; there being but two narrow En-
trances, both well guarded by Forts. It would therefore be impossible to find
anywhere, a more secure Retreat for Students" (Berkeley 1948–57: 7:352
[*A Proposal*]). As a matter of fact, in doing so, Berkeley followed a pattern
of thought that had been brilliantly illustrated by Thomas More. More set
his Utopia on a remote, well-protected, inaccessible island. One has to be a
Utopian, already an insider, to know how to enter Utopia safely; otherwise,
any attempt at forcing the entrance proves fatal. Utopia has its secret traps,
gates, and paths; it is not for everybody to enter it unharmed:

Other rocks there be lying hid under the water, which therefore be dangerous. The channels be known only to themselves [Utopians], and therefore it
seldom chanceth that any stranger, unless be he guided by an Utopian, can
come into this haven, insomuch that they themselves could scarcely enter
without jeopardy, but that their way is directed and ruled by certain land-
marks standing on the shore. By turning, translating, and removing these

marks into other places they may destroy their enemies' navies, be they never so many. (More 1974: 55–56)

Berkeley's strong emphasis (following in the footsteps of More) on this aspect of his project is perfectly justified when considered in light of the utopian tradition, and of the canons of utopian thinking: remoteness, difficulty of access, and isolation are necessary not only for keeping young innocent students safe from the corrupting profane world, or for preventing it from interfering with the normal course of the academic/utopian affairs, but also for conferring a high prestige and esteem on this scholarly community. Remoteness causes fascination; inaccessibility is what gives birth to, and increases, desire. The strength of such an ideal scholarly community does not consist only in the intrinsic nature, in, say, the volume and quality of its learning or in its scientific accomplishments, but also—maybe more importantly—in its publicly and socially recognized image, in the wide fascination that it holds.

Once all the specific requirements are met, Berkeley's "soft" utopia is ready to make its debut:

Among a People [the inhabitants of Bermuda] of this Character, and in a Situation thus circumstantiated, it would seem that a *Seminary of Religion* and Learning might very fitly be placed. The Correspondence with other Parts of *America*, the Goodness of the Air, the Plenty and Security of the Place, the Frugality and Innocence of the Inhabitants, all conspiring to favour such a Design. Thus much at least is evident, that young Students would be there less liable to be corrupted in their Morals; and the governing Part would be easier, and better contented with a small Stipend, and a retired academical Life, in a Corner from whence Avarice and Luxury are excluded. (Berkeley 1948–57, 7:353 [*A Proposal*])

As it appears, life—of course, private life included—in such an "ideal community" is dominated by a certain degree of artificiality: as it were, life is not allowed to take its natural course, but it is very carefully and in detail "regulated," ordered, surveyed, controlled, kept far away from any possible "unnatural" vices and temptations—in short, life is thoroughly rationalized and engineered. As Giuseppe Mazzotta has observed, utopians "are necessary for many reasons." One of these reasons is that "there is always a need to accommodate the excess of private desires to the public good, politics to ethics, moderation to freedom" (Mazzotta 2001: 60). The utopia works as a most efficient machine: its input is the raw, uneducated, unformed humans, still in a "natural state" and driven by primary instincts, and its output is nothing other than a wonderfully designed, perfectly civilized, and smoothly working human community.

This process of "rationalization" is an essential characteristic of any utopian organization, starting with its very outset: recruitment of its members. As has been remarked about the recruitment of new members in Hesse's *Das Glasperlenspiel*, "an exchange between Castalian institutions and their surroundings persists: since all Castalians are celibate men and since they do not have any alternative form of perpetuating their ascetic community (immortality, regeneration, cloning, and so forth), lay children are recruited on the basis of their intellectual and artistic performance by thoroughly combing the schools of the real world" (Antohi 2000: xi). In a similar fashion, Berkeley's ideal scholarly society regularly needs new members. Its main intention is to produce worthy priests and missionaries who are to be involved in the propagation of the Gospel, and the conversion of Indians; consequently, there is a need for an established way of replacing them and permanently renewing the utopian community. It is at this point that Berkeley's system differs significantly from that envisaged by Hesse. For, while the new members of Castalia were "elected," being invited to join the utopian community only as the final result of a difficult process of selection, in Berkeley's Bermuda among the toughest procedures are those related to the recruitment of future members of the scholarly community. Basically, if peaceful methods fail, Berkeley recommends the kidnapping of young Indians and forcing them into his utopian machine:

> The young *Americans* necessary for this Purpose, may in the beginning be procured, either by peaceable Methods from those savage Nations, which border on our Colonies, and are in Friendship with us, or by taking captive the Children of our Enemies. (Berkeley 1948–57, 7:347 [*A Proposal*])

This controversial aspect of Berkeley's Bermuda project has long been discussed among Berkeley scholars. David Berman openly regards this violent solution as "chilling" and, despite his constantly sympathetic consideration of George Berkeley, he cannot help being very sarcastic at this point: "The Indian children are to be kidnapped. Why? No doubt, for their spiritual advantage" (Berman 1994: 132–33). On the other hand, when he comes to discuss this issue, Harry Bracken advances an interesting millennialist hypothesis which I will examine later in this chapter.

Apart from the provision about recruitment, there are in Berkeley's *Proposal* clear and detailed regulations with regard to the schooling itself. Just as in other utopias, for example in Plato's *Republic*, so in Berkeley's college there are rationalized and detailed procedures regarding access to the utopian community, starting age, precise subject matters to be taught, and so on:

> It is proposed to admit into the aforesaid College only such Savages as are under ten Years of Age, before evil Habits have taken a deep root; and yet not so early as to prevent retaining their Mother Language, which should be preserved by Intercourse among themselves.
>
> It is further proposed, to ground these young *Americans* thoroughly in Religion and Morality, and to give them a good Tincture of other Learning; particularly of Eloquence, History and practical Mathematics; to which it may not be improper to add some skill in Physics. (Berkeley 1948–57: 7:347–48 [*A Proposal*])

This is the only reference Berkeley makes to the specifics of the curriculum to be used in his college. Had he got the necessary funds from the British authorities, he would, of course, have had to offer a much more detailed curriculum and an ampler description of the academic programs to be undertaken in the college. Sketchy as it is, the *Proposal* does not go into more detail about Berkeley's educational doctrines. It is interesting to notice at this point that Berkeley does not see the study of his own philosophy as playing any role in shaping his utopian project. He did not explicitly build his utopian project on principles derived from his own philosophical system, nor did he mention that students should study it. Rather, he simply followed in general the traditional utopian way of thinking, broadly conceived. The details he provides in his *Proposal* are derived not from such and such Berkeleian immaterialist theses, but from the inner logic of utopianism itself.

Several of Berkeley's commentators and admirers have been seriously embarrassed in coming across such tough statements in his writing. The conventional image of the "good Bishop" would rather exclude all these unpleasant procedures, regulations, or "brutalities." Yet, it seems to me at this point that, in light of the utopia-based hypothesis I am advancing, such procedures, however cruel or "totalitarian" they might appear, are to some extent understandable, or at least made intelligible: they do not pursue severity for its own sake, but belong to a certain pattern of utopian thought, to a particular way of considering the relationship between private life and public life, between what we are and what we should be, and, in general, they betray a certain understanding of what it means to be human and what "the Good" means. In this context, in the mind of the utopian authors who propose them, tough procedures lose their seeming "cruelty" and "totalitarianism" if considered as mere means for obtaining a much greater good: an obvious improvement, or transfiguration, of the fellow humans' way of life. According to such a line of thought, which can be easily followed from Plato to Marx, the impressive, overwhelming "advantages" that such a transfiguration would bring about are much greater and more important than any of the possible "local inconveniences" it might cause to those who happen to be involved. In More's Utopia, for example, there are specific rules and codes of conduct regulating all aspects of private and social life. For More, these regulations are not about the production and reproduction of power, but are simply intended to help utopians live a happy and simple life: "After supper they bestow one hour in play, in summer in their gardens, in winter in their common halls where they dine and sup. There they exercise themselves in music, or else in honest and wholesome communication"; "to the intent the prescript number of the citizens should neither decrease nor above measure increase, it is ordained that no family . . . shall at once have fewer children of the age of fourteen or thereabout than ten or more than sixteen"; "if any be desirous to visit either their friends dwelling in another city or to see the place itself, they easily obtain licence of their Syphogrants and Tranibores" (More 1974: 65, 69, 75). It is exactly like bitter medicine: it might be unpleasant now, but it brings a greater good (and, consequently, a greater pleasure) in the future. It is, ultimately, the benevolence, noble motivations, and generosity of the utopian projects that result in these unpleasant side effects.

Obviously, it is not here for me to agree or disagree with Berkeley's violent utopian procedures: I am simply trying to place them in a wider context of the tradition of utopian thought, and see how are they derived and explained. For, insofar as it is possible to talk about a "perennial utopian theme," as Frank Manuel has put it (Manuel 1965: 70), I think that Berkeley's Bermuda project could be better understood if regarded as belonging to the long tradition of those similar projects through which this utopian theme has been approached, developed, and made famous. Seen in such a light, all these detailed and unpleasant provisions, regulations, and tough measures Berkeley envisaged are, as it were, born out of a genuine ardent desire to see his neighbors happier, less distressed, and more virtuous, just as in any other utopian project. Besides, unlike us, Berkeley lived in a rather "innocent" age, one that had not witnessed any serious attempts at putting utopian projects into practice.

The "Incongruity"

If a "state of mind is utopian when it is incongruous with the state of reality within which it occurs" (Mannheim 1936: 192), then Berkeley's state of mind when conceiving and proposing his Bermuda project was certainly utopian. The huge and unbridgeable gap (or "incongruity," in Mannheim's terminology) between the real (geographical, natural, and social) situation of the islands of Bermuda and their ideal situation in Berkeley's mind (that is, the way he misrepresented them) is revealed by both some of the contemporary opponents of his plan and—maybe more importantly—by several accounts of the real Bermuda from the first colonists there, dated some decades before Berkeley's project was conceived. Some of these accounts are still extant.

Arthur Aston Luce, who studied the whole affair thoroughly, found that—when the issue of giving the project financial support came to be discussed in the British Parliament—the opposition to Berkeley's Bermuda project was not always malevolent or unjustified. There were realistic people ("enlightened opposition") who criticized Berkeley's project on the basis of their own knowledge of the real situation of the islands. Among them, William Byrd of Virginia, for example, "who with local knowledge opposed the project, not as undesirable, but as impracticable," brought—in remarkably ironic form—pertinent and solid arguments against Berkeley's project. He regarded George Berkeley as "a Don Quixote in zeal" and his project as a "visionary scheme." A. A. Luce summarizes Byrd's argument:

> There is no bread in Bermuda; there is nothing fit for the sustenance of man but onions and cabbages; its inhabitants are healthy, because, forsooth, they have so little to eat; the air is pure because swept by storms and hurricanes. . . . There are no Indians in Bermuda, "nor within two hundred leagues of it upon the continent, and it will need the gift of miracles to persuade them to leave their country and venture themselves upon the great ocean, on the temptation of being converted." The Dean must take the French way and dragoon them into Christianity. He must take half a dozen regiments, and "make a descent upon the coast of Florida, and take as many prisoners as he can." Behind the sarcasm . . . is the assurance of the man with local knowledge. (Luce 1949: 137)

On the other hand, there are those accounts from the first colonists in Bermuda, mainly private letters which were edited some time ago under the title *The Rich Papers: Letters from Bermuda 1615–1646: Eyewitness Accounts Sent by the Early Colonists to Sir Nathaniel Rich*, describing both the exact natural circumstances under which the islands were then planted and administrated, but also the numerous other problems encountered, for example, the serious troubles caused by the drunkenness, immorality, and general unreliability of the inhabitants. The sharp contrast between the poor "state of reality" in Bermuda and Berkeley's too enthusiastic "state of mind" is marked at times by such chilling fragments as the following one: "If the Adventurers [the company then administrating the islands] send noe clothes to this poore people before this time 12 months, many of them wilbe naked if not dead" (Ives 1984: 14). Undoubtedly, some of the serious problems might have been solved by Berkeley's time, but it is unreasonable to believe that the unfriendly climate, for example, had changed very much in the meantime.

These accounts depict a small world, with its fortunes and misfortunes, with its happy and unhappy events, all of them bearing apparently no resemblance to any earthly paradise. At least not more than any other corner (or island) of the known world. Life in Bermuda was taking its course in a more or less bearable manner, but sometimes there were events so terrific that seriously jeopardized the very minimal conditions of living there. For example, as it is recorded, one such event was a tremendous invasion of rats:

> Rattes have been and are a great judgement of God upon us. All the Ilands have been in a manner like so many Cunny [coney, rabbit] warrens, which did put the people much out of heart. It is incredible how they did swimme from Iland to Iland, and suddainly like an armie of men did invade the Ilands from one end to an other, devouring the fruites of the earth in strange manner. (Ibid.: 14)[10]

As for the morals of the inhabitants, highly praised by Berkeley, they were not, at the time of writing of these accounts, as exemplary as one could wish. For example, some of the Bermudans seem to have often resorted to the virtues of wine. To the extent that, far from being overwhelmed by innocence, moderation, and other noble virtues, some of them had come to be seriously fond of drinking. A Bermuda priest wrote once to Sir Nathaniel Rich:

> Good sir, for God sake do what you can to send hither godly preachers, before sinne hath got the upper hand. It is lamentable to see how sinne aboundeth every day more and more as the people do increase. I am not able

to expresse the abhominable drunkeness, loathsome spuing [spewing, vomiting] swearing, swaggering and quarrelling, while the ship is in harbour with any wine or strong waters in her. (Ibid.: 161–62)

In conclusion, from most points of view, the Bermuda islands were at that time a place of exile and hard life, rather than anything else.

ESCHATOLOGY

The Millennialist Context

It is worth recalling that Berkeley's college in Bermuda was not designed as an end in itself, as a solely educational institution, but simply as a means. Its ultimate mission was to produce worthy priests and theologians, "missionaries" able to persuade the "savage Indians" to accept Christianity.

Such a mission had at that time some rather special connotations. More precisely, what I suggest is that, in close connection to the topics of the earthly paradise and utopianism discussed above, a consideration of Berkeley's *Proposal* within the context of the religious (apocalyptic, millennialist, and eschatological) ideas and attitudes that lay behind the early transoceanic voyages of discovery (and then of colonization) of America would be of great importance for a better understanding of his project. As Mircea Eliade and especially Harry Bracken and David Berman have shown, Berkeley's American Project is hardly understandable without taking seriously into account its messianism. In a paper titled "Bishop Berkeley's Messianism" (Bracken 1988: 65–80),[11] Bracken suggests that in his *Proposal* Berkeley embraced the then-popular analogy between the American Indians and the "Lost Tribes of the Israel," whose conversion would have had a special value according to St. Paul. As such, Berkeley's eagerness to convert the Indians might be regarded as an attempt to prepare for the Second Coming. And it is precisely this messianic feature of Berkeley's project that is much indebted to the religious and theological background against which the first transatlantic voyages, and then the early colonization of America, occurred.

There is some agreement among many historians and religious scientists nowadays that an important factor in realizing the new geographic discoveries was in fact, as Mircea Eliade has put it, "the nostalgia for the earthly paradise that the ancestors of the American nations had crossed the Atlantic to find" (Eliade 1965: 261). According to such a line of thought, the deeper causes and motivations of the transatlantic voyages undertaken by the early discoverers and colonists were not only of an economic or political nature,

but they also had to do with a certain religious atmosphere that characterized the European world toward the end of the Middle Ages. More precisely: it was an atmosphere marked by eschatological expectations,
millennialist dreams, and by a need for a radical "moral transformation" and
"regeneration." And it was within "this messianic and apocalyptic atmosphere that the transoceanic expeditions and the geographic discoveries that
radically shook and transformed Western Europe took place. Throughout
Europe people believed in an imminent regeneration of the world" (ibid.:
262).

Mircea Eliade and Jean Delumeau[12] are among the historians who endorse this line of thought, and in doing so they exhibit an impressive knowledge and a deep understanding of the whole cultural, religious, and
intellectual context of that wonderfully confused and multifaceted age:

> Scholars have long pointed out how the search for paradisal islands was an
> important stimulus to voyages of discovery from the fourteenth to the seven-
> teenth centuries. Nostalgia for the garden of Eden; the conviction of Chris-
> topher Columbus and missionaries that the end time was at hand; the will to
> bring religion to new lands; and the desire to find gold, precious stones, and
> other rare commodities: all these combined to spur travelers, religious, sail-
> ors, and conquerors on to new horizons. Their culture and the dreams it
> brought with it led them, at least in the beginning, to see in the strange lands
> opening up before them the characteristics of those blessed countries that
> had haunted the Western imagination since antiquity. (Delumeau 1995:
> 109–10)

Eliade's and Delumeau's interpretations are abundantly confirmed by what
the discoverers and first colonists themselves thought about what they were
then doing, seeing, experiencing, and so on. There is plenty of textual evidence available, pointing to a close relationship between the tradition of the
search for the earthly paradise in Europe and the way in which the first
travelers and colonists experienced their encounter with the New World.
For example, in a letter sent by Amerigo Vespucci to Lorenzo de Medici,
sometime between 1499 and 1502, the famous navigator talks about

> the friendly land, covered with countless very tall trees that do not lose their
> leaves and emit sweet and fragrant odors and are loaded with tasty fruits that
> promote the body's health; the fields of thick grass that are filled with flowers
> which have a wonderfully delightful perfume; the great throng of birds of
> various species, whose feathers, colors, and songs defy description. . . . For
> myself, I thought I was near the earthly paradise. (Quoted in ibid.: 110)

If in the case of Vespucci these things were veiled in a poetic and somewhat vague form, Christopher Columbus openly considered his transoceanic enterprise in terms of sacred history, and saw his mission as definitely belonging to a divine plan. He "did not doubt that he had come near the Earthly Paradise" and consequently—however strange this might appear today—he considered his adventurous navigation in theological and mystical rather than secular terms. Columbus was convinced, for example, that the fresh water currents that he came across in the Gulf of Paria originated nowhere else than in the Garden of Eden. The discovery of the New World had for him a clear "eschatological implication." He was

> persuaded that the prophecy concerning the diffusion of the Gospel throughout the whole world had to be realized before the end of the world—which was not far off. In his *Book of Prophecies,* Columbus affirmed that this event, namely, the end of the world, would be preceded by the conquest of the new continent, the conversion of the heathen, and the destruction of the Antichrist. (Eliade 1965: 262)

Then, what is equally important is that such a state of mind not only persisted even after the establishment of the colonies, but it also increased in intensity, developed, and spread widely throughout America.[13] The first colonists' dreams and fantasies proved to be so intense that it was as if what they found out after crossing the ocean confirmed literally all their eschatological expectations and millenarian ideas: "the most popular religious doctrine in the Colonies was that America had been chosen among all the nations of the earth as the place of the Second Coming of Christ, and the millennium, though essentially of a spiritual nature, would be accompanied by a paradisiacal transformation of the earth, as an outer sign of an inner perfection" (ibid.: 264). The awareness of their being "chosen," the sense of their blessing, election, and mission—and the corresponding "responsibilities"—made them feel in some way "associates" or "partners" of God, trustful implementers of his plans. As it were, theirs were not simply human enterprises, their doings were not just facts of social history; they perceived themselves as being deeply involved in the unfolding of an apocalyptic process, in affairs of a clearly divine nature:

> The first English colonists in America considered themselves chosen by Providence to establish a "City on a Mountain" that would serve as an example of the true Reformation for all Europe. They had followed the path of the sun toward the Far West, continuing and prolonging in a prodigious

fashion the traditional passing of religion and culture from East to West. . . .
The first pioneers did not doubt that the final drama of moral regeneration
and universal salvation would begin with them, since they were the first to
follow the sun in its course toward the paradisiacal gardens of the West.
(Ibid.)

Broadly speaking, this was the religious context within which Berkeley's
Proposal emerged. Keeping this fact in mind when considering the "bold-
ness," "savagery" or "unrealistic" character of his project would be, I think,
of some help.

Berkeley's Messianism

Since one of the main aims of his projected college was to supply the colonies with virtuous, well-prepared priests and missionaries,[14] some Berkeley
scholars—based also on the last stanza of that famous poem that Berkeley
dedicated to America—concluded that his motivation in initiating and pursuing the project was ultimately one of an eschatological and millennialist
nature. The poem is called *America; or, the Muse's Refuge: A Prophecy*, and is
an excellent piece of poetry that he disseminated in order to get more support for his project. At the beginning, it was circulated anonymously, but
eventually Berkeley published it in the *Miscellany* (1752) under his own
name. David Berman discusses in some detail "the eschatological aspect of
Berkeley's poem and project" in his book on Berkeley (Berman 1994: 116),
and one of his conclusions is that it is "evident that his poem is apocalyptic
and eschatological" (ibid.: 118). As a matter of fact, Berman generally follows Bracken's interpretation, which I will be summarizing below. (Let me
also add that Mircea Eliade has a rather similar interpretation of this poem.)

I reproduce here only the last stanza of the poem, namely, that which has
received special interest from commentators:

Westward the Course of Empire takes its Way,
The four first Acts already past.
A fifth shall close the Drama with the Day,
The world's great Effort is the last. (Berkeley 1948–57: 7:370 [*America*])

In trying to interpret the symbolism of the five acts Bracken resorts to the
Old Testament, namely, to the book of Daniel: "I take the symbolism of the
final stanza, the four plus one Acts, to be from *Daniel*, chapter 2, where the
four kingdoms, usually taken to be Babylon, Persia, Greece and Rome, shall
be succeeded by a fifth: 'And in the days of these kings shall the God of

heaven set up a kingdom, which shall never be destroyed . . .' (2: 44)"
(Bracken 1988: 71). Given the complex millennialist and apocalyptic context depicted above, with all its great expectations, intensely religious feelings of—and preparations for—the Millennium, an interpretation like this
certainly acquires a certain degree of reasonableness. Bracken epitomizes his
demonstration with a decisive scriptural argument. According to him, "the
key to this extraordinary proposal is that Berkeley accepts the [then] popular
view that the American Indians are the Lost Tribes of Israel. As Jews, their
conversion is especially dear to God and each conversion promises, as Paul
tells us in *Romans xi*, to bring closer the Second Coming" (ibid.: 73). Then,
he undertakes a detailed research of some of the beliefs then current in
America, beliefs according to which the American Indians were—in some
way or other—of Jewish origin. Of course, it is not the truthfulness of those
beliefs that is important here, but simply their sheer existence, and what
Berkeley made of them.

Following Bracken's hypothesis, by converting the native Indians the
theology graduates from Berkeley's college would have converted the Lost
Tribes of Israel, which—according to St. Paul—was a clear sign of the
much-expected, triumphal end of the world: the *Apocalypsis*. Thus, in
Berkeley's mind the propagation of Gospel in America and the conversion
of the Indians living there would have had a highly spiritual value as they
would have been at the same time preparation for, and a sign of, the approaching Second Coming. Hence the ardent necessity of building a missionary college in Bermuda: "Given what we know about Berkeley, we
must find a reason not only for his committing himself so completely to his
American dream, but especially for the savagery he was prepared to inflict
on Indian children" (ibid.: 80). The Messianic interpretation gives us such
a reason, allowing us to see Berkeley's project in a different light.

Harry Bracken's documented interpretation, even if one does not accept
it entirely,[15] has the merit of underlining the theological complexity of the
Bermuda project, and suggesting some ways of explaining several of the
confused aspects of Berkeley's enterprise. More than that, it is perfectly consistent with the complex religious context sketched above. Then, almost
needless to say, Bracken's interpretation fits pretty well into—and, to a great
extent, is supported by—my own attempt, earlier in this chapter, to place
Berkeley in the tradition of the search for an earthly paradise and of the
educational utopias. In fact, Bracken's reconstruction of Berkeley's way of
thinking as far as this particular issue is concerned might also be applied to
the way in which many of his contemporaries were then thinking. For, as it

has been said, in "the eyes of the English . . . the colonization of America merely prolonged and perfected a Sacred History begun at the outset of the Reformation. Indeed, the push of the pioneers toward the West continued the triumphal march of Wisdom and the True Religion from East to West. For some time already, Protestant theologians had been inclined to identify the West with spiritual and moral progress" (Eliade 1965: 263).

At least two fundamental Christian ideas were inextricably interwoven in Berkeley's Bermuda project: a nostalgia for an earthly paradise and the "the expectation of a kingdom of happiness that is to be established on our earth and to last for a millennium" (Delumeau 1995: 1). The "happy islands" of Bermuda, despite their imaginary, utopian nature—if not simply because of that—have been the chosen space for such an enterprise, its privileged environment. They have played a central role in this story: their isolation from the outside world, their purity (as they are surrounded by the water of the endless ocean), their difficult accessibility, exoticism, paradisical appearance, beauties, innocence of the inhabitants, and so on—all these are attributes enabling us to consider those islands as some unearthly or unnatural place, a place where the marvels or such supernatural events as the Second Coming and Millennium are at any time possible.

On the other hand, the millennialist interpretation of Berkeley's Bermuda project presented above adds to his utopia a character somehow different from that of a simply political/social project. Berkeley's utopia has a certain theological flavor that we do not find in other utopias. Of course, it remains a utopia in the tradition of Plato, Campanella, and Thomas More, but—in addition to that—Berkeley's utopia is also characterized by certain chiliastic elements. Berkeley's is a religiously modeled utopia, an educational utopia with a clear soteriological mission. Even if the main emphasis is not placed, in his project, upon messianism, the chiliastic features are present and have something to say about the ultimate specificity of the Bermuda project. To be more precise, this messianism belongs not so much to the project itself (explicitly and essentially) as to its unspoken presuppositions, to the intellectual and religious background against which it was conceived. As it were, the Millennium is rapidly approaching: under such circumstances, getting ready (*praeparatio*) is the crucial and most urgent thing to do. Hence the imperative of preparing a body of worthy, well-trained, and dedicated people, ready to prepare, in turn, their neighbors for the great event, which is to say, to save their souls *in aeternum*. Instructing such special people is an extremely difficult and demanding job. In fact, it is a job that is made possible only within the firm boundaries of a highly disciplined educational utopia. And this is where Berkeley's project comes in.

MAKING SOME (PHILOSOPHICAL) SENSE OF THE BERMUDA PROJECT

Philosophy and Biography

Bishop Atterbury made a telling remark about George Berkeley that, I think, shows the way Berkeley was perceived by some of his contemporaries: "So much understanding, so much knowledge, so much innocence, and such humility, I did not think had been the portion of any but angels till I saw this gentleman" (quoted in Luce 1949: 63). In light of Bishop Atterbury's generous remark, as well as of other similar ones, I think it would be interesting to see Berkeley's biography as being marked by a certain form of "angelism."[16] By Berkeley's "angelism" I mean here a dominant tendency, manifest throughout his life, toward seeing the best in people, toward an idealization of real facts and situations and seeing them as transfigured, a drive toward generosity, benevolence, and self-sacrifice—a tendency easily recognizable in Berkeley's everyday behavior, as well as in his initiatives, projects, undertakings, deeds, and so on. There is a sense in which George Berkeley's biography was touchingly marked by various dreams of universal salvation and idealistic enterprises: the tar-water and Bermuda episodes, which have been dealt with in some detail in this book, being only the most famous of them. There are numerous writings and documents attesting to Berkeley's "unusual generosity," kindness, philanthropy, good nature, benevolence, care for others, and enthusiastic dedication to the public good. He was not satisfied with enlightening people with his philosophy; he also tried to improve their lives, to leave a mark of generosity and philanthropy on them. I just quoted above Bishop Atterbury's eulogy. Similarly, in a poem, Pope wrote that famous line: "To Berkeley, ev'ry virtue under heav'n" (quoted in Berman 1994: 120), just as Arthur Aston Luce's *Life of George Berkeley, Bishop of Cloyne*—probably the most important biography of Berkeley ever written—ends in this vein: "He was clearly something of a saint" (Luce 1949: 225).

The most touching and detailed account of this kind, however, revealing to an admirable extent the angelism of his character, comes from Berkeley's wife. Of course, there was something deeply personal in her statement, and we should consider it with some caution. Yet, beyond its personal character, one can easily discover a realistic and believable portrait of Bishop Berkeley. In a letter to one of their sons, she remembers how Berkeley's "instructive conversation was delicate" and when he dealt directly with religion he

> did it in so masterly a manner, that it made a deep and lasting impression. You never heard him give his tongue the liberty of speaking evil. Never did he reveal the fault or secret of a friend. . . . an universal knowledge of men, things, and books prevented the greatest wit of his age from being at a loss for subjects of conversation; but had he been as dull as he was bright, his conscience and good nature would have kept close the door of his lips rather than to have opened them to vilify or lessen his brother. . . . Now he was not born to all this, no more than others are, but in his own words, his industry was greater; he struck a light at twelve to rise and study and pray, for he was very pious; and his studies were not barren speculations, for he loved God and man. (Quoted in Luce 1949: 181–82)[17]

The most significant thing that a comment like this conveys is, I believe, the sense of continuity, and the admirable consistency, between what Berkeley thought, wrote and professed as a philosopher, and the way in which he lived his life. As his wife's letter suggests, there is no gap, no "incongruity" between Berkeley's thinking and his way of living: his religious and ethical thought pervaded his entire life, conferring upon it meaning, greatness, and exemplarity. What is more important, as she says: "he was not born to all this," but he had to make efforts and painstakingly fight with himself in order to attain such a state of ethical transparency and exemplarity.

Now, in this context, Berkeley's Bermuda project, as it was presented in detail above, might serve as a good illustration of the notion of a Berkeleian angelism that I am trying to advance here. The American project, failed as it was, was deeply marked precisely by a tendency toward seeing the best in people, toward idealization of real situations and state of affairs[18] that I mentioned above when advancing the notion of Berkeley's angelism. Berkeley's Bermuda project represented, in a sense, the culmination of his angelism, being its most remarkable and expressive embodiment. It was precisely in this project that all his idealistic pursuits and utopian dreams were put to work and given a unique meaning. The Bermuda project played an excellent catalytic role in the unfolding of Berkeley's angelism. True, even before this daring enterprise there had been numerous occasions on which Berkeley's outstanding character manifested itself, but the Bermuda project played an essential role in the formation and dissemination of Berkeley's renown as a "modern apostle."[19] To the extent that, at a given moment, some of his contemporaries knew him not as a philosopher, but first of all as the eccentric promoter of the Bermuda project, while others were quite certain that his philosophy would in the future be decisively overshadowed by the significance of his missionary enterprises: "His eminent Talents, by which he shines in the learned World, will not give him so much Lustre and Distinction in the annals of future Times, as that Apostolic Zeal which he is so confessedly endowed," wrote an anonymous author (quoted in Berman 1994: 105).

Based on much of what I said above about Berkeley's enthusiastic commitment to the utopian ways of thinking, and on his readiness to put the rest of his life in the service of a missionary cause, I would suggest here that Berkeley's Bermuda project might be seen as a remarkable instantiation of the ancient conception of philosophy as a way of life.[20] In this concept the aim of philosophy is not so much producing and disseminating knowledge about the world as it is that an existential transformation take place within the philosopher himself. Berkeley's whole Bermuda project, even if failed, points to the fact that he regarded philosophy not only as simply an academic discipline to be taught in schools and discussed in specialists' writings or journals, but rather as a reflexive exercise that must result in some improvement in people's lives: first, a self-improvement occurring in the philosopher himself, and then an improvement of his neighbors' lives. Berkeley's design of, and then enthusiastic embarking on, the Bermuda project suggests that, at a given point in his life, he felt that it was not enough for him to teach philosophy at Trinity College in Dublin, and that he had to make his philosophical preoccupations, in some way or other, useful for life, useful in some broader sense and for a larger community of people than simply the group of scholars involved. As such, he embarked on various practical projects, sailing to America to establish a utopian theology college, then becoming a dean, then a bishop, then, in the alchemists' footsteps, searching for a panacea with which to cure the sick and improve his neighbors' lives. The entire alchemical way of thinking, which I briefly examined in a previous chapter, is also about such a transformation of philosophy into a way of living: as I showed there, the alchemist's preparation for performing the "great work" is not only in terms of specific knowledge or specific technical skills, but it should also be in ethical and existential terms. The alchemist has to transmute his knowledge into a better life, for himself and for the others. If he does not do that, he fails, even if he succeeds in transmuting base metals into gold. To conclude, it must have been something of Berkeley's conception of philosophy as a form of (ascetic) life that

his friend Jonathan Swift meant when saying that he was "an absolute philosopher with regard to money, titles, and power" (quoted in Luce 1949:
100).

My view here that Berkeley's Bermuda project betrays a commitment to
a concept of philosophy as a way of life is supported by, among other Berkeley scholars, David Berman, who even draws a more specific parallel between the Bermuda project and Berkeley's theological writings (especially
Alciphron, discussed in the previous chapter):

> The benevolent Bermuda project of 1724–31 and the theological writings of
> 1732–5 fit and support each other perfectly, especially if one subscribes . . .
> to the orthodox view on the connection between religion and morality. . . .
> the fact that Berkeley himself was one of the most zealous adherents of this
> position helped to complete the picture. Dean Berkeley could therefore be
> seen as an almost perfect instantiation of the orthodox position. As Marcus
> Aurelius is often seen as the exemplification of the ideal Stoic sage, so Berke-
> ley came to be seen as a paradigmatic Christian: perfectly moral and religious.
> (Berman 1994: 122)

Berman's reference, in this context, to the Stoics, with their constant emphasis upon the "utility for life" that must characterize any philosophical
exercise, endorses my interpretation. I find another confirmation in the
above-quoted letter by Berkeley's wife. At a given moment, she makes this
remarkable statement: "Humility, tenderness, patience, generosity, charity
to men's souls and bodies, was the sole end of all his projects, and the business of his life" (quoted in Luce 1949: 182). When a philosopher decides to
embrace a worldview according to which "charity to men's souls and bodies" is "the business of his life," this is certainly an indication that he wants
to leave in the world not only the books he writes or the various philosophical doctrines he invents, but some other kind of "traces" as well. And, as all
Vitae sanctorum show, the most efficient way of influencing others' lives, and
leaving visible "traces" upon their souls, is by one's own example: If one
succeeds in guiding one's own life according to what one teaches, this is the
best validation of one's teachings, and the surest confirmations that those
teachings will not die with the one who professed them.

Immaterialism and Utopianism

Finally, I am wondering whether it would not be possible to talk about an
even more specific, if somehow speculative, parallel between certain features of Berkeley's "Bermuda project" and certain tenets of his philosophy.

More precisely, my question is: to what extent is such a utopian and, so to speak, unearthly mode of thinking as that revealed by the Bermuda project consistent, or kindred, with the immaterialist character of Berkeley's philosophy? In other words, to what extent is it possible to follow some deeper continuities, some common patterns of thinking and living, connecting his utopian propensities with the essence of his main philosophical message? This is, of course, too large and complex a topic to be dealt with exhaustively here. It is not my intention to do so now, at the end of this chapter, but simply to point to the possibility of such questioning.

A utopia would be, according to such a tempting analogy, an immaterialism "applied" to the social order, some sort of practical idealism. To put it otherwise, the utopianism of Berkeley's Bermuda project would be with regard to social things the mirror of what his immaterialism is with regards to natural things. Just as Berkeley's natural world lacks solid and dense materiality, so his utopian project lacks those basic features that generally characterize "realistic" projects. Just as, in Berkeley's immaterialism, the cosmos we see around is but the sophisticated interplay between our mind and God's, our uninterrupted "conversation" with God, articulated according to a certain grammar, so Berkeley's utopia is a careful rational construction, a complex "narrative" woven according to certain rules established in the course of the utopian tradition. Just as the ontological precariousness of the things in the world is compensated for by their being perceived, and "cared for," by God himself, so the fragility of the social constructions and actors is compensated for, on the utopian island, by their playing a part in a redeeming whole. As it were, Berkeley's being a "dreamer" in social affairs might well be associated with his being an immaterialist in philosophical matters. And his utopian, "impossible" proposals might be regarded as some social or civic reflection of, say, his paradoxical claims that matter does not exist and only spirits and minds exist. It is basically the same dissatisfaction with the current states of (both natural and social) affairs, and the same tendency toward replacing the existing state of things with an ideal one, that might be seen as manifesting in both cases, an attempt at somehow bridging the huge gap between the two ("there is a gap between the transparent solarity of utopian discourses and the murkiness or danger of the unsayable in the world of history" [Mazzotta 2001: 67]). Alexander Campbell Fraser, one of Berkeley's editors at the beginning of the twentieth century, even uses the term "social idealism" with reference to Berkeley's project: "It [*The Proposal*] is the lamentation of an ardent social idealist over the corrupt civilization of Britain and the Old World. Soon after a social enterprise of romantic benevolence presented itself to his imagination" (Fraser 1901, 4:342). In some connection with this possible paralleling, William Butler Yeats insightfully realized that Berkeley's world is ultimately dependent on our "dreaming" it:

> God-appointed Berkeley that proved all things a dream,
> That this pragmatical, preposterous pig of a world, its farrow that so solid
>   seem
> Must vanish on the instant if the mind but changes its theme. (Yeats 1965:
>   268)

7.   *George Berkeley and Catharism*

In this final chapter I take a slightly different approach to George Berkeley's thought. Whereas in the other chapters, I have traced the roots of Berkeley's thinking to a number of ancient traditions or schools of thought, pointing to a (stronger or weaker) relation of genealogy between them, what I want to do now is to look at Berkeley's denial of matter experimentally, from the standpoint of the Cathar doctrines on matter. I am in no way saying that Catharism is at the origin of Berkeley's denial of matter; however, it is theoretically interesting to undertake a comparative analysis of some of the ideas professed by the medieval Dualistic heresies (Catharism in particular), on the one hand, and George Berkeley's (philosophically scandalous and controversial) denial of the existence of matter, on the other hand. The central notion of this comparative approach is the idea that, in both cases, matter comes to be regarded, in some way or other, for some reason or other, as the source of evil. Based on this central insight other comparative considerations will also be advanced, pointing at the same time to the major difference that exists between the Cathar ideas and Berkeley's doctrine of the nonexistence of matter.

In what follows I will first offer a very brief historical introduction to the problem of Catharism; the Cathar doctrine about the material world will be presented here, in an attempt to offer a new perspective from which to look at Berkeley's immaterialism. Then, I will (re)tell the "story" of Berkeley's refutation of the material world as it appears from the vantage point of the Cathar doctrine on matter. Finally, I will place both Berkeley's refutation of matter and Catharism within a broader theoretical framework, and will attempt to connect both of them to a recurring archetypal Dualistic pattern employed in facing the "evil realm of matter" by other thinkers or artists, living in other cultural epochs.

THE CATHARS

The Cathar Heresy

The reason I have chosen Catharism out of all the Dualistic heresies as a comparison in this chapter is twofold. On the one hand, Cathar history and doctrines are relatively well known, with a great deal of scholarship dedicated to the subject, and with a multitude of approaches to it: over the centuries (and especially during the twentieth century) Catharism has, to various degrees, preoccupied historians of religion, politics, art, and literature, as well as theologians and philosophers. On the other hand, Catharism is the last important (and probably the most consequential) embodiment of the Dualistic tendency in the Western Christian world, marking to a certain extent—directly or indirectly and more or less traceably—some of its mentalities, intellectual and emotional perspectives, favorite topics, and ways of thinking. Catharism did not simply disappear from European culture along with the last occupants of the Montségur castle: it only changed its mode of existence, from a troubling heresy into a fascinating cultural topic that was to captivate many people's minds over the next centuries. Thus, as has been remarked, the disappearance of Catharism as a heresy from the Western world coincided with the emergence of a new source of inspiration for the European imagination:

> The saga of the collision between Catharism and Catholicism has long been one of the most favoured subjects for research, myth-making, romance and controversy. The fall of the Cathar citadel of Montségur and the ensuing mass burning of the Cathar *perfecti* . . . is often deemed to represent what Lawrence Durrell called "the Thermopylae of the Gnostic soul," and the Cathars, whether maligned or romanticised, still retain their peculiar mystique and long-lasting hold on the European imagination. (Stoyanov 2000: 292)

This being said, I am hopeful that, within a broader context of history of ideas, a consideration (even an experimental one) of Berkeley in view of the Cathar doctrines on matter might cast an interesting light on his immaterialism.

In the absence of a comprehensive corpus of Cathar writings it is difficult enough to establish, when investigating what the Cathars actually professed, which were the specifically Cathar beliefs and not Dualistic beliefs in general. This is why we should rely to a great extent on what the Cathars' Catholic opponents (and especially the Inquisition) attributed to them. (In such a context, Emmanual Le Roy Ladurie's book [1978], based on the direct access to the confessions of the Cathar heretics in the Inquisition's archives becomes an invaluable source for any researcher of Catharism.) As a number of studies suggest, it is reasonable to suppose that the core Cathar ideas regarding matter and the material world—and which properly form the subject of my comparison—are not necessarily the Cathars' invention, but are derived from mainstream teachings of the Dualistic tradition. The persistence of religious Dualism in the Western world over the centuries,[1] even if influenced from time to time by similar ideas from the East, is nowadays a received fact among many historians and religious scientists: "Western scholars tend to stress the existence of a Dualist tradition in the West throughout the Dark Ages and to regard the Balkan influence on the heretical movement, which no one now denies, as coming in rather late in the story. Certainly a Western Dualist tradition persisted from early times; but I believe that it was continually reinforced from the East, through Italy, where connections with the East were always maintained" (Runciman 1982: viii).

First of all, Catharism was undoubtedly "a Christian heresy." It appeared in France and Italy in the twelfth century, as an attempt at "reforming" the Catholic Church from within. The Cathars "considered and proclaimed themselves 'true Christians', 'good Christians', as distinct from the official Catholic Church which according to them had betrayed the genuine doctrine of the Apostles" (Ladurie 1978: viii). There are authors who even associate the emergence of Catharism in Europe with a series of other major developments that took place in Western culture in the twelfth and thirteenth centuries. Yuri Stoyanov, for example, places Catharism within the same context as Gothic art and architecture and the new ascetic and reform movements within the Catholic world: "Along with Gothic art and architecture, the renewed ideals of monasticism, asceticism and apostolic life, the advent of the dualist heresy in the west was symptomatic of the religious enthusiasm and permutations of the twelfth century" (Stoyanov 2000: 184). On the other hand, we should constantly bear in mind that, even if Catharism was born within a Catholic context, it brought with itself numerous heretical elements and foreign ideas, unorthodox ways of thinking, and an exotic theology, enough so to draw the Catholic Church's attention immediately:

> Catharism stood at some distance from traditional Christian doctrine, which was monotheist. Catharism accepted the (Manichaean) existence of two opposite principles, if not of two deities, one of good and the other of evil.

One was God, the other Satan. On the one hand was light, on the other dark. On one side was the spiritual world, which was good, and on the other the terrestrial world, which was carnal, physical, corrupt. (Ladurie 1978: viii)

Expectedly enough, in the absence of an established and inflexible corpus of doctrines, and of an authority responsible for keeping and monitoring its "orthodoxy," Catharism was naturally predisposed to numerous interpretations, deviations, and versions. Indeed, it was most probably not only the spontaneous and uncontrollable nature of the heresy itself that played so important a part in the emergence of these conflicting interpretations, but also the natural inclination of Gnosticism—inherent in all these Dualistic movements—toward endless speculation, luxuriant imagination, and spectacular mythology and narratives. Consequently, there is a long and interesting history of the various smaller heresies that appeared here and there within the Dualistic heresy itself, to the extent that, in the tenth century, an ironic remark was made about the Bulgarian Bogomils that each of them "invented something for himself" (Loos 1974: 133). And this was the case with almost all the Dualistic heretics:

> the Benedictine Eckbert reproached the German Cathars for the same variety of opinions. Already in the Byzantine world the teaching of the sect were constantly enriched by the results of free speculation on the texts of the New Testament, and by the creations of the folk-imagination, inspired by apocryphal writings. In the West the variety and permutations of the dualist doctrines can be traced quite distinctly, although of course it is difficult to say what has been taken over from the eastern branches of the sect and what is the later contribution of the western Cathar groups. (Ibid.)

Given some of the Cathar accounts of the precise relationships between the two principles (God and Devil), historians have distinguished two main versions, or tendencies, of Catharism: a "radical" one (in France) and a "moderate" one (in Italy). As Emmanual Le Roy Ladurie has concisely put it: "On the one hand there was absolute dualism, typical of Catharism in Languedoc in the twelfth century: this proclaimed the eternal opposition between the two principles, good and evil. On the other hand was the modified dualism characteristic of Italian Catharism: here God occupies a place which was more eminent and more 'eternal' than that of the Devil" (Ladurie 1978: viii). These two branches of Catharism constantly fought each other, and it is rather ironic that one of the few Cathar writings still extant, *Liber de duobus principiis* (Thouzellier 1973), is in fact a polemical, "radical" tract directed against the "moderate" Cathars.

Yet, for the purposes of the present comparative research, these divisions within Catharism do not matter too much. What is really significant about the Cathars, from the point of view of my present approach, is the strong contempt they permanently and unreservedly showed to all that belonged to the material world. Such a contempt was their distinctive feature, and, so to speak, *le point d' honneur* of all Cathar adherents: "All 'Cathars'—men of the pure life—were united in their revulsion against all that binds the human being to his material body" (Loos 1974: 251). And indeed it is precisely this feature that makes Catharism so symptomatic, illustrative, and appealing as to the subsequent developments of European cultural history. The Cathars offer a radical worldview, a vision of the material world as a corrupted and corrupting realm, something from which we could not expect anything positive and should keep safely apart. "In this dualist theodicy the cosmos is viewed as the outcome and the battleground of two opposed principles, good and evil or light and darkness" (Stoyanov 2000: 2) and it is precisely the siding with the principle of light, and putting one's life into its service, that confers meaning on one's life.

Due precisely to its peculiar doctrines about the material world, Catharism, despite the terrible and finally fatal prosecutions from the Catholic Church (if not, indeed, because of them) has over the centuries come to be considered, in many scholarly circles, with great sympathy and interest, and seen as an important ingredient of Western literature, music, art, and other forms of sensibility or social life.[2] I will in the following examine in some detail the Cathar doctrine on matter.

The "Prince of This World"

Matter had always troubled thinkers, theologians, and scholars (whether ancient or medieval) as to the conceivability of its origin, nature, composition, constitution, or movements, but the Cathar (or, more generally, Dualistic) response, by attributing matter's origin, existence, and maintenance to the Devil (or the Evil God), was certainly one of the most intriguing solutions ever found: Characteristically, it was a simple solution and a sophisticated one at the same time. It was simple because it appealed to a universal, manifold, and abstract principle answering a large number of philosophical and theological questions;[3] and it was sophisticated because, at the psychological and ethical level of the individual, it brought about a terrible complexity: the soul was now regarded as some sort of "metaphysical" battlefield between the "ultimate principles" themselves. The individual soul was dramatically and uninterruptedly disputed by God and the Devil in person:

"The battle was fought on a cosmic scale, but also within the human breast. One Cathar tract asserted that 'every day the evil god effects great evil against him [the good god] . . . and the latter god, our god, exercises great power in combating the former one'" (Fichtenau 1998: 161). It was probably this marked sense of self-importance, "election," and immense pride that, among other factors, made Catharism so attractive for many medieval audiences: at every moment of his life, man felt he was wanted by and fought over by God and the Devil. Everything in the surrounding world acquired now a new significance, just as all man's doings could not be indifferent or neutral any longer. Consequently, the current setting of his earthly life, that is, the material world around (and within) him played a new role: it was an essential *datum* involved in the cosmic battle, by means of which (more precisely, by the human attitudes adopted to it), he could be rescued or lost forever.

> It was of little importance for the attitude adopted towards this material world whether one or another force created amorphous matter *ex nihilo*. Views on the ultimate origin of the material being might change, the decisive point was that the Devil or the evil God had made (*fecit*) this world of ours and all that it contains. This was one of the fundamental theses acknowledged by all branches of the sect. . . . all that we see around us is the work of the Devil; he is the creator and ruler of all earthly things; it is he who gave the command to lie with women, to eat meat and to drink wine. (Ibid.: 253)

The notion that the creation of the material world should be attributed precisely to the Devil must have resulted from a process of theological systematization, a process unfolded in several phases. First, there is the empirical, everyday-life evidence that there is evil in the world. Then, under the circumstances of a peculiar theological sensibility, this evidence tends more and more to be perceived as overwhelming, and to result in an argument as follows: there is such a consistent, widespread, and deeply rooted negative side of our earthly world that attributing its creation to God raises embarrassingly insoluble theological problems; there is nothing in the world resembling God, whereas there are so many things reminiscent of the nature and the works of the Devil. It must have been this very special theological sensibility that explains why Cathars were in general so uneasy and anxious about the (material) world: "Sorrow and darkness permeate everything, the world contains more evil than good, and hence it belongs to the devil rather than God. Since our days are also marked by fear, illness, hardship, and misfortune, things that we humans must suffer in this life, 'We say that the days of this present world are evil'" (ibid.: 160). Under such circumstances, attributing the creation and maintenance of the material world to the Devil has come to be regarded as a somehow natural conclusion. Jesus Christ himself had named the Devil "the Prince of this world." Hence the Cathar interpretation of this particular biblical passage as supporting their own beliefs: "this world" is the material world of the Devil, and we should make all efforts to stay away from it.

Given the fact that within the medieval Christian frame of the theological (and philosophical) conceptualization, the notion of God always implies a maximum of existence (God is always seen as the Supreme Being, or Essence, bearing the positive attributes of plenitude, eternity, perfection, and so on), it is self-evident that a principle opposed to God, "the principle of darkness," together with all his workings, modalities, and agents, must be necessarily characterized by a minimum of existence, eventually by nonexistence. On the other hand, at the personal psychological level and under the circumstances of the peculiar theological sensibility mentioned above, the negative terms in which Cathars considered the material world (overwhelmed as it was by sorrow, darkness, illness, misfortune, suffering, and so forth) tend, by contamination, to be associated with negativity itself. As a result, it happens that the lack of value tends to be increasingly perceived as a lack of real existence. (However "fallacious" and illegitimate such a step might appear to us today, within the framework of an intensely religious movement, marked by impatience and urgency, it acquires a certain psychological justification: as it were, what does not deserve to exist, does not properly and truly exist.) Therefore, the next natural step for the Cathars to take was to consider this "wicked" material world in terms of nonbeing and nothingness: and they immediately took this step. Following is a short fragment from a theological conversation between a Cathar, one Peter, and a Catholic, William, who is trying to learn from him as much as he can about the Cathar theology:

> A crucial text from the first chapter of St. John's gospel emerged: "All things were made by him; and without him was not anything made that was made." In the vulgate, the term used is *nihil*, "*Sine ipso factum est nihil.*" Peter followed a tradition of interpreting the *nihil* to mean visible things, turning John's poetic phrase into support for their crucial tenet that the visible world was not the creation of the good God. "Visible things," he said, "are *nothing.*" (Lambert 1998: 160)

Peter reveals a great ability in countering his Catholic opponent's opinions, and he does so in an interesting, and theologically documented and ingenious, manner. The fragment strengthens the idea that Catharism is a Christian heresy, Peter's way of defending his opinions being deeply marked by the style of the theological debates of the day. Peter "had a clear understanding of the basic Cathar rejection of the whole visible world and sexuality as evil" and the ability to refute

> counter-texts which did not support dualism. . . . When he [William] objected [with] the Colossians text "In Him were all things created in heaven and earth, visible and invisible," Peter replied "Visible to the heart and invisible to the eyes of the flesh." William showed him his hand and asked if his flesh would rise again; Peter struck a wooden post and said, "Flesh will not rise again except as a wooden post." (Ibid.)

Catharism was a rather pessimistic religious movement, but not a completely desperate one: however evil the world might be, there is nevertheless a way to escape it, there are means for Cathar adherents to "purify" themselves and "save" their souls from the corrupted and corrupting world within which they were "incidentally" born and forced to live. These means include specific practices (fasts and abstinence from eating certain foods, such as meat, eggs, and milk and from drinking wine, and so on), rituals (first of all, of course, the *consolamentum*, which is the proper entrance in the rank of the "elect," the Cathar elite) and, underlying all these, the comprehensive and detailed knowledge of the Cathar doctrines, the acute awareness that the world is created, constituted, and maintained precisely in the way in which Cathar theologians say it is. This was a redeeming knowledge, which of course betrays, once again, the Gnostic character of Catharism.

The Gnostic character of Catharism has been repeatedly highlighted by historians. Heinrich Fichtenau, to take only one recent example, offers an excellent account of the way in which Catharism "flows" from Gnosticism, and of their close "structural" relationships. Fichtenau puts together "the Gnostics, Bogomils, and Cathars," and talks about their commitment to the theology of the Dualist tradition. In their hands, says Fichtenau,

> dualism became the key to unlocking the meaning of the universe. It was said of the Cathars that "they . . . maintain . . . there are two ages of the world (*saecula*), a good one and an evil one; similarly, there are two worlds

(*mundos*), two realms, two heavens, two earths, and in this way they maintain that there are two of everything." While this remark is not strictly accurate, it still illustrates a fundamental tendency inherent to this ontology. And only a story that did not rest content with the Gnostic idea of an emanating good principle could measure up to this view. The prosaic Gnostic myth was supplanted by one that played upon human emotions to greater dramatic effect, involving as it did the fall of angels, imprisonment, liberation, and re-ascendance. (Fichtenau 1998: 161)

Catharism took over from Gnosticism the notion that we, as spiritual substances, are only temporarily in this world and have to make every effort to find our way back to the "principle of light." Our soul is, in Catharism as well as Gnosticism "a stranger and an exile in the body." The Cathars learned from the Gnostics that "the souls of men were 'precious pearls', divine sparks from this spiritual realm and had descended into the wicked material world of the 'howling darkness' to be imprisoned in material bodies and could be released only through the redeeming mediation of *gnosis*" (Stoyanov 2000: 87). According to this line of thought, therefore, there is nothing, in this life, more important than learning how to fight the realm of matter and to recover the original lightness of light.

BERKELEY'S DENIAL OF THE EXISTENCE OF MATTER

The Problem

George Berkeley's denial of the existence of matter is seen not only as the most important part of his philosophy, but also as one of the greatest challenges he left to his commentators, whether critical or apologetic. Most Berkeley scholars have considered his refutation of matter in terms of the strength (or weakness) of his rational arguments against the material world, paying much attention to his abolition of the distinction between primary and secondary qualities, his refutation of the Lockean abstract ideas, his detailed accounts on the inconceivability, meaningless, and superfluity of matter, and so forth. There are consequently many excellent and comprehensive monographs and studies on Berkeley's immaterialist philosophy, considered from this particular point of view, revealing either the ingenuity and justification of Berkeley's arguments or the inconsistencies and weak points he showed in refuting matter. Those by J. O. Urmson, A. C. Grayling, D. Berman, I. Tipton, G. Pitcher, J. Dancy, and G. J. Warnock being only the best known and most influential.

Nevertheless, it seems to me that, at the present stage of Berkeley studies, a shift from the strictly logical and analytical consideration of his argumentation against matter to a discussion of it in terms of religious studies, cultural history, and the history of ideas is as necessary as it is fruitful. Such a shift in Berkeley's scholarly reception might bring about a supplementation of the current logic-analytical approaches with a better and more powerful historical contextualization of the Berkeleian immaterialist philosophy, and indeed offer us a deeper and maybe more complete understanding of it. My suggestion is that placing Berkeley within a broader framework of religious traditions (a framework within which Platonism, the alchemical tradition, and the topic of the book of nature, as well as the Cathar doctrines on matter, all form parts) would result in the fact that Berkeley's immaterialism would make more sense.

The interesting thing here is that it is George Berkeley himself who, in a way, points out the necessity of such an interpretative shift, in the *Principles of Human Knowledge*:

> Matter being expelled out of Nature, drags with it so many sceptical and impious notions, such an incredible number of disputes and puzzling questions, which have been thorns in the sides of the divines, as well as philosophers, and made so much fruitless work for mankind; that *if the arguments we have produced against it, are not found equal to demonstration* (as to me they evidently seem) yet I am sure *all friends to knowledge, peace, and religion, have reasons to wish they were.* , (Berkeley 1948–57: 2:82 [*Principles* § 96], emphasis added)

From such a passage at least two important ideas might be inferred. First, it is obvious that there is something Berkeley considers to be superior to the mere strength or soundness of the logical argumentation: namely, the utility and efficiency of the philosophical ideas in terms of some broader existential benefits, that is, in Berkeley's words, in terms of their long-term contribution to the consolidation and advancement of "knowledge, peace, and religion." Berkeley's fragment confirms excellently what has already been said, in the previous chapter, about a possible consideration of Berkeley's thought from the standpoint of a conception of philosophy as a way of life.

Secondly, this fragment implies that the nonexistence of matter is not necessarily, in Berkeley, the logical conclusion, or outcome, of a lengthy reasoning approach, but—perhaps on the contrary—a presupposition, an "intuition" that Berkeley had possibly had from the outset of his intellectual enterprise, prior to, and independent of, any logical, argumentative procedure. I suggest that the ultimate nature of this "intuition" is a theological or religious one, and by the means of his writings George Berkeley tried to justify it logically and offer it a respectable philosophical, even "scientific," appearance.

As clearly follows from the passage just quoted, Berkeley's primary aim is to supply his philosophical teachings with an immediate character of social and ethical-practical efficacy. As it were, to him philosophy is not simply a matter of arguing, counterarguing, reasoning, or persuading people for philosophy's own sake, but rather it is, so to speak, a matter of life (and death), of improving and enlarging the conditions of human living, and of "healing" others' minds and souls; eventually, philosophy is to look for some practical horizon as its real place of manifestation. In other words, Berkeley intended to consider his philosophy in terms of public and political (in the original sense of *polis*) relevance, rather than strictly scholarly or academic relevance (although he never neglected the scholarly significance and fate of his writings). But I do not want to insist anymore on this aspect of Berkeley's work as I have already dealt with it in some detail in some of the previous chapters.

Matter and Evil

Once Berkeley started seeing philosophy as having to be—in some way or other—useful for life, his intellectual approach acquired, apart from its specifically metaphysical character, a marked religious-practical character. And it is precisely at this point that he might be seen in some proximity with the Cathar (Dualistic, in fact) search for the "origin of evil." One of my main objectives in this chapter is to show that a consideration (however experimental) of Berkeley's refutation of matter in view of the Cathar ideas presented above would cast a new light on this most scandalous and provocative of his theses and contribute to a better understanding of it. My central argument for such a consideration is that, by his trying to locate the source of his neighbors' alienation (in the shapes of atheism, skepticism, disbelief, and so on), Berkeley was in fact asking the same question as the Cathars did. The question is, to use the famous Latin phrasing: Unde malum et qua in re? ("Whence came Evil, and in what does it exist?"). Moreover, both Berkeley and the Cathars gave the ancient question comparatively the same answer: matter. In both cases matter is regarded as related to the source of evil. Of course, there are numerous elements distinguishing Berkeley's philosophy from the Cathar theology, but there are at least this common central idea. And this fact is, both for Berkeley and for the Cathars, accompanied by specific theological anxieties and concerns and by the arduous desire to stay away from the world of matter.

Almost needless to say, George Berkeley is not a Dualist thinker in the proper and full sense of the word, as he clearly and repeatedly says that "only minds and spirits" exist. Therefore, I am not saying that Berkeley could be related to the Cathars by virtue of some fundamental similarity of their ultimate metaphysical principles. However, a certain parallel between Berkeley and the Cathars is possible as far as their attitudes to matter are concerned, no matter if matter is allowed to have a positive existence or not. For the interesting thing about Berkeley's denial of the existence of matter is that, even if denied philosophically, there is a sense in which matter has a marked psychological existence in his philosophical thinking: it bothers and embarrasses him, it troubles and concerns him, and it always puzzles and obsesses his mind. Matter occupies an essential position in most of his philosophical writings, just as it is present in the very name he gave his philosophy: immaterialism. It would be difficult to say about Berkeley, otherwise than very metaphorically, that he is a modern Cathar. Nevertheless, there is something in his case echoing, even if in a remote fashion, a certain set of Cathar attitudes: his underlying psychology, his radical refutation of matter, and his overall attitudes to the material world, his intense anxiety about the intellectual and ethical dangers that the recognition of matter brings about, and—above all—his passionate advocacy of the spiritual side of human life. All these point to the existence in Berkeley's philosophy of a mentality that one encounters when studying the Cathar phenomenon.

Although the "gentle Bishop" was in general an example of polite manners and mild temper, when coming to talk about the upholders of matter, he could not help using rather strong language, with adjectives and phrases that are reminiscent of the most passionate of the Christian apologists:

> upon the same foundation [the doctrine of matter] have been raised all the impious schemes of *atheism* and irreligion. . . . How great a friend material substance hath been to *atheists* in all ages, were needless to relate. All their monstrous systems have so visible and necessary a dependence on it, that when this corner-stone is once removed, the whole fabric cannot choose but fall to the ground; insomuch that it is no longer worth while, to bestow a particular consideration on the absurdities of every wretched sect of *atheists*. (Berkeley 1948–57: 2:81 [*Principles* § 92])

A fragment like this, betraying, on the philosopher's side, so intense a concern and deep interest in the disastrous effects that the recognition of matter might have on people's faith and morals, leads us to what is probably one of the most interesting and spectacular elements revealed by a comparison of Catharism and Berkeley's denial of the existence of matter: their similar shift from depreciating matter to considering it nonexistent. Somehow paradoxically, matter, although responsible for such numerous destructive consequences, is in fact nonexistent; matter, although so dangerous for any human knowledge, serenity, and virtue, is actually nothing—which means, exactly in the same way as it did to the Cathars, that the lack of value comes to be perceived as a lack of real existence. And it is especially this shift that proves sufficiently the religious nature of Berkeley's "intuition" of the nonexistence of matter: this paradoxical solution cannot be "explained" in logical terms at all, but only as an extreme result of a peculiar theological vision of the world, a vision whose inner articulations and modes of manifestation are, even if in a strange way, similar to those of the Cathar theology examined above. There is a fragment in *Alciphron* that brings forth, in a remarkably expressive manner, some of the key features of Berkeley's Cathar-like vision: religious pessimism, bitter awareness of the human imperfections and weaknesses, and a deep contempt to the earthly world. The fragment runs as follows: "To me it seems the man can see neither deep nor far who is not sensible of his own misery, sinfulness, and dependence; who doth not perceive that this present world is not designed or adapted to make rational souls happy" (ibid.: 3:178). And there are, of course, numerous other similar fragments in Berkeley attesting to a certain theological sensibility that might be seen in some relation to that of the Cathars.

Berkeley's impatience and ardent desire to offer his neighbors an immediate and efficient solution for their uneasiness and alienation make him extremely hostile to all partisans of matter, no matter their epochs, schools, or philosophical arguments and justifications. In his extreme view, even the slightest recognition of the existence of matter makes possible the triumph of materialism, which for him is more or less the same as atheism, which, by the same token, means the explicit encouragement of immorality, selfishness, public corruption, and the ruin of every human society. In short, to him, materialist philosophers attack the very foundations of the Christian faith:

> Nay hath it [matter] not furnished the *atheists* and *infidels* of all ages, with the most plausible argument against a Creation? That a corporeal substance,

which hath an absolute existence without the minds of spirits, should be produced out of nothing by the mere will of a spirit, hath been looked upon as
a thing so contrary to all reason, so impossible and absurd, that not only the
most celebrated among the ancients, but even divers modern and Christian
philosophers have thought matter coeternal with the Deity. Lay these things
together, and then judge you whether materialism disposes men to believe
the creation of things. (Ibid., 2:256 [*Three Dialogues*])

On the other hand, there is a significant difference between Berkeley and
the Cathars in seeing matter as the origin of evil. While Catharism considered matter a principle of evil as to man's nature (avoidable only through
specific religious practices, prayers, and ritual gestures), Berkeley saw the
existence of matter as a source of evil in terms of man's culture (avoidable
only through the theoretical denial of matter): namely, in religion and theology, philosophy, the sciences (physics and even mathematics), everyday
moral life, and so forth. This is probably one of the most important differences between Berkeley's doctrine of the nonexistence of matter and the
Cathars' ideas. In most of his philosophical writings, Berkeley deals not so
much with, say, the way in which the "human condition" is affected by its
"materiality," that is, he pays comparatively little theoretical attention to the
fact that, by their nature, humans are essentially "embodied souls," but he
is very much concerned with the way in which the strictly theoretical recognition of the existence of matter by philosophers, theologians, scientists,
and scholars in general affects human intellectual products, vitiates the sciences, and fatally "contaminates" man's beliefs and wisdom.

In the *Three Dialogues between Hylas and Philonous*, he talks extensively
about "the great advantages that arise from the belief of immaterialism, both
in regard to religion and human learning" (ibid.: 257). These theoretical
advantages are numerous, impressive and, thinks he, easily and immediately
recognizable. Berkeley traces them in various fields, but he implies that, beyond any possible enumeration, the denial of the existence of matter necessarily brings benefits for any imaginable human enterprise. I will give only
a few examples.

In the field of theology, the advantages brought about by the refusal of
matter are among the greatest. As Berkeley says, the "being of a God," the
"incorruptibility of the soul,"

those great articles of religion, are they not proved with the clearest and most
immediate evidence? When say the being of a *God*, I do not mean an
obscure general cause of things, whereof we have no conception, but *God*,

in the strict and proper sense of the word. A being whose spirituality, omnipresence, providence, omniscience, infinite power and goodness, are as conspicuous as the existence of sensible things, of which . . . there is no more reason to doubt, that of our own being. (Ibid.)

Also, in the sphere of the physical sciences ("natural philosophy") the refutation of matter would produce, however paradoxical this might appear to us, benefits very difficult to overvalue. Once the existence of matter is denied, many difficult, if not completely insoluble, problems and many scholarly disputes and conflicts would instantly disappear forever. For, according to Berkeley, it is precisely the embracing of the notion of matter that leads natural philosophers into error:

> what intricacies, what obscurities, what contradictions, hath the belief of matter led men into! To say nothing of the numberless disputes about its extent, continuity, homogeneity, gravity, divisibility, &c. do they not pretend to explain all things by bodies operating on bodies, according to the laws of motion? and yet, are they able to comprehend how any one body should move another? . . . Can they account by the laws of motion, for sounds, tastes, smells, or colours, or for the regular course of things? . . . But laying aside matter and corporeal causes, and admitting only the efficiency of an all-perfect mind, are not all the effects of Nature easy and intelligible? If the phenomena are nothing else but *ideas*; God is a *spirit*, but matter an unintelligent, unperceiving being. (Ibid.)

It is worth noting at this point that Berkeley can coherently advance an entire system of "philosophy of science" without supposing at all the existence of matter. In today's Berkeley scholarship this is considered an important and quite original characteristic of his thought. As Urmson has pointed out, what makes Berkeley's thinking interesting from the point of view of today's philosophy of science is precisely the fact "that he claims that his ontology is perfectly compatible with both common sense and religious beliefs and that . . . he can give a satisfactory account of the nature and value of the sciences without invoking the hypothesis of matter" (Urmson 1982: 33).

One encounters the same important advantages in ethics if matter is expelled. The immediate presence and manifestation of God, without the useless interposition of matter, would be of the greatest help in supporting people's moral endeavors. As Berkeley says, "the apprehension of a distant Deity, naturally disposes men to negligence in their moral actions, which they would be more cautious of, in case they thought Him immediately present, and acting on their minds without the interposition of matter, or unthinking second causes" (Berkeley 1948–57, 2:257 [*Three Dialogues*]).

By the same token, in metaphysics, the notion that matter does not exist, once generally accepted by scholars and philosophers, would have wonderful effects for the solving of numerous traditional philosophical problems, puzzles, and disputes. As a result of the denial of the existence of matter, metaphysics would become much sounder, more commonsensical, and reasonable:

> what difficulties concerning entity in abstract, substantial forms, hylarchic principles, plastic natures, substance and accident, principle of individuation, possibility of matter's thinking, origin of ideas, the manner how two independent substances so widely different as *spirit* and *matter*, should mutually operate on each other? What difficulties, I say, and endless disquisitions concerning these and innumerable other like points, do we escape by supposing only spirits and ideas? (Ibid.)

However strange it might appear, the recognition of matter has disastrous effects even in mathematics, and only thanks to its refutation would it be possible to put an end to the numberless paradoxes, perplexities, and intellectual sufferings that matter has always caused to mathematicians: "Even the *mathematics* themselves, if we take away the absolute existence of extended things, become much more clear and easy; the most shocking paradoxes and intricate speculations in those sciences, depending on the infinite divisibility of finite extension, which depends on that supposition" (ibid.).

Even the worst and most unimaginable mistakes, fallacies, and sins have had the belief in matter as their main cause. As a matter of fact, it would be hard to talk about any false ideas, prejudices, or other dangerous beliefs without immediately noticing the recognition of matter as their ultimate source. The acceptance of matter is for Berkeley at the root of all evil. For example, the ultimate sources of idolatry are to be found in the fact that we take the visible things for material, which is thus not only an error in theoretical terms, but also a serious religious offence:

> on the same principle [doctrine of matter] doth *idolatry* likewise in all its various forms depend. Did men but consider that the sun, moon, and stars, and every other object of the senses, are only so many sensations in their minds, which have no other existence but barely being perceived, doubtless they would never fall down, and worship their own *ideas*; but rather address their homage to that Eternal Invisible Mind which produces and sustain all things. (Berkeley 1948–57, 2:82 [*Principles* § 94])

It is easy to see that matter comes to play a central role in George Berkeley's account of the nature (and forms of manifestation) of evil in the entire sphere of human culture. From all these fragments I quoted it becomes manifest that Berkeley tends, as it were, to demonize matter. And it is precisely this demonization of the material world that, once again, reminds us of how close his ideas sometimes are to the doctrines of those Cathars who formerly thought that the Devil ("father of matter") was the cause of all human unhappiness and imperfection.

A Broader Framework

The aim of these final speculative considerations is to place both Catharism and Berkeley's denial of the existence of matter within some broader theoretical framework. For some of the possible questions a critical reader might ask now, once my experimental comparative exercise is completed, are the following: How is it possible to undertake, legitimately, such a comparative approach as this one? How justified is the parallel drawn between these two phenomena, so remote in space and time, and how can it be sustained theoretically?

One possible, though somehow still speculative, answer to such questions may be found in the following thoughts. The legitimacy of a comparative approach of this nature comes from the fact that both Catharism and Berkeley's "intuition" of the nonexistence of matter might be regarded as deriving from the same unique source. Namely: from a fundamental archetypal Dualistic pattern, to which both of them, even if in different ways, belong, and which—it can be further speculated—seems to be recurrent in the religious and intellectual history of numerous other cultures. The existence of such an archetypal pattern has been observed and discussed, or at least presupposed, by numerous historians, religion scientists, and theoreticians of culture. Its roots are various—anthropological, mythical, social, empirical—just as its manifestations are far from being limited to the field of religious life: they are manifest, too, in philosophy, literature, mentalities, and visual arts.

Originally, there were a number of fundamental pairs of opposites ("left-right," "up-down," "day-night," "life-death," and so on) that, according to some authors (for example, Cassirer), might to some extent have contributed an anthropological Dualistic element to the formation of some *Weltanschauung* or other, beginning with the most primitive mythical thought. As Ernst Cassirer said, the development of "the mythical feeling of space always starts from the opposition of *day* and *night*, *light* and *darkness*. The dominant power which this antithesis exerts on the mythical consciousness can be followed down to the most highly developed religions" (Cassirer 1955: 96). Thus, according to this line of thought, seeing and considering the things in the world in a Dualistic manner have gradually come to stay at the roots of various cultural behaviors, known under various guises and names. A synthetic and precise account of how this archetypal Dualistic pattern originally formed and how it uses different expressions is given by Heinrich Fichtenau, who in fact takes over Cassirer's approach:

> Whoever perceives the world as a maelstrom of incomprehensible phenomena will try to impose some order. The simplest mode of organisation is a 'binary' system that characterises things as either "on" or "off," being or non-being, or in the dualistic terms common to the worldviews and religious concepts of the most divers peoples. (Fichtenau 1998: 160–61)

Subsequently, based on the internalization of such a fundamental anthropological and mythical set of distinctions, more elaborate and diverse forms of Dualism were brought into being and developed. For example, in philosophy Dualism has played an essential role, even from its inception. Philosophical Dualistic tendencies can be traced as far back as the pre-Socratics, but it was in Plato's thought, "with its dualities between the mortal body and the immortal soul, or the world perceived by the senses and the world of eternal ideas, comprehended by the mind" (Stoyanov 2000: 2), that the philosophical dualism was to be given one of its most sophisticated and durable expressions. The Platonic dualism would then stay at the heart of almost all subsequent philosophical dualisms in Western thought. The "Platonic type of soul-body duality" enjoyed an outstanding posterity. It came to influence

> important Jewish and Christian traditions. A dualist spirit-matter opposition along with a rigorous asceticism was cultivated in the esoteric-initiatory trends of Orphism and Pythagoreanism. . . . The Orphic-Pythagorean teaching which explains the physical body as a tomb for the divine and immortal soul is shared in the Gnostic type of religiosity with its implicit focus on the rescue of the "divine spark" in man from the bodily prison . . .—a preoccupation shared by the medieval Bogomil and Cathar heresies. (Ibid.: 5)

As such, the detailed Gnostic accounts of the nature and origin of man occupied a crucial position and successfully provided the source of inspiration for several subsequent Dualistic religious (and even intellectual) movements.[4] From this standpoint, the Cathar theology did almost nothing but

take over, clarify, and develop some of the main cosmological and anthropological ideas professed within the various branches of ancient Gnosticism.
Milan Loos offers an excellent summary of the Gnostic accounts of man's
nature, fate, and possibilities of salvation. According to him, in Gnosticism,
man's soul is imprisoned in

> this dungeon of the world, confined in the darkness of matter; but it origi-
> nated in a very different place, in a timeless world, in the bright abode of
> another God of whom the earthly world and its rulers have no conception.
> The soul partakes of the very substance of this Unknown God, but in the
> material world it has lost the consciousness of its identity. . . . Only *gnosis* can
> awaken it, knowledge which comes from above and is really only the reviv-
> ing memory of the soul's origin. (Loos 1974: 21–22)

Besides its numerous occurrences in the field of religion, theology, or
(religious) philosophy, this archetypal Dualistic pattern might also be found
in various other areas, some of them remote enough from the religious. Indeed, there are several secular forms through which it manifests and reveals
itself: Romantic nihilism, to take only a modern and better known example,
might be to some extent regarded as one of these forms. A close and special
relationship between the Dualistic outlooks and the idea of nothingness has
been observed both in Catharism and in Berkeley's immaterialism. Dualism
may presuppose the idea of nothingness as an extreme form of "existence"
of one of its terms. As such, with respect to this particular relationship, we
can see how some of the modern European nihilists sometimes expressed
views echoing ideas of a peculiarly Dualistic or Gnostic character, even if
they considered themselves outside the religious sphere, if not simply atheists. Here is Giacomo Leopardi's dramatic confession: "I was terrified finding myself in the midst of nothingness, and myself nothing. I felt as if I were
stifled believing and feeling that everything is nothing, solid nothingness"
(quoted in Schenk 1979: 53).

As a matter of fact, this nihilism is the distinctive mark of a broader modern sensibility, whether Romantic or post-Romantic, a sensibility characterizing a large number of modern artistic, philosophical, and intellectual
movements. As Hans Georg Schenk has excellently shown, Schopenhauer's
thought, for instance, might be regarded as one of the most significant philosophical embodiments of this sensibility. It is not difficult to see how
human existence is often associated in Schopenhauer with the idea of meaningless, absurd suffering and useless sacrifice, which is, of course, strongly

reminiscent of the traditional Dualistic perception of the earthly world as deeply corrupted, valueless, and not deserving to exist:

> As with Leopardi and Senancour, so with Schopenhauer, the idea of man's utterly senseless existence produces gloom and despondency. . . . From the very start the philosopher's mind is focused on man's torments and agonies, which . . . he depicts in all their manifold shapes. Enjoyment and happiness, on the other hand are sadly dismissed as a mirage, and thus the whole course of life seems to be oscillating between the two poles of suffering and *ennui*. . . . the world appears as the worst of possible worlds. (Ibid.: 59)[5]

Finally, we might find numerous significant differences between the ancient Gnostics or medieval Cathars, on the one hand, and the modern nihilists and Schopenhauer, on the other. Nevertheless, despite all these differences, even in the most elaborate modern cases, it is often possible to discern some traces of that primordial Dualistic tendency to contest the established, commonly received state of things, in an attempt to transcend it. For it is ultimately the same fundamental attitude of the isolated individual facing the hostile universe that appears either in the form of a need for spiritual, religious elevation (and escape from it) or, perhaps more sophisticatedly, in the form of a feeling of nothingness and universal vanity.

This lengthy divagation should not necessarily be seen as part of my main argument in this chapter for a look at George Berkeley's immaterialism from the standpoint of the Cathar doctrines on matter. The only reason I have advanced these speculations here is the need I felt to point out a possible broader, more comprehensive, theoretical framework within which not only Berkeley's immaterialism and the Cathars' doctrines of matter, but also a number of other cultural phenomena and numerous other thinkers, artists, religious figures, and myth-makers might well be placed, interpreted, and given some transhistorical meaning, outside and beyond their specific historical settings.

Conclusion

As I have shown throughout the seven chapters of this book, there are in Berkeley a number of important topics, notions, and concerns that are not dealt with—sometimes, not even mentioned *en passant*—in today's mainstream Berkeley scholarship. In other words, for various reasons, this scholarship is not interested in recognizing and taking aboard the entire intellectual universe that is Berkeley's philosophy. Moreover, as it happens, sometimes Berkeley scholars are even embarrassed when coming across, in some of Berkeley's writings, such out-of-fashion issues as alchemy, the search for the *elixir vitae,* the quest for the earthly paradise, utopianism, archetypal knowledge, God as narrator of the world, the *liber mundi,* or Cathar-like attitudes to the material world. These topics are not generally present in our current philosophical debates, but—as I have shown—they are massively present in Berkeley, and if one hopes to know "things as they are," one cannot simply pass over the existence of such topics in Berkeley's thought. They cannot be surgically removed from the rest and dismissed as useless "historical stuff." In fact, in the very texture of Berkeley's thought they are organically intermingled with those of his ideas that still interest us today; they put their indelible imprint on the latter. Understanding what Berkeley (or, for that matter, any other historical figure) meant to say means precisely reconstructing the whole of what was said, and thinking about it on its own terms, not on ours. Studying a past figure goes beyond considering what that figure might have to say about our present philosophical concerns; studying a past figure, event, or system of thought, must be undertaken for his or its own sake, and not only for ours.

It has not been my intention in this book to replace the existing (predominantly analytic) manner of treating Berkeley's philosophy with what I propose in this book. As I said in the introduction, the analytic Berkeley scholars do a good job in constantly relating Berkeleian arguments and ideas to important issues in our contemporary debates. And this linking of the needs of the present with the resources that the past can offer us is a very important factor for the advancement of any form of human knowledge.

Instead, what I have tried to do in this book is to show that it is not only necessary, but also possible, legitimate, and meaningful to supplement the existing analytically minded scholarship with a sense of historical awareness, with an understanding of the remarkable intellectual richness and cultural complexity behind Berkeley's thinking, and with the notion of a much larger framework of cultural and religious-metaphysical traditions. In this framework, Berkeley's philosophy has to be considered and interpreted in close connection with a number of kindred ways of thought characterizing the European intellectual world. To put it differently, George Berkeley's philosophy has been systematically dealt with in this book as the privileged meeting point of various currents of thought, manners of philosophizing, religious/theological movements, spiritual/soteriological techniques, traditional *topoi*, and cultural representations.

Nevertheless, my objective here has not been to account for all these strictly from the point of view of an antiquarian, but to make a deeper sense of them by investigating the significance of their presence in Berkeley, and the role they played in the constitution of Berkeley's thought. I have followed in detail how they became essential elements of Berkeley's thinking and inserted themselves into its intimate texture. In parallel, I have tried to see how Berkeley's thinking emerged, worked, and made sense from the specific perspectives of these other currents of thought. Whether I succeeded in my enterprise is not up for me to judge, but what I can say, for my part, is that this has been a most fascinating and rewarding experience.

What has been said in this book so far is sufficient, I hope, for pointing out the possibility of a new way of looking at Berkeley's thought, one better articulated historically and more intelligible than what today's mainstream Berkeley scholarship offers. Mine is a reading derived from broad historical associations and flexible interpretations; it is a reading born out of the idea that going beyond differences and looking for what things have in common is a profitable intellectual enterprise, even a necessity of a scholarly life. Driven by this idea, I have been looking in this book for common patterns of thought, understanding, and feeling; for patterns within which thinkers and authors belonging to different epochs and cultures find their natural place and spontaneously establish a conversation with each other, a conversation that defies the ages, countries, languages, religions, and various other particularisms. Throughout the book I have been looking for the existence of those transhistorical patterns through which people—of different times and of different mentalities—come to perform the miracle of understanding themselves, their world, and God, in the same (or in a similar) way. In terms of cultural history, the miracle of likeness is as awe-inspiring as the miracle of diversity. I have always been looking in this book for what people have in common, even in those cases in which they did not seem to have very much in common. On the other hand, an essential argument that this book has made is that, in order to understand better what this conversation is about, one should first study the actual historical backgrounds against which the conversing figures emerged. Then, once this has been established, one can go into the heart of the matter. This is why such an approach is not at all about using the past (which I was very critical about in the introduction), but is about making (better) sense of the past. In this way the history of thought ceases to be an incomprehensible mass of ancient books and useless doctrines, and asserts itself, in a fundamental way, as an ongoing project.

This book is an answer to the ironic question that Martin Heidegger asks in the quotation I chose as the epigraph. In my attempt to discover whence Berkeley's philosophy comes, I have constantly endeavored to "bracket" what I knew about Berkeley's importance for some of today's philosophical debates, and to focus mainly on the possible roots of his thought, without even asking whether a discussion of those roots is or is not "interesting" from the point of view of contemporary philosophical discussions. I openly acknowledge that, say, showing how *Siris* was based on an alchemical mode of thought might not contribute a great deal to solving what passes today as "genuinely philosophical problems." Nor does placing Berkeley's Bermuda project in the tradition of the quest for the earthly paradise answer many of our fashionable philosophical interrogations.

What I do nevertheless believe is that there are also other questions, and that my approach in the present book offers a proper way of asking and, I hope, answering them: What is Berkeley's relationship with the past? What role does the ancient and medieval heritage play in the constitution of his philosophy? To what extent is he indebted to various traditional modes of thought and to what extent is his philosophy "novel"? To what extent was he aware of the modeling influence of the past on his own way of philosophizing? Did he try to resist it? These questions (and other similar ones) are important because they are nothing other than specific instantiations of a set of other—ampler and more difficult—questions, of whose theoretical significance it is difficult to doubt seriously, and which my approach, in the long run, is essentially about, questions such as these: How does a given philosophy articulate itself? To what extent is it possible for an individual thinker to escape the dominating influence of the past when designing his own philosophy? Considering this influence, why and when is a given philosophy "new"? What precisely renders it so? How is it that novelty appears against a certain intellectual background? Does philosophical novelty consist of proposing new solutions to old problems or, rather, of proposing—inventing—new problems? And, in general, how is novelty possible in the history of philosophy? Given the philosophers' constant desire to challenge the established views, and propose their own views instead, how is any *philosophia perennis* possible?

Yet—it might still be asked—do these questions indeed have philosophical significance? My belief, a belief on which this entire book is founded, is that the answer is yes. What pervades all these questions is the fundamental and perennial need to understand what the past is, and what the favorite ways through which the past is shaping our present lives are. In other words, all these questions, and any other similar ones, are but instantiations of one and the same fundamental interrogation: Where do we (that is, our ideas, our modes of thought, the current workings of our minds) come from?

If philosophy is to convey the Socratic advice "know yourself" successfully, it cannot do it otherwise than by its own example: by taking the advice seriously and "knowing itself," whatever the price might be.

Notes

Introduction

1. See, for example, Karl Popper's article "A Note on Berkeley as Precursor of Mach" (Popper 1956).

2. I will give only few examples, out of very many possible: A. C. Grayling's *Berkeley: The Central Arguments* (Grayling 1986), Jonathan Dancy's *Berkeley: An Introduction* (Dancy 1987), David Berman's *Berkeley: Idealism and the Man* (Berman 1994), George Pappas's *Berkeley's Thought* (Pappas 2000), etc.

3. Let me say here that this is not necessarily the position defended by Rorty, Schneewind, and Skinner. They just try to make a case for it, and compare this position with its rivals. I use their description of this position simply because of its remarkable clarity and precision.

4. "There is knowledge—historical knowledge—to be gained which one can only get by bracketing one's own better knowledge about, e.g., the movements of the heavens or the existence of God" (Rorty 1984: 50).

5. In a recent book, Bernard Williams makes the same point about historical research being based upon an idea of truth and an ideal of truthfulness. He, too, uses the example offered by Orwell's masterpiece (Williams 2002).

6. I am making here repeated references to Rorty, Schneewind, and Skinner (1984), finding their work particularly useful for my purposes in this book, but there are numerous other contemporary authors who hold similar views about this crisis in today's philosophy.

7. "'Philosophy' is a sufficiently flexible term so that no one is greatly surprised when a philosopher announce that half of the previous canon of 'great philosophers' must be thrown out because the problems of philosophy have been discovered to be different than had previously been thought. Such a philosopher usually explains that the slack will be taken up by something else ('religion' or 'science' or 'literature')" (ibid.: 8–9).

8. The complete fragment runs as follows: "We would urge that, in Britain and America, the historiography of philosophy has recently been less conscious than it ought to have been. In particular, the influence of analytic philosophy has worked against self-consciousness of the desired sort. Analytical philosophers have seen no need to situate themselves within Gadamer's 'conversation which we are' because they take themselves to be the first to have understood what philosophy is, what questions are the genuinely philosophical ones" (ibid.: 11).

9. "On the analytic philosophers' own account of the situation, indeed, there is nothing which can properly be called 'the history of philosophy,' but only a history of almost-philosophy, only a pre-history of philosophy" (ibid.: 12).

10. For Popkin the (analytic) philosophers "are often willing to eliminate the study of the history of philosophy, since what called itself philosophy in the past was just confusion and error. They are willing to curtail access to the historical past through what they encourage and discourage as proper activities of students, professors and publishers" (Popkin 1992: 325).

11. A more commonsensical and refreshing criticism is brought by MacIntyre: "for any particular philosophical generation its occupation of the present can only be temporary; in some not too distant future it will have been transmuted into one more part of the philosophical past" (MacIntyre 1984: 39).

Chapter 1   George Berkeley and the Platonic Tradition

1. "The Neoplatonists stressed and developed certain aspects of Plato's metaphysics and of the resulting view of man. For them the important part of man is his soul and any discussion of the soul's abilities and aspirations must be seen in the context of the universe as a whole" (Sheppard 1994: 6).

2. This issue will be amply developed in chapter 5, which is dedicated precisely to placing Berkeley in the Christian tradition of apologetic philosophy.

3. Obviously, the relationship was more complex than it might appear at first sight. Christianity borrowed certain ideas from Platonism, at the same time criticizing or openly rejecting others: "Certain Platonic doctrines were fairly uniformly rejected, notably the doctrine of the Pre-existence of Souls; gradually the Christian doctrine of *creatio ex nihilo* came to distinguish Christian theology from developments in Platonism, notably in Neoplatonism. . . . This piecemeal adaptation of Platonism makes it, in fact, difficult to put one's finger on unambiguously Platonic elements in Christianity" (Louth 1994: 53).

4. For example, on the particular problem of the archetypes in Berkeley's philosophy there are already a number of studies by Peter S. Wenz (1976), Charles J. McCracken (1971), C. C. W. Taylor (1985), Stephen H. Daniel (2001), and others.

5. "As he grows older he gains confidence; he conceals less from prudential motives; he makes less and less use of the current (and confusing) jargon of the philosophers; and he widens his horizon and finds his kinship more surely with the ancient philosophers" (Ardley 1968: 10).

6. See chapter 5 in this book for a detailed discussion of this problem.

7. He constantly claimed that his immaterialist view is, and should be considered, perfectly compatible with the basic principles of the Christian *Weltanschauung*: "to a Christian it cannot surely be shocking to say, the real tree existing without his mind is truly known and comprehended by (that is, *exists in*) the infinite mind of God. Probably he may not at first glance be aware of the direct and immediate proof there is of this, inasmuch as the very being of a tree, or any other sensible thing, implies a mind wherein it is." (Berkeley 1948–57, 2:235 [*Three Dialogues*]).

8. For more about this issue and its other occurrences in the history of Western philosophy, see my essay " 'God is dreaming you.' Narrative as *Imitatio Dei in Miguel de Unamuno*" (Bradatan 2004b).

9. See, for example, the criticisms brought by Robert McKim to Wenz's arguments (McKim 1982).

10. More about the Platonic dualism will be said in chapter 7.

11. Dillon speaks of a series of "philosophical procedures to « deconstruct » the objective material world [pour 'déconstruction' du monde matériel objectif] that the two philosophers [Berkeley and Plotinus] shared" (Dillon 1997: 100).

12. Since another chapter of this book—chapter 3—is dedicated precisely to the place that George Berkeley occupies in the tradition of *liber mundi*, I will deal here with this topic only insofar as is necessary for a better understanding of the Platonic character of Berkeley's early philosophical writings.

12. Some twenty years later, in *Alciphron; or, The Minute Philosopher* (1732) he reaffirms the importance of the *liber mundi* topic: "God speaks to men by the intervention and use of arbitrary, outward, sensible signs, having no resemblance or necessary connexion with the things they stand for and suggest; . . . by innumerable combinations of these signs, an endless variety of things is discovered and made known to us; . . . we are thereby instructed or informed in their different natures; . . . and we are directed how to regulate our motions, and how to act with respect to things distant from us, as well in time and place" (Berkeley 1948–57, 3:149).

Chapter 2   Philosophy as Palimpsest: Archetypal Knowledge in Siris

1. And this explains why it has been difficult to reach agreement among Berkeley scholars as to the Platonism of his early writings, some of these authors being utterly opposed to accepting such an idea.

2. If Berkeley is still considered today simply as another representative of the "new philosophy," and nothing else, this is possible only through the dismissal of his *Siris*, a writing in which he put years of intense work and which he highly valued to the last days of his life.

3. The front page of the auction catalogue reads:

A Catalogue of the Valuable Library of the late Right Rev. Dr. Berkeley, Lord Bishop of Cloyne.

Together with the Libraries of his Son and Grandson, the late Rev. George Berkeley, D.D., Prebendary of Canterbury, and the late George Monk Berkeley, Esq.

Including a good Collections of Books in *Divinity, Foreign* and *English Domestic History, Voyages, Travels, Classics, Belles Lettres, Miscellanies, Poetry,* and in almost in every Branch of Polite Literature, in both modern and dead Languages.

N.B. Several *Editiones Principes* in the fifteenth and sixteenth Centuries.
Which will be Sold by Auction,

by *Leigh* and *Sotheby*, Booksellers, At their House in York-Street, Covent-Garden, On Monday, June 6, 1796, and the Five following Days.

Beginning each Day at Twelve o'Clock.

To be viewed to the Time of Sale.

4. For a detailed discussion of the fortunes and contents of this catalogue, see Aaron's article "A Catalogue of Berkeley's Library" (Aaron 1932).

5. The library in question was a family library, containing also books purchased after Berkeley's death, by his son and grandson. But I think that Jessop's following remark is applicable not only to the books by Plato, but also to those by the Platonic authors: "The sale-catalogue of Berkeley's family library (1796) lists four different editions of the works of Plato. If we may judge from the directions of interest of Berkeley's son and grandson, the volume had probably not been theirs" (T. E. Jessop in Berkeley 1948–57, 2:156 n. 1 [*Three Dialogues*]).

6. "[I]nsofar as an act (or an object) acquires a certain reality through the repetition of certain paradigmatic gestures, and acquires it through that alone, there is an implicit abolition of profane time, of duration, or 'history': and he who reproduces the exemplary gestures thus finds himself transported into the mythical epoch in which its revelation took place" (Eliade 1971: 35).

Chapter 3   George Berkeley and the Liber Mundi *Tradition*

1. Let me also add at this stage that Berkeley never uses the phrase "book of nature" as such: he only talks of the "language of nature" or "natural language," just as he talks of the "optic" or "visual language," of nature as a "Discourse of God," and so forth. This is why, in this chapter, I take the topic of the book of nature in a rather broad sense, as an umbrella topic including all these subtopics.

2. Let us note in passing that this theological grounding of *liber mundi*, as it is revealed here, is similar to the theological justification of the representation of divine figures (*icons*): theologically speaking, the icon is not simply a "painting"; it can "grasp" God's image because, by Incarnation, God has decided to make Himself visible to earthly eyes. The icon is not made only of wood and paint, but it also contains a "hidden" side: God's image as a spiritual unseen reality. Thus the icon has a double nature, just as Christ has a dual nature. Just as, to return to my topic, the "book of the world" itself has: *signum* and *signatum*.

3. Let us also quote, to illustrate, some titles of medieval encyclopedic books: *Speculum quadruplex* (Vincent of Beauvais), *Speculum humanae salvationis* (Hugues of Saint-Cher), *Speculum humanae conditionis*, and so forth.

4. For a recent discussion of the relationship between book and mirror in the Middle Ages and beyond see, for example, Peter Harrison's study "The 'Book of Nature' and Early Modern Science" (Harrison 2006).

5. It is interesting to see how this metaphor of the "invisible hand" changed its meaning along the centuries, to the extent that, for example, in Adam Smith's economic theory, it would mean nothing divine or theological at all, but simply the laws of free market.

6. Needless to say, the topic is also present within the other "religions of the Book." For instance, as far as the Islamic world is concerned, Mohhyddin ibn-Arabi considers that "this Universe is an immense book" (Chevalier and Gheerbrandt 1969: entry "Livre"). But an inquiry, however sketchy, into how the topic appears, not only in Christianity, but also in the other "religions of the Book" would have gone much beyond the scope and purpose of the present chapter.

7. "The old traditional religions of the Greeks and the Romans were not embodied in sacred books. Judaism and Christianity and, later, Mohammedanism were religions of the book. The name, Bible, may come from *biblion*, papyrus rolls, or from Byblus, a town in Syria famous as a papyrus market; as we have it, the Bible was written down between 1000 B.C. and A.D. 150" (Artz 1980: 39–40).

8. See, for example, Eric Jager's fascinating recent book on "the book of the heart" (Jager 2000).

9. See, for this discussion, chapter 16 ("The Book as Symbol") of Curtius's book (Curtius 1979: 302–47).

10. This process is, of course, much more complex than presented here, the "reading" of *liber creaturarum* being only a first stage. As a matter of fact, in Gilson's summarization, "this elevation is marked by three main stages. The first one consists in finding again God's traces within the sensible world; the second one consists in searching for God's image in our souls; and the third one consists in transcending all created things and finding the mystical delights of the knowledge and adoration of God" (Gilson 1944: chap. 8, § 2).

11. For a discussion of Sebonde's doctrine see Gilson's book (Gilson 1944: 465–67).

12. Jesse Gellrich's book, referred to already many times in this chapter is specifically concerned with the idea of book in relation to the many "cultural forms" (language theory, mythology, fiction, manuscript painting, sacred architecture, music, etc.) of the Middle Ages (Gellrich 1985).

13. It is not difficult to see that a certain "Platonic" dimension is present in this principle of imitation. Some authors, for example, see the climactic point of this tendency in the thirteenth century: "The perception of the earthly society as an ordered structure reflecting the greater harmonies of the universe was . . . a basic pillar supporting the thirteenth-century world view" (Barber 1993: 475).

14. See David Berman's discussion of this problem (Berman 1994: 22–28).

15. Published in answer to a newspaper criticism against *An Essay towards a New Theory of Vision*. Adam Smith described this short work as "one of the finest examples of philosophical analysis that is to be found, either in our own, or in any other language" (Quoted in Berman 1994: 136).

16. For a detailed discussion of the "natural language" in the seventeenth century, and of the entire literary, philosophical, and linguistic context, see, for example, Margreta de Grazia's and Thomas C. Singer's articles (Grazia 1980 and Singer 1989).

17. "For in him we live and move and exist" (Acts 17.28). The idea is also present in Cleanthes.

18. See, for the use of these two metaphors in the Middle Ages and in the modern period, Mills' excellent article (Mills 1982).

19. For Leonardo da Vinci's mechanics, as well as for the specific relationship between his conceptions and Descartes's mechanical conceptions, see, for instance, the book that Paul Valéry wrote about Da Vinci (Valéry 1957).

Chapter 4   George Berkeley and the Alchemical Tradition

1. "Tar is a black and sticky substance with none too good a name in letters, and the very idea of a bishop discarding his white lawn sleeves and handling it and extracting a nasty medicine from it is too much for our sense of gravity, and Berkeley's tar-water has become a jest" (Luce 1949: 197).

2. Nevertheless, besides the Bermuda Project, *Siris* was, as I already mentioned, one of the main sources of Berkeley's popularity during his lifetime, and even after his death: "Berkeley's philosophical writings have suffered a curious fate. In his own day the earlier works, such as his *Principles of Human Knowledge*, were little read and had even less influence, but his *Siris* enjoyed great popularity; if not for the philosophy, at least for the tar-water" (Ritchie 1954: 41).

3. "In his last work, *Siris*, he reverted to earlier modes of thought, to those of the seventeenth century, so far as it had not yet come under the influence of Descartes, Hobbes and Locke" (ibid.).

4. "One alchemist complained that, falling under this suspicion [that he had discovered the secret of the *elixir vitae*] because he had happened to effect some rather spectacular cures during an epidemic, he had to disguise himself, shave off his beard, and put on a wig before he was able to escape, under a false name, from a mob howling for his elixir" (Holmyard 1990: 16).

5. One of Paracelsus's most important alchemical works is even entitled *De vita longa*.

6. See, for example, Lee Stavenhagen's commentary on Morienus's *Testament of Alchemy*: "While Greek writers on this topic were inclined to employ allegory as their main technique, the great Islamic theorists generally moved in a more experimental direction, ingeniously combining astrology and number magic with patterns observed in metallurgical reactions" (Stavenhagen 1974: 64–65).

7. For more about Paracelsus's doctrine of signatures see Peter Harrison's book *The Bible, Protestantism, and the Rise of Natural Science* (Harrison 1998: 251–55).

8. This is, of course, a rather simplified view of the medieval alchemist for the sake of the argument. Actually, he played several social roles, and, as historians show, had a polymorphous, though picturesque appearance: "Au XIVe siècle, de toute façon, l'alchimiste présente des aspects divers: il y a le médicin de cour, le franciscain dissident, les opérateurs présents à la cour anglaise, le savant spécialisé qui se croit digne, puisque sa recherche rentre entre les sciences (*scientiae*), de s'insérer dans l'institution universitaire" (Crisciani and Gagnon 1980: 73).

9. "Quia istam rem, quam tu diu quesivisti, non poterit aliquis perpetrare nec perfectare, nec potuerit ad istam applicare ab aliquo sapiente nisi per dilectionem et

humilitatem molliciem et amorem perfectum atque verum. Et est ista res quam deus adducit suis fidelibus quibus illam adducere disposuit cum fortitudine maiori usquedum sibi parat hominem a quo eam sciat et eam sibi detegat a suis secretis. Nec ista res aliquid est nisi donum dei, qui eam cui vult ex suis servis demonstrat, qui sibi sunt humiles et in omnibus subditi (Morienus 1974: 10).

10. "In this aspect of the alchemical enterprise (sometimes reffered to as 'esoteric' alchemy), the would-be adept considered his materials and apparatus as elements in a spiritual metaphor, an inner process brought to a successful fruition only by those with no crass motive such as personal gain" (Kren 1990: vii).

11. For example, T. E. Jessop, *Siris*'s editor, says in his introduction: "In claiming that it was probably a panacea . . . , he belonged to his age: in his time even physicians of standing had their 'catholicons,' and there was very little science against them, and the old alchemistic faith behind them" (Jessop 1953: vi–ii).

12. As a matter of fact, A. D. Ritchie makes exactly the same point: "One of the most ancient and widespread types of cosmological system is the theory of the Great Chain of Being. The central doctrine, in the form in which it is the basis of alchemy, is summarized in a sentence quoted by Berkeley from one of the *Hermetic* works: 'All parts of the world vegetate by a fine subtle aether which acts as an engine or instrument subject to the will of the supreme God.'" (Ritchie: 1954: 46–47). Once again, what is regrettable about Ritchie's article is that he did not develop the idea as much as he could have, just as he did not sufficiently discuss its consequences.

13. As A. D. Ritchie suggests, Berkeley possibly had some sort of personal affinity with this particular theory: "The fundamental tenet of the Great Chain Theory is that all things in heaven and earth are interconnected. Whatever else Berkeley may or may not have believed, that he believed with all his heart. His favourite text was 'In God we live and move and have our being'" (Ritchie 1954: 41).

14. One of these is T. E. Jessop, who, in his introduction to *Siris* says: "The lowest link could have been anything in the sensible world, but at the time of writing Berkeley was thinking much of vegetable tar, and it is from this that he follows the chain to the Trinity—starting with empiric medicine, seeking a theory for it in vegetable and animal physiology old and new, finding the physical Aether as the quickening force in all things" (Jessop 1953: 6–7).

15. "Judged in the light of the then prevailing concepts the alchemists were engaged in an exact science, basing as they did their assumptions on the teaching of Aristotle. According to him all substances are but differing forms of one and the same prime matter, and it was thus theoretically possible to change one substance into another. This possibility seemed close at hand, as was the splitting of the atom in the early decades of our century, for Aristotle's teachings were as axiomatic in those days as is the theory of relativity today. . . . This is one of the main reasons alchemy enjoyed such long life" (Federman 1969: 4).

16. Let us take only one example: "Mr. Homberg, the famous modern chemist, who brought that art to so great perfection, holds the substance of light or fire to be the true chemic principle sulphur, and to extend itself throughout the whole universe. It is his opinion that this is the only active principle; that mixed with various

things it formeth several sorts of natural productions; with salt making oil, with earth bitumen, with mercury metal; that this principle, fire, or substance of light, is in itself imperceptible, and only becomes sensible as it is joined with some other principle." (Berkeley 1948–57, 5:95 [*Siris*]).

17. C. G. Jung, for example, advocates this view.

18. "To make the mental journey with him is to leave the screeching of this bustling age, and to enjoy the effortless movement of one of our rarest minds gently expanding its practiced powers, carrying strange learning lightly, oscillating with ease between minute observations of natural history and the large visions of cosmology and theology, rising and falling freely through the several dimensions of reality and thought—such was the charm of this voyaging mind—insufflating the narrative of it all with a breadth as aromatic as the balsam with which it began" (Jessop 1953: 7).

Chapter 5   Philosophy as Apologetics

1. Though this chapter is not dedicated to what might be called Berkeley's theology, references will nevertheless be made here and there to some of Berkeley's theological ideas and arguments; it is not possible to deal with an apologetic gesture properly without constantly taking into account the specific theological suppositions on which it is based, and whose visible and social expression it is. For the theological dimension of Berkeley's thought see, for example, Stephen Clark's *God, Religion, and Reality*, especially the chapter "Communities of Faith" (Clark 1998: 123–34); Edward Sillen's *George Berkeley and the Proofs for the Existence of God* (Sillen 1957); and Hedenius's *Sensationalism and Theology in Berkeley's Philosophy* (Hedenius 1936).

2. Some of the ideas in this section might slightly overlap with what has been already said in the chapter "George Berkeley and the Platonic Tradition" or elsewhere.

3. One of the major theoretical consequences that the existence of such a metaphysical supposition has upon a theistic philosophy consists in the advantage "of principle," so to speak, that it has over an atheistic one in offering much "bolder," more comprehensive, and more synthetic explanations, or, as has been said, "a greater coordinating and synthesizing power" (Copleston 1974: 69). A theistic philosopher may—safely and consistently—cluster around his notion of God a whole system of suppositions and hypotheses based on which he would be able to make sense of things otherwise very difficult to explain: "a theistic world-view is capable of accommodating within itself the forms of human experience and the aspects of reality which other world-visions take account of, and that, in addition, it makes better sense of certain forms of experience, such as religious experience, than can be made by a non-theistic world-vision" (ibid.: 88).

4. "Atheism is necessarily dependent upon theism for its vocabulary, its meanings, and its embodiments. Atheism has often been dependent upon theism for its evocation and its existence" (Buckley 1987: 17).

5. "It is reasonable to believe what we cannot 'prove'; it is even reasonable to believe, and feel, what we can't understand. Both theses depend upon a further 'religious' axiom, that the Origin is to be trusted. If we could not sensibly believe the testimony of ages, nor trust our common sense or 'natural taste,' we should have no escape from chaos. To that extent, we *must* live on faith. If we could not sensibly believe that what is now obscure may still have a solution, and may guide our hearts, we must remain '*minute* philosophers'" (Clark 1998: 132).

6. The corresponding passage in *Three Dialogues* reads as follows:

But allowing matter to exist, and the notion of [its] absolute existence to be as clear as light; yet was this ever known to make the Creation more credible? Nay hath it not furnished the *atheists* and *infidels* of all ages, with the most plausible argument against a Creation? That a corporeal substance, which hath an absolute existence without the minds of spirits, should be produced out of nothing by the mere will of a spirit, hath been looked upon as a thing so contrary to all reason, so impossible and absurd, that not only the most celebrated among the ancients, but even divers modern and Christian philosophers have thought matter coeternal with the Deity. Lay these things together, and then judge you whether materialism disposes men to believe the creation of things. (Berkeley 1948–57: 2:256)

7. In *Alciphron* Crito remarks about the two free-thinkers: "they will please themselves with the prospect of leaving a convert behind them, even in a country village" (ibid., 3:33).

8. More will be said about George Berkeley's denial of the existence of matter in chapter 7.

9. Moreover, "*Alciphron* is a model of the psychology and logic of controversy, and to a large degree of the ethics of it too. No other apologetic work known to me has stated the objections to Christianity so fully, cogently and pungently, met them so directly, and kept the logical principles of decent discussion so clearly to the fore" (Jessop 1950: 8).

10. "If free-thinking had lost some of its novelty by the time Berkeley wrote *Alciphron*, its proponents had lost none of their energy. Both Collins's *Discourse Concerning Ridicule and Irony* and the second volume of Mandeville's *Fable* were first published in 1729, and in 1730 Tindal's exhaustive *Christianity as Old as Creation* appeared. Berkeley's satiric purpose in *Alciphron* is the exposure of this social phenomenon; Lysicles and Alciphron are not just reflections of the moral and religious ideas they propound, but renderings of a recognizable social type" (Walmsley 1990: 110).

11. "While Euphranor's method seems radically different from Crito's, its effect is surprisingly similar—an ironic rereading of the free-thinkers' words. As with Crito's parodies, the end is a comic self-negation in which the voice of free-thought is made to contradict itself" (Walmsley 1990: 114).

12. "[H]aving observed several sects and subdivisions of sects espousing very different and contrary opinions, and yet all professing Christianity, I rejected those points wherein they differed, retaining only that which was agreed to by all, and so

become a Latitudinarian. Having afterwards, upon a more enlarged view of things, perceived that Christians, Jews, and Mahometans had each their different system of faith, agreeing only in the belief of one God, I became a deist. Lastly, extending my view to all the other various notions which inhabit this globe, and finding they agreed in no one point of faith, but differed one from another, as well as from the forementioned sects, even in the notion of God, in which there is as great diversity as in the methods of worship, I thereupon became an atheist." (Berkeley 1948–57, 3:43–44)

13. "As a matter of fact, the most enlightened among free-thinkers are not people who have dedicated themselves to the academic study. As the character Alciphron sees it, "our philosophers . . . are of a very different kind from those awkward students who think to come at knowledge by poring on dead languages and old authors, or by sequestering themselves from the cares of the world to meditate in solitude and retirement. They are the best bred men of the age, men who know the world, men of pleasure, men of fashion, and fine gentlemen" (ibid.: 47).

14. For the proper education of the freethinker the crucial thing is not to attend universities, but to find out "good company." Finding "good company" is the key to every successful education, as only by the means of such company does the freethinker's formation properly take place: "much is to be got by conversing with ingenious men, which is short way to knowledge, that saves a man the drudgery of reading and thinking" (ibid.: 165). But where precisely do these sages teach their learning? Where can these embodiments of wisdom be found and attended? The answer comes from Crito: "in a drawing-room, a coffee-house, a chocolate-house, at the tavern, or groom's porter. In these and the like fashionable places of resort, it is the custom for polite persons to speak freely on all subjects, religious moral, or political. . . . Three or four sentences from a man of quality, spoke with a good air, make more impression and convey more knowledge than a dozen dissertations in a dry academic way" (ibid.: 48).

15. "Your free-thinkers . . . seem to mistake your talent. They imagine strongly, but reason weakly; mighty at exaggeration, and jejune in argument" (ibid.: 209).

16. "Those who think of themselves as 'scientists,' and especially those who most despise the dogmas of religion, are often willfully dogmatic" (Clark 1998: 131).

17. "[I]n the process of faith seeking understanding of itself—in the development, that is to say, of theological reflection—use was made of concepts, or at any rate of terms, taken from the philosophy of the ancient world" (Copleston 1974: 26).

18. Actually, one of the writings of St. Augustine is called *De utilitate credendi (On the usefulness of belief)*.

19. Quoted by Dulles (1971: 64).

20. See Dulles (op. cit.) for this discussion.

Chapter 6   George Berkeley's Bermuda Project

1. "For whatever reasons, Berkeley seems to have lost confidence in the Old World and was looking hopefully to America. For it was probably in the early

months of 1722 that he conceived his plan for a missionary and art college in Bermuda, which was to engage him for the next decade" (Berman 1994: 100).

2. Berkeley's Bermudians have many things in common with the inhabitants of Thomas More's Utopia. The utopians "embrace chiefly the pleasures of the mind, for them they count the chiefest and most principal of all. The chief part of them they think doth come of the exercise of virtue and conscience of good life" (More 1974: 92).

3. Of course, he says several times that he was informed about the islands by very trustful persons ("the best Information I could get"), but, as we shall see below, his description did not fit the real situation of the islands at all. He was either misinformed or—more probably—the trustful persons conveyed to him something of the popular medieval view of the paradisical islands.

4. It is true that, later on, when the project had already started to fail, Berkeley showed himself ready to build the college somewhere on the American mainland. But what I am particularly interested in here is his first, genuine, impulse and intention, as recorded in the letters mentioned and in the *Proposal*.

5. "Distance lends enchantment, and isolation preserves things in existence. Later on, many 'utopias,' among them that of Thomas More, would be located on islands" (Delumeau 1995: 98).

6. Kappler's book, cited by Delumeau, is *Monstres, démons, et merveilles à la fin du Moyen Âge* (Paris: Payot, 1980).

7. Sometimes his enthusiasm infected others. For example, one of his contemporaries said: "Young and old, learned and rich, all desirous of retiring to enjoy peace of mind and health of body, and of *restoring the golden age* in that corner of the world" (a contemporary [Dan Dering] quoted in Luce 1949: 97, emphasis added).

8. Many people "found the entire enterprise absurd. . . . those with first-hand experience of the American Church or educational scenes were profoundly distressed with Berkeley's ignorance. It is clear that for many years, Berkeley was seen as something of a nut" (Bracken 1988: 68).

9. According to some authors, this remoteness of the island from the American mainland was in fact one of the main causes of the failure of the entire project. A. Luce, for example, considers that "the tragedy of the Bermuda project was just Bermuda. Six hundred miles of ocean separate it from the nearest point of the mainland. Students might have come sixty miles, but not six hundred. The romance of Bermuda won support for the scheme, the facts of Bermuda killed it" (Luce 1949: 99).

10. Then, far from being "the best air in the world," as Berkeley claimed in a private letter (Berkeley 1948–57, 8:156), Bermuda's air was often violently agitated by "terrible winds," causing much trouble and many falls to the Bermudans: "Mr Lewis [a settler] . . . hath taken a greate hurt by a fall, which hath bruised him much, and his [he is] att this instant very weake, the force of the wind beeing soe terrible. Att the same tyme the like was never seen. Mr Lewis, goeing to the governors, the wind beeing so strong that it bente hime to the ground. And the same day there were many of our howses blowne downe. We have hadd a very unseasonable summer and winter that it hath hinred [hindered] much labour, which otherwise might hadd been performed" (Ives 1984: 85).

11. And, as Bracken openly recognizes, messianism was not unique to Berkeley. Even if for different reasons, "there is hardly a single great mind of the period which is not involved in millennial thinking. Henry More, Sir Isaac Newton, and Sir Robert Boyle may be the names best known to academic philosophers" (Bracken 1988: 78).

12. Of course, Eliade and Delumeau are not the only scholars to endorse and follow this idea. I have chosen to discuss them only because they offer a rather synthetic view of the phenomenon. There are numerous other authors who have, over the last decades, discussed the discovery of the New World in relation to the tradition of the search for the earthly paradise. See, for example, Joseph Duncan's *Milton's Earthly Paradise: A Historical Study of Eden* (Duncan 1972); and George Williams's *Wilderness and Paradise in Christian Thought* (Williams 1962).

13. Certain pioneers already saw Paradise in the various regions of America. Traveling along the coast of New England in 1614, John Smith compared it to Eden: "heaven and earth never agreed better to frame a place for man's habitation. . . . we chanced in a lande, even as God made it." George Alsop presents Maryland as the only place seeming to be the "Earthly Paradise." Its trees, its plants, its fruits, its flowers, he wrote, speak in "Hieroglyphicks of our Adamitical or Primitive situation." Another writer discovered the "future Eden" in Georgia—a region located on the same latitude as Palestine: "That promis'd *Canaan*, which was pointed out by God's own choice, to bless the Labours of a favorite People." For Edward Johnson, Massachusetts was the place "where the Lord will create a new Heaven and a new Earth." Likewise, the Boston Puritan, John Cotton, informed those preparing to set sail from England for Massachusetts that they were granted a privilege of Heaven, thanks to "the grand charter given to *Adam* and his posterity in Paradise." (Eliade 1965: 264–65)

14. "[T]o provide, in the first Place, a constant Supply of worthy Clergymen for the *English* Churches in those Parts; and in the second Place, a like constant Supply of zealous Missionaries, well fitted for propagating Christianity among the Savages" (Berkeley 1948–57, 7:345 [*A Proposal*]).

15. In general, he is very careful and scrupulous in his analysis. He admits that his is only a partial and possible interpretation, with the possibility of other points of view: "*if* it is granted that Berkeley hoped to use the traditional symbolism of Daniel so that he might characterize America in messianic terms then we have a *partial* answer to the point of the American Project" (Bracken 1988: 73, emphasis added).

16. Jacques Maritain in his book *Three Reformers* uses this term with reference to Descartes. He talks about Descartes's "sin of *angelism*": "He turned Knowledge and Thought into a hopeless perplexity, and abyss of unrest, because he conceived human Thought after the type of angelic Thought" (Maritain 1950: 54). Needless to say, unlike Maritain, I use here the term in a positive and appreciative sense.

17. Certainly, some of these phrases belong, to a certain degree, to the specific rhetoric and general polite formulae of the age, but the convergence of so many

witnesses, from so many different people, tends nevertheless to confirm and "validate" them. Such a portrait and excellent "public image" could have hardly been built up in the absence of a set of actual character traits and biographical facts enabling Berkeley's contemporaries to see and describe him in the way in which they did.

18. Of course, one of the probable reasons the project eventually failed was Berkeley's tendency toward idealizations and his "lack of realism."

19. "Berkeley's moral character had been eulogized before the Bermuda project—by, for example, Richard Steele and Bishop Atterbury. But their praise would hardly have been well known. It was, above all, the Bermuda project that gave their remarks prominence and substance. . . . Bermuda was the river that powered Berkeley's moral reputation" (Berman 1994: 120–21).

20. There have been some interesting discussions dedicated to this topic recently. I will give only two examples here: Pierre Hadot in his *Philosophy as a Way of Life: Spiritual Exercises from Socrates to Foucault* (1995) and Alexander Nehamas's *The Art of Living: Socratic Reflections from Plato to Foucault* (2000).

Chapter 7   George Berkeley and Catharism

1. For a discussion of the Dualists sects and Dualist religion in the West, see Stoyanov's book (2000: 287).

2. To take only an indirect and modern example, the great success that Denis de Rougemont's book *L'amour et l'Occident* has enjoyed over the years proves this sufficiently.

3. Referring to Dualism in general Steven Runciman makes relatively the same point:

> Dualism, for all its claims, does not, any better than Orthodoxy, solve the problem of good and evil. The Orthodox might be unable to explain [why] God the Omnipotent should have permitted such a thing as evil to be and to enter into the world of His creation. But the Dualists only answered the question by raising a new difficulty. If Satan created the world, how and why did God allow any good to be imprisoned in it? For the Dualists had to admit that Man possesses the consciousness of good; otherwise there could be no such thing as religion at all. To solve this problem they had to invent innumerable stories to explain the presence of good in the world. (Runciman 1982: 175)

4. As far as the influences of Gnosticism on Western literature are concerned, Harold Bloom, in a recent book, talks of Gnosticism as the "religion of literature" *par excellence*: "From Valentinus through the German Romantic poet Novalis, the French Romantic Nerval, and the English William Blake, Gnosticism has been indistinguishable from imaginative genius. I venture . . . the judgment that it is pragmatically *the religion of literature*" (Bloom 2002: xviii).

5. Moreover, it is not only in literature or philosophy that this view appears. There are also works in the visual arts that express it. Schenk has some interesting considerations on the way in which the idea of the absurd and meaninglessness makes itself "visible" in some of Goya's paintings. In some way, the Devil is, if not its proper creator, at least the powerful master of Goya's world, echoing, if you wish, that Cathar association of the visible material world with the rule of the demon and nothingness: "as in Schopenhauer's case, Goya's almost exclusive preoc- cupation with the dark side of life helps to produce a diabolical picture of the world. It has been observed that while Hieronymus Bosch, the fifteenth-century Flemish artist, introduces men into his infernal world, Goya introduced the infernal into the world of man. In the end it is no longer human beings, however vile or insane, but gruesome monsters that haunt his 'Disparates' and, with a vengeance, his 'Pinturas Negras.' Their inexpressible horror, as Aldous Huxley has pointed out, is based on their 'mindlessness, animality and spiritual darkness'" (Schenk 1979: 63).

References

Aaron, R. I. 1932. "A Catalogue of Berkeley's Library." *Mind* 41:465–75.

Alighieri, Dante. 1984. *Dante's Paradise*. Trans., notes, and commentary by Mark Musa. Bloomington: Indiana University Press.

Anselm, St. 1962. *Basic Writings*. 2d ed. Trans. Sydney N. Deane. LaSalle: Open Court.

Antohi, Sorin. 2000. "Commuting to Castalia: Noica's 'School': Culture and Power in Communist Romania." Preface to *The Păltiniş Diary*, by Gabriel Liiceanu, trans. James Christian Brown, vii–xxiii. Budapest: Central European University Press.

Aquinas, Thomas, St. 1955–56. *On the Truth of the Catholic Faith*. Trans. A. C. Pegis. 4 vols. Garden City: Doubleday Image.

Ardley, Gavin. 1968. *Berkeley's Renovation of Philosophy*. The Hague: Martinus Nijhoff.

Arsić, Branka. 2003. *The Passive Eye: Gaze and Subjectivity in Berkeley (via Beckett)*. Stanford: Stanford University Press.

Artz, Frederick B. 1980. *The Mind of the Middle Ages A.D. 200–1500: An Historical Survey*. Chicago: University of Chicago Press. (Original edition: 1953)

Ashmole, Elias. 1968. *Theatrum Chemicum Britannicum*. Preface by C. H. Josten. Hildesheim: Georg Olms. (Original edition: 1652)

Augustine, Aurelius. 1877. *On the Christian Doctrine*. Vol. 9, *The Works of Aurelius Augustine, Bishop of Hippo*, ed. Marcus Dods, trans. J. F. Shaw. Edinburgh: Clark.

———. 1963. *The Confessions of Saint Augustine*. Trans. Rex Warner. New York: New American Library.

Baldwin, Anna, and Sarah Hutton, eds. 1994. *Platonism and the English Imagination*. Cambridge: Cambridge University Press.

Barber, M. 1993. *The Two Cities: Medieval Europe, 1050–1320*. London: Routledge.

Becker, Carl L. 1967. *The Heavenly City of the Eighteenth-Century Philosophers*. New Haven: Yale University Press. (Original edition: 1932)

Bergson, Henri. 1959. *Œuvres*. Notes by André Robinet. Introduction by Henri Gouhier. Paris: PUF

Berkeley, George. 1948–57. *The Works of George Berkeley Bishop of Cloyne*. Ed. A. A. Luce and T. E. Jessop. 9 vols. London: Thomas Nelson.

———. 1989. *Philosophical Works, Including the Works on Vision*. Introduction and notes by M. R. Ayers. London: Dent.

Berman, David, ed. 1985. *George Berkeley: Essays and Replies*. Dublin: Irish Academic Press and Hermathena.

———. 1994. *George Berkeley: Idealism and the Man*. Oxford, Eng.: Clarendon Press.

Bloom, Harold. 2002. *Genius: A Mosaic of One Hundred Exemplary Creative Minds*. New York: Warner.

Boethius, Thomas à Kempis, Thomas Browne. 1943. *The Consolation of Philosophy: Boethius, "The Consolation of Philosophy"; Thomas à Kempis, "The Imitation of Christ"; Sir Thomas Browne, "Religio Medici."* Introduction by Irwin Edman. New York: The Modern Library.

Bonaventure, St. 1998. *Itinerarium mentis in Deum*. Vol. 2, *Works of Saint Bonaventura*. Trans., introduction, and commentary by Philotheus Boehner. New York: Franciscan Institute of St Bonaventura University.

Bracken, Harry. 1988. "Bishop Berkeley's Messianism." In *Millenarianism and Messianism in English Literature and Thought, 1650–1800*, ed. Richard H. Popkin, 65–80. Leiden: Brill.

Bradatan, Costica. 2003. "Waiting for the *Eschaton*: Berkeley's 'Bermuda Project' between Earthly Paradise and Educational Utopia." *Journal of Utopian Studies* 14, no.1 (spring): 36–50.

———. 2004a. "Philosophy as Palimpsest: In Search for an Immemorial Wisdom." *Existentia An International Journal of Philosophy* 14, nos. 3–4 (fall): 337–44.

———. 2004b. " 'God Is Dreaming You': Narrative as *Imitatio Dei* in Miguel de Unamuno." *Janus Head: A Journal of Interdisciplinary Studies in Continental Philosophy, Literature, Phenomenological Psychology, and the Arts* 7, no. 2 (winter): 453–67.

———. 2005a. "Alchemists or Ecologists? Some Remarks on the Philosophy of Alchemical Transmutation." *Acta Philosophica: Rivista Internazionale di Filosofia* 14, no. 2: 261–74.

———. 2005b. " 'One Is All, and All Is One': The Great Chain of Being in Berkeley's *Siris*." In *Ordering the World in the Eighteenth Century*, ed. Frank O'Gorman and Diana Donald, 63–82. New York: Palgrave Macmillan

———. 2006a. "Rhetoric of Faith and Patterns of Persuasion in Berkeley's *Alciphron*." *Heythrop Journal* 47, no. 4: 544–61.

———. 2006b. Introduction to *George Berkeley's Treatise Concerning the Principles of Human Knowledge*. New York: Barnes and Noble, vii–xv.

———. 2006c. "George Berkeley's 'Universal Language of Nature.'" In *The Book of Nature in Early Modern and Modern History*, ed. Arjo Vanderjagt and Klaas van Berkel, 69–82. Leuven: Peeters.

Buckley, Michael J. 1987. *At the Origins of Modern Atheism*. New Haven: Yale University Press.

Cassirer, Ernst. 1953. *The Platonic Renaissance in England*. Trans. James P. Pettergrove. London: Thomas Nelson. (Original edition: 1932)

———. 1955. *Mythical Thought*. Vol. 2, *Philosophy of Symbolical Forms*, trans. Ralph Manheim, introductory note by Charles W. Hendel. New Haven: Yale University Press. (Original edition: 1925)

Charles, Sébastien. 2000. "La *Siris* au siècle des Lumières: Panacée ou imposture?" *Hermathena. Trinity College Dublin Review* 168 (summer): 55–69.

Chevalier, Jean, and Alain Gheerbrandt. 1969. *Dictionnaire des Symboles*. Paris: Ed. Robert Laffont.

Clark, Stephen R. L. 1984. *From Athens to Jerusalem: The Love of Wisdom and the Love of God*. Oxford, Eng.: Clarendon Press.

———. R. L. 1998. *God, Religion, and Reality*. London: SPCK.

Clayton, Philip. 2000. *The Problem of God in Modern Thought*. Grand Rapids, Mich.: Eerdmans.

Collingwood, R. G. 1957. *The Idea of History*. Oxford: Oxford University Press. (Original edition: 1946)

Collins, James. 1972. *Interpreting Modern Philosophy*. Princeton: Princeton University Press.

———. 1978. *God in Modern Philosophy*. Westport, Conn.: Greenwood Press.

Collins, Randall. 1998. *The Sociology of Philosophies: A Global Theory of Intellectual Change*. Cambridge: Harvard University Press.

Colón, Fernando. 1992. *The Life of the Admiral Christopher Columbus by his Son, Ferdinand*. Trans. and annotated by Benjamin Keen. New Brunswick, N.J.: Rutgers University Press. (Original edition: 1571)

Cooper, David E. 1996. *World Philosophies: An Historical Introduction*. Oxford, Eng.: Blackwell.

Copleston, Frederick Charles. 1974. *Religion and Philosophy*. Dublin: Gill and Macmillan.

———. 1993–94. *A History of Philosophy*. 9 vols. New York: Doubleday. (Original edition: 1946–74)

Creery, Walter, ed. 1991. *George Berkeley: Critical Assessments*. 3 vols. London: Routledge.

Crisciani, Chiara, and Claude Gagnon. 1980. *Alchimie et philosophie au Moyen Âge: Perspectives et problèmes*. Québec: L'Aurore/Univers.

Curtius, Ernest Robert. 1979. *European Literature and the Latin Middle Ages*. Trans. Willard R. Trask. London: Routledge and Kegan Paul. (Original edition: 1948)

Dancy, Jonathan. 1987. *Berkeley: An Introduction*. Oxford, Eng.: Blackwell.

Daniel, Stephen H. 2001. "Berkeley's Christian Neoplatonism, Archetypes, and Divine Ideas." *Journal of the History of Philosophy* 39, no. 2: 239–58.

Danaher, James P. 2002. "Is Berkeley's World a Divine Language?" *Modern Theology* 18, no. 3 (July): 361–73.

Delumeau, Jean. 1995. *History of Paradise: The Garden of Eden in Myth and Tradition*. Trans. Matthew O'Connell. New York: Continuum.

Derrida, Jacques. 1976. *Of Grammatology*. Trans. Gayatri C. Spivak. Baltimore: Johns Hopkins University Press. (Original edition: 1967)

Descartes, René. 1905. *Principia philosophiae*. Vols. 8 and 9. *Œuvres*. Paris: Cerf. (Original edition: 1644)

———. 1956. *Discourse on Method*. Trans. Laurence J. Lafleur. New York: Liberal Arts Press. (Original edition: 1637)

———. 1954. *Philosophical Writings*. Trans. and ed. Elizabeth Anscombe and Peter Thomas Geach. Introduction by Alexandre Koyré. London: Open University Press.

Dillon, John M. 1990. *The Golden Chain: Studies in the Development of Platonism and Christianity*. Aldershot, Eng.: Ashgate.

———. 1997. *The Great Tradition: Further Studies in the Development of Platonism and Early Christianity*. Aldershot, Eng.: Ashgate.

Donne, John. 1952. *The Divine Poems*. Ed. Helen Gardner. Oxford, Eng.: Clarendon Press. (Original edition: 1633)

Dreves, Guido Maria, ed. 1909. *Ein Jahrtausend lateinischer Hymnendichtung*. 2 vols. Leipzig: Reisland.

Dulles, Avery. 1971. *A History of Apologetics*. London: Hutchinson. New York: Corpus.

Duncan, Joseph Ellis. 1972. *Milton's Earthly Paradise: A Historical Study of Eden*. Minneapolis: University of Minnesota Press.

Eco, Umberto. 1994. *La Recherche de la langue parfaite*. Paris: Seuil.

———. 1995. *The Search for the Perfect Language*. Trans. James Fentress. Oxford, Eng.: Blackwell.

Edwards, Mark, Martin Goodman, Simon Price, and Christopher Rowland, eds. 1999. *Apologetics in the Roman Empire: Pagans, Jews, and Christians*. Oxford: Oxford University Press.

Eliade, Mircea. 1965. "Paradise and Utopia: Mythical Geography and Eschatology." In *Utopias and Utopian Thought*, ed. Frank E. Manuel, 260–80. Boston: Beacon Press.

———. 1971. *The Myth of the Eternal Return; or, Cosmos and History*. Trans. Willard R. Trask. Princeton: Princeton University Press. (Original edition: 1949)

Evans, Gillian Rosemary. 1993. *Philosophy and Theology in the Middle Ages*. London: Routledge.

Federmann, Reinhardt. 1969. *The Royal Art of Alchemy*. Trans. Richard H. Weber. Philadelphia: Chilton. (Original edition: 1964)

Feibleman, James Kern. 1971. *Religious Platonism: The Influence of Religion on Plato and the Influence of Plato on Religion*. Westport, Conn.: Greenwood Press.

Fichte, Johann Gottlieb. 1970. *Science of Knowledge* (*Wissenschaftslehre*). Ed. and trans. Peter Heath and John Lachs. New York: Meredith. (Original edition: 1794/95)

Fichtenau, Heinrich. 1998. *Heretics and Scholars in the High Middle Ages, 1000–1200*. Trans. Denise A. Kaiser. University Park: Pennsylvania State University Press.

Ficino, Marsilio. 1985. *Commentary on Plato's Symposium on Love*. Trans. Sears Jayne. Dallas: Spring.

———. 1989. *Three Books on Life*. Trans., introduction, and notes by Carol V. Kaske and John R. Clark. Binghamton, N.Y.: Center for Medieval and Early Renaissance Studies.

Foster, John, and Howard Robinson, eds. 1985. *Essays on Berkeley: A Tercentennial Celebration*. Oxford, Eng.: Clarendon Press.

Foucault, Michel. 1971. *Les Mots et les choses*. Paris: Gallimard. (Original edition: 1966)

Fraser, Alexander Campbell, ed. 1901. *The Works of George Berkeley, D. D.; Formerly Bishop of Cloyne: Including his Posthumous Works*. 4 vols. Oxford, Eng.: Clarendon Press.

Frye, Northrop. 1965. "Varieties of Literary Utopias." In *Utopias and Utopian Thought*. Ed. Frank E. Manuel, 25–49. Boston: Beacon Press.

Furst, L. R. 1979. *The Contours of European Romanticism*. London: Macmillan.

Gellrich, Jesse M. 1985. *The Idea of the Book in the Middle Age*. Ithaca: Cornell University Press.

Gilson, Étienne. 1939. *Reason and Revelation in the Middle Ages*. London: Charles Scribner.

———. 1955. *History of Christian Philosophy in the Middle Ages*. London: Sheed and Ward.

———. 1944. *La Philosophie au Moyen Âge des origines patristiques à la fin du XIVe siècle*. Paris: Payot. (Original edition: 1922)

Grazia, Margreta de. 1980. "The Secularization of Language in the Seventeenth Century." *Journal of the History of Ideas* 41, no. 2: 319–29.

Grayling, A. C. 1986. *Berkeley: The Central Arguments*. London: Duckworth.

Hadot, Pierre. 1995. *Philosophy as a Way of Life: Spiritual Exercises from Socrates to Foucault*. Oxford, Eng.: Blackwell. (Original edition: 1981)

Harrison, Peter. 1998. *The Bible, Protestantism, and the Rise of Natural Science*. Cambridge: Cambridge University Press.

———. 2006. "The 'Book of Nature' and Early Modern Science." In *The Book of Nature in Early Modern and Modern History*, ed. Arjo Vanderjagt and Klaas van Berkel, 1–26. Leuven: Peeters.

Hazard, Paul. 1961. *La Crise de la conscience européenne, 1680–1715*. Paris: Fayard. (Original edition: 1935)

Hausman, David B., and Alan Hausman. 1997. *Descartes's Legacy: Minds and Meaning in Early Modern Philosophy*. Toronto: University of Toronto Press.

Hedenius, Ingemar. 1936. *Sensationalism and Theology in Berkeley's Philosophy*. Uppsala, Sweden: Almqvist and Wiksells.

Heidegger, Martin. 2002. *The Essence of Truth: On Plato's Cave Allegory and* Theaetetus. Trans. Ted Sadler. New York: Continuum. (Original edition: 1930)

Hesse, Herman. 1990. *The Glass Bead Game: Magister Ludi*. Trans. Richard and Clara Winston. Foreword by Theodore Ziolkowski. New York: Picador. (Original edition: 1943)

Holland, Alan John, ed. 1984. *Philosophy: Its History and Historiography*. Dordrecht: Reidel.

Holmyard, Eric John. 1990. *Alchemy*. New York: Dover. (Original edition: 1957)

Hutton, Sarah. 1994. "Introduction to the Renaissance and Seventeenth Century." In *Platonism and the English Imagination*, ed. Anna Baldwin and Sarah Hutton, 65–75. Cambridge: Cambridge University Press.

Inge, W. R. 1926. *The Platonic Tradition in English Religious Thought: The Hulsean Lectures at Cambridge, 1925–1926*. London: Longman.

Ives, Vernon Arthur, ed. 1984. *The Rich Papers: Letters from Bermuda, 1615–1646: Eyewitness Accounts Sent by the Early Colonists to Sir Nathaniel Rich*. Toronto: University of Toronto Press.

Jager, Eric. 2000. *The Book of the Heart*. Chicago: University of Chicago Press.

Jessop T. E. 1949a. Introduction to *Principles of Human Knowledge*. Vol. 2, *The Works of George Berkeley, Bishop of Cloyne*, ed A. A. Luce and T. E. Jessop, 3–17. London: Thomas Nelson.

———. 1949b. Introduction to *Three Dialogues between Hylas and Philonous*. Vol. 2, *The Works of George Berkeley, Bishop of Cloyne*, ed A. A. Luce and T. E. Jessop, 149–61. London: Thomas Nelson.

———. 1950. Introduction to *Alciphron*. Vol. 3, *The Works of George Berkeley, Bishop of Cloyne*, ed. A. A. Luce and T. E. Jessop, 1–20. London: Thomas Nelson.

———. 1953. Introduction to *Siris*. Vol. 5, *The Works of George Berkeley, Bishop of Cloyne*, ed. A. A. Luce and T. E. Jessop, 1–30. London: Thomas Nelson.

Johnston, G. A. 1923. *The Development of Berkeley's Philosophy*. London: Macmillan.

Joussain, André. 1921. *Exposé critique de la philosophie de Berkeley*. Paris: Boivin.

Jung, Carl Gustav. 1953. *Psychology and Alchemy*. Vol. 12, *The Complete Works of C. G. Jung*. Ed. Herbert Read, Michael Fordham, and Gerhard Adler. Trans. R. F. C. Hull. London: Routledge and Kegan Paul. (Original edition: 1944)

Justin Martyr, St. 1997. *The First and Second Apologies*. Trans. Leslie William Barnard. New York: Paulist Press.

Kamenka, Eugene, ed. 1987. *Utopias*. Oxford: Oxford University Press.

Kenny, Anthony, ed. 1986. *Rationalism, Empiricism, and Idealism: British Academy Lectures on the History of Philosophy*. Oxford, Eng.: Clarendon Press.

Kingston, F. T. 1992. *The Metaphysics of George Berkeley, 1685–1753: Irish Philosopher*. Lewiston. N.Y.: Edwin Mellen.

Koselleck, Reinhart. 2002. *The Practice of Conceptual History: Timing History, Spacing Concepts*. Trans. Todd Samuel Presner et al. Foreword by Hayden White. Stanford: Stanford University Press.

Kren, Claudia. 1990. *Alchemy in Europe: A Guide to Research*. New York: Garland.

Ladurie, Emmanuel Le Roy. 1978. *Montaillou: Cathars and Catholics in a French Village, 1294–1324*. Trans. Barbara Bray. London: Scholar Press. (Original edition: 1975)

Lambert, Malcolm. 1998. *The Cathars*. Oxford, Eng.: Blackwell.

Leroy, A. 1959. *George Berkeley*. Paris: PUF.

Loos, Milan. 1974. *Dualist Heresy in the Middle Ages*. Trans. Iris Lewitova. Prague: Czechoslovak Academy of Sciences. The Hague: Martinus Nijhoff.

Louth, Andrew. 1981. *The Origins of the Christian Mystical Tradition: From Plato to Denys*. Oxford: Oxford University Press.

———. 1994. "Platonism and the Middle English Mystics." In *Platonism and the English Imagination*, ed. Anna Baldwin and Sarah Hutton, 52–64. Cambridge: Cambridge University Press.

Lovejoy, Arthur O. 1964. *The Great Chain of Being: A Study of the History of an Idea.* Cambridge: Harvard University Press. (Original edition: 1936)

Luce, Arthur Aston. 1934. *Berkeley and Malebranche: A Study in the Origins of Berkeley's Thought.* Oxford: Oxford University Press.

——. 1968. *Berkeley's Immaterialism: A Commentary on His Treatise Concerning the Principles of Human Knowledge.* New York: Russell and Russell.

——. 1949. *The Life of George Berkeley, Bishop of Cloyne.* London: Thomas Nelson.

MacIntyre, Alasdair. 1984. "The Relation of Philosophy to Its Past." In *Philosophy in History: Essays on the Historiography of Philosophy,* ed. Richard Rorty, J. B. Schneewind, and Quentin Skinner, 31–48. Cambridge: Cambridge University Press

Malley, William J. 1978. *Hellenism and Christianity: The Conflict between Hellenic and Christian Wisdom in the* Contra Galilaeos *of Julian the Apostate and the* Contra Julianum *of St. Cyril of Alexandria.* Rome: Università Gregoriana Editrice.

Mannheim, Karl. 1936. *Ideology and Utopia: An Introduction to the Sociology of Knowledge.* Trans. Louis Wirth and Edward Shils. New York: Harcourt. (Original edition: 1929)

Manuel, Frank Edward, ed. 1965. *Utopias and Utopian Thought.* Boston: Beacon Press.

Maritain, Jacques. 1950. *Three Reformers: Luther—Descartes—Rousseau.* Westport, Conn.: Greenwood Press. (Original edition: 1925)

Mazzotta, Giuseppe. 1993. *Dante's Vision and the Circle of Knowledge.* Princeton: Princeton University Press.

——. 2001. *Cosmopoiesis: The Renaissance Experiment.* Toronto: University of Toronto Press.

McCabe, Mary Margaret. 2000. *Plato and His Predecessors: The Dramatisation of Reason.* Cambridge: Cambridge University Press.

McCracken, Charles J., and Ian C. Tipton, eds. 2000. *Berkeley's "Principles" and "Dialogues": Background Source Materials.* Cambridge: Cambridge University Press.

McCracken, Charles J. 1971. "What *Does* Berkeley's God See in the Quad?" *Archiv für Geschichte der Philosophie* 61: 280–92.

McKim, Robert. 1982. "Wenz on Abstract Ideas and Christian Neo-Platonism in Berkeley." *Journal of the History of Ideas* 43, no. 4: 665–71.

Mead, George H. 1929. "Bishop Berkeley and His Message." *Journal of Philosophy* 26: 421–30.

Miles, L. 1962. *John Colet and the Platonic Tradition.* London: George Allen and Unwin.

Mills, William J. 1982. "Metaphorical Vision: Changes in Western Attitudes to the Environment." *Annals of the Association of American Geographers* 72, no. 2: 237–53.

More, Thomas. 1974. *Utopia.* Introduction by John Warrington. London: Dent. (Original edition: 1516)

Morienus. 1974. *A Testament of Alchemy: Being the revelations of Morienus, ancient adept and hermit of Jerusalem, to Khalid ibn Yazid ibn Mu'awiyya, King of the Arabs, of the divine secrets of the magisterium and accomplishment of the alchemical art.* Ed. and trans. from the oldest manuscripts, with commentary by Lee Stavenhagen. Hanover, N.H.: University Press of New England.

Muirhead, John H. 1931. *The Platonic Tradition in Anglo-Saxon Philosophy: Studies in the History of Idealism in England and America.* London: George Allen and Unwin.

Nehamas, Alexander. 2000. *The Art of Living: Socratic Reflections from Plato to Foucault.* Berkeley and Los Angeles: University of California Press.

Nelli, René. 1964. *Le Phénomène cathare: Perspectives philosophiques, morales et icono-graphiques.* Paris: PUF.

Origen. 1953. *Contra Celsum.* Trans., introduction, and notes by Henry Chadwick. Cambridge: Cambridge University Press.

Orwell, George. 1987. *Nineteen Eighty-Four.* London: Penguin. (Original edition: 1949)

Panofsky, Ernst. 1968. *Idea: A Concept in Art Theory.* Trans. Joseph J. S. Peake. Columbia: University of South Carolina Press. (Original edition: 1924)

Pappas, George S. 2000. *Berkeley's Thought.* Ithaca: Cornell University Press.

Paracelsus. 1975. *The Archidoxes of Magic.* Trans. Robert Turner. London: Askin. New York: Samuel Weiser. (Original edition: 1655)

Patrides, C. A., ed. 1969. *The Cambridge Platonists.* London: Edward Arnold.

Pelikan, Jaroslav. 1993. *Christianity and Classical Culture: The Metamorphosis of Natural Theology in the Christian Encounter with Hellenism.* New Haven: Yale University Press.

Pétrement, Simone. 1946. *Le Dualisme dans l'histoire de la philosophie et des religions.* Paris: Gallimard.

Pico della Mirandola, Giovanni. 1986. *Commentary on a Poem of Platonic Love.* Trans. Douglas Carmichael. Lanham, Md.: University Press of America.

Plato. 1961. *The Collected Dialogues of Plato including the Letters.* Ed. Edith Hamilton and Huntington Cairns. Trans. J. B. Skemp. Princeton: Princeton University Press.

———. 1997. *Complete Works.* Ed. John M. Cooper and D. S. Hutchinson. Trans. G. M. A. Grube. Indianapolis: Hackett.

Plotinus. 1966–88. *Plotinus with an English Translation.* Ed. and trans. A. H. Armstrong. 6 vols. London: Loeb Classical Library.

Popper, Karl. 1956. "A Note on Berkeley as Precursor of Mach." *British Journal for the Philosophy of Science* 4 (May): 26–36.

Popkin, Richard H., ed. 1988. *Millenarianism and Messianism in English Literature and Thought, 1650–1800.* Leiden: Brill.

———. 1992. *The Third Force in Seventeenth-Century Thought.* Leiden: Brill.

Price, Simon. 1999. "Latin Christian Apologetics: Minucius Felix, Tertullian, and Cyprian." In *Apologetics in the Roman Empire: Pagans, Jews, and Christians.* Ed. Mark Edwards, Martin Goodman, Simon Price, and Christopher Rowland, 105–30. Oxford: Oxford University Press.

Priest, Stephen. 1990. *The British Empiricists.* London: Penguin.

Raine, Kathleen. 1977. *Berkeley, Blake, and the New Age*. Ipswich, Eng.: Golgo-nooza.

Read, John. 1947. *The Alchemist in Life, Literature, and Art*. London: Thomas Nelson.

Richardson, Alan. 1947. *Christian Apologetics*. London: S. C. M. Press.

Ritchie, A. D. 1954. "George Berkeley's *Siris*: The Philosophy of the Great Chain of Being and the Alchemical Theory." *Proceedings of the British Academy* 40: 41–55.

Roberts, Gareth. 1994. *The Mirror of Alchemy: Alchemical Ideas and Images in Manuscripts and Books from Antiquity to the Seventeenth Century*. London: British Library.

Roberts, James D. 1968. *From Puritanism to Platonism in Seventeenth Century England*. The Hague: Martinus Nijhoff.

Rorty, Richard. 1984. "The Historiography of Philosophy: Four Genres." In *Philosophy in History: Essays on the Historiography of Philosophy*, ed. Richard Rorty, J. B. Schneewind, and Quentin Skinner, 49–75. Cambridge: Cambridge University Press.

Rorty, Richard, J. B. Schneewind, and Quentin Skinner, eds. 1984. *Philosophy in History: Essays on the Historiography of Philosophy*. Cambridge: Cambridge University Press.

Rosen, Stanley. 1989. *The Ancients and the Moderns: Rethinking Modernity*. New Haven: Yale University Press.

Rougemont, Denis de. 1972. *L'amour et l'Occident*. Paris: Plon. (Original edition: 1939)

Runciman, Steven. 1982. *The Medieval Manichee: A Study of the Christian Dualist Heresy*. Cambridge: Cambridge University Press. (Original edition: 1947)

Schenk, Hans G. 1979. *The Mind of the European Romantics: An Essay in Cultural History*. Oxford: Oxford University Press. (Original edition: 1966)

Sallis, John. 1999. *Chronology: On Beginning in Plato's "Timaeus."* Bloomington: Indiana University Press.

Sambur, S., and S. Pines, eds. 1987. *The Concept of Time in Late Neoplatonism*. Jerusalem: Israel Academy of Science and Humanities.

Sebonde, Raymond (Sabundus, Raimundus). 1966. *Theologia naturalis seu liber creaturarum*. Stuttgart: Frommann.

Sheppard, Anne. 1994. "Plato and the Neoplatonists." In *Platonism and the English Imagination*, ed. Anna Baldwin and Sarah Hutton, 3–18. Cambridge: Cambridge University Press.

Shorey, Paul. 1938. *Platonism: Ancient and Modern*. Berkeley and Los Angeles: University of California Press.

Sillen, Edward A. 1957. *George Berkeley and the Proofs for the Existence of God*. London: Longman.

Singer, T. C. 1989. "Hieroglyphs, Real Characters, and the Idea of Natural Language in English Seventeenth-Century Thought." *Journal of the History of Ideas* 50, no. 1: 49–70.

Skorupski, Jan. 1993. *English-Language Philosophy*. Oxford: Oxford University Press.

Smith, John. 1969. "The True Way or Method of Attaining to Divine Knowledge." In *The Cambridge Platonists*, ed. Patrides London: Edward Arnold., 128–44. (Original edition: 1660).

Steinkraus, Warren E., ed. 1966. *New Studies in Berkeley's Philosophy*. New York: Holt, Rinehart, and Winston.

Stavenhagen, Lee, ed. and trans. 1974. *A Testament of Alchemy: Being the revelations of Morienus, ancient adept and hermit of Jerusalem, to Khalid ibn Yazid ibn Mu'awiyya, King of the Arabs, of the divine secrets of the magisterium and accomplishment of the alchemical art, by Morienus*. Hanover, N.H.: University Press of New England.

Stoyanov, Yuri. 2000. *The Other God: Dualist Religions from Antiquity to the Cathar Heresy*. New Haven: Yale Nota Bene and Yale University Press.

Taylor, Alfred E. 1963. *Platonism and Its Influence*. New York: Cooper Square Publishers.

Taylor, Charles. 1984. "Philosophy and Its history." In *Philosophy in History: Essays on the Historiography of Philosophy*, ed. Richard Rorty, J. B. Schneewind, and Quentin Skinner, 17–30. Cambridge: Cambridge University Press.

Taylor, Charles C. W. 1985. "Berkeley on Archetypes." *Archiv für Geschichte der Philosophie* 67: 65–79.

Taylor, Sherwood F. 1951. *The Alchemists: Founders of Modern Chemistry*. Melbourne: Heinemann.

Thomas, Kenneth. 1983. *Man and the Natural World: Changing Attitudes in England, 1500–1800*. New York: Penguin.

Thouzellier, Christine, trans. 1973. *Livre des deux principes (Liber de duobus principiis)*. Introduction, critical text, notes, and index by Christine Thouzellier. Paris: Cerf.

Tripton, Ian C. 1974. *Berkeley: The Philosophy of Immaterialism*. London: Methuen.

Turbane, Colin M., ed. 1982. *Berkeley: Critical and Interpretive Essays*. Minneapolis: University of Minnesota Press.

Turner, John D., and Ruth Majercik, eds. 2000. *Gnosticism and Later Platonism: Themes, Figures, and Texts*. Atlanta: Society of Biblical Literature.

Urmson, J. O. 1982. *Berkeley*. Oxford: Oxford University Press.

Valéry, Paul. 1957. *Introduction à la méthode de Léonard de Vinci*. Paris: Gallimard. (Original edition: 1895)

Vanderjagt, Arjo, and Klaas van Berkel, eds. 2006. *The Book of Nature in Early Modern and Modern History*. Leuven: Peeters.

Walmsley, Peter. 1990. *The Rhetoric of Berkeley's Philosophy*. Cambridge: Cambridge University Press.

Wenz, Peter S. 1976. "Berkeley's Christian Neo-Platonism." *Journal of the History of Ideas* 37, no. 3: 537–46.

Willey, Basil. 1949a. *The Seventeenth Century Background: Studies in the Thought of the Age in Relation to Poetry and Religion*. London: Chatto and Windus. (Original edition: 1934)

———. 1949b. *The Eighteenth Century Background: Studies on the Idea of Nature in the Thought of the Period*. London: Chatto and Windus. (Original edition: 1940)

Williams, Bernard. 2002. *Truth and Truthfulness: An Essay in Genealogy.* Princeton: Princeton University Press.

Williams, George. 1962. *Wilderness and Paradise in Christian Thought.* New York: Harper.

Winkler, Kenneth P. 1989. *Berkeley: An Interpretation.* Oxford, Eng.: Clarendon Press.

Wippel, J. F., and A. B. Wolter. 1969. *Medieval Philosophy: From St. Augustine to Nicholas of Cusa.* New York: Free Press. London: Collier-Macmillan.

Wisdom, John O. 1953. *The Unconscious Origins of Berkeley's Philosophy.* London: Hogarth Press.

Woolhouse, R. S. 1988. *A History of Western Philosophy: The Empiricists.* Oxford: Oxford University Press.

Yates, Frances A. 1966. *The Art of Memory.* London: Routledge and Kegan Paul.

Yeats, William B. 1965. *The Collected Poems of W. B. Yeats.* London: Macmillan.

Zumthor, Paul. 1997. *Babel; ou, L'Inachèvement.* Paris: Seuil.

Index

Aaron, Richard Ithamar, 200n4
Alan of Lille, 4, 60, 68–69
alchemy
   in Christian world, 95–100
   in Islamic world, 94–95, 98, 202n6
   Jung on, 94, 98, 100, 109, 204n17
   mystic alchemy, 95, 99, 100
   as perennial wisdom, 109–12
   See also Berkeley, George, and alchemy
Al-Razi (*See* Razi)
Ambrose, Saint, 98
Anselm, Saint, 25, 35, 118, 119
Antohi, Sorin, 156
apologetics, 7, 21, 24, 76, 77, 116
   in Christianity, 116, 118, 122, 130, 138, 140, 143–45
   as a genre, 127, 128–29
   See also Berkeley, George, and the Christian apologetic
Aquinas, Thomas, 144
Ardley, Gavin, 198n5
Aristotle, 46, 86, 103, 104, 138, 203n15
Arsić, Branka, 3, 33, 75
Artz, Frederick, 201n7
Ashmole, Elias, 93
atheism, 25, 116, 118, 120–23, 127, 128, 129, 130, 132, 191, 204nn3, 4, 205n6, 206n12
   belief in the existence of matter as the source of, 123, 125–26, 183, 184, 185
   paradoxes of, 120–21, 126, 135–36
   See also Berkeley, George, on atheism

Augustine, Saint, 4, 27, 36, 61, 62, 63, 64, 65, 74, 119, 124, 139, 144, 206n18
Avicenna, 94, 95

Barber, Malcolm, 201n13
Bergson, Henri, 71
Berkeley, George
   angelism of, 85, 167–68, 208n16
   archetypes in, 18, 22–23, 29–34, 35, 36, 37, 39
   and alchemy, 5, 7, 49, 87–92, 100–2, 103–9, 112–15, 152, 169, 182, 193, 195, 203nn11, 12, 15. *See also* alchemy
   Alciphron (1732), 7, 37, 78, 83, 84, 113, 116, 123, 127; Christian apologetic in, 127–45 passim.
   on atheism, 25, 122–23, 125–26, 127, 128, 129, 130, 132, 183, 184, 185, 191, 205n6, 206n12. *See also* atheism
   and Catharism, 4, 8, 125, 173, 182, 183–89, 191, 192. *See also* Catharism
   apologetics, 7, 24, 76–77, 116, 118, 122, 125, 127–42 passim. *See also* apologetics
   An Essay towards a New Theory of Vision (1709), 39, 72, 81, 201n5; *Siris* (1744), 5, 6, 7, 18, 21, 22, 23, 30, 73, 136, 195, 199n2, 202nn2, 3, 203nn11, 14, 204n16; alchemy in, 87–92, 108, 112–15